THINKING ACROSS THE AMERICAN GRAIN

THINKING ACROSS THE AMERICAN GRAIN

Ideology, Intellect, and the New Pragmatism

★

GILES GUNN

THE UNIVERSITY OF CHICAGO PRESS
CHICAGO AND LONDON

Giles Gunn is professor of English at the University of California, Santa Barbara.

The University of Chicago Press, Chicago 60637
The University of Chicago Press, Ltd., London
© 1992 by The University of Chicago
All rights reserved. Published 1992
Printed in the United States of America

00 99 98 97 96 95 94 93 92   5 4 3 2 1

ISBN (cloth): 0-226-31076-0
ISBN (paper): 0-226-31077-9

Library of Congress Cataloging-in-Publication Data

Gunn, Giles B.
    Thinking across the American grain : ideology, intellect, and the
new pragmatism / Giles Gunn.
        p.   cm.
    Includes bibliographical references and index.
    1. United States—Intellectual life—20th century.   2. Pragmatism.
3. Criticism—United States.   I. Title.
E169.12.G864   1992
973.92—dc20   91-23913
                                                              CIP

♾ The paper used in this publication meets the minimum requirements of the
American National Standard for Information Sciences—Permanence of Paper for
Printed Library Materials, ANSI Z39.48–1984.

For Deborah, Adam, and especially Abigail

To say more than human things with human voice,
That cannot be; to say human things with more
Than human voice, that also, cannot be;
To speak humanly from the height or from the depth
Of human things, that is acutest speech.

Wallace Stevens

Contents

★

Acknowledgments

★

Several chapters in this volume were originally composed as essays and published elsewhere, but all have been revised substantially to fit the purposes of this book. Portions of chapter 2 were published under the title "Beyond Transcendence or Beyond Ideology: The New Problematics of Cultural Criticism in America," *American Literary History,* 2 (Spring 1990), 1–18, and is reprinted by permission of Oxford University Press. Different versions of chapter 3 were published under the titles "Henry James, Senior: American Eccentric or American Original?" *The Journal of Religion,* 54 (July 1974), 218–43, © 1974 by The University of Chicago, and "An Introduction," in *Henry James, Senior: A Selection of His Writings,* edited by Giles Gunn (Chicago: American Library Association, 1975), 3–29, © 1974 by the American Library Association. Chapter 4 appeared in a somewhat different version as "John Dewey and the Culture of Criticism, *Works and Days,* 5 (Fall 1987), 7–26. Chapter 6 is an expanded version of an article entitled "Rorty's *Novum Organum*" and is reprinted by permission from *Raritan: A Quarterly Review,* 10, no. 1 (Summer 1990), © 1990 by *Raritan,* 165 College Ave., New Brunswick, NJ, 08903. Chapter 7 is a much expanded version of "The Kingdoms of Theory and the New Historicism in America," which appeared in the *Yale Review,* 77 (March 1988), 207–36, © Yale University; the chapter also contains excerpts from "Perception at the Pitch of Passion," *Yale Review,* 74 (Autumn 1984), 135–42, and "Authority and Its Distractions," *Yale Review,* 78 (Spring 1989), 119–27, © Yale University. Various passages in chapter 9 have appeared in somewhat different form in, respectively, the "Introduction" to *The Bible and American Arts and Letters,* edited by Giles Gunn (Philadelphia and Chico, Calif.: Fortress Press and Scholars Press, 1983), pp. 1–9, and the Introduction to *Church, State, and American Culture,* edited by Giles Gunn (Chapel Hill: University of North Carolina at Chapel Hill, 1984), pp. 1–7. I wish to thank all these publishers and institutions for their willingness to grant permission to reprint this material here.

I have received assistance in this project from a number of individuals and other sources. Though they are in no way responsible for my judgments, I have benefitted in various important ways from conversations and correspondence with Denis Donoghue, Jeffrey Stout, Richard Poirier, Henry Samuel Levinson, Richard J. Bernstein, Thomas Bender, Leo Marx, Peter Vasile, David Carrasco, Nataša Ďurovičová, John and Joy Kasson, Peter Kaufman, Rowland Sherrill, James Egan, Shannon Miller, Neysa Turner, Schubert M. Ogden, Louis Montrose, Gerald Graff, H. Porter Abbott, Paul Hernadi, Everett Zimmerman, Alan Trachtenberg, Cecilia Tichi, Alan Liu, Stephen Greenblatt, Walter Capps, and Forrest G. Robinson. This manuscript has also profited immensely from the sympathetic but searching readings it received from R.W.B. Lewis, Michael Denning, and Andrew Delbanco. My colleague Garrett Stewart gave the penultimate draft of this manuscript a critique so acute and helpful that it led to a recasting of significant portions of my whole argument. Barbara Herrnstein Smith inadvertently saved me from the embarrassment of including in this book something not entirely consistent with the thinking in which it eventuated. My thanks go as well to Robin Craig for help in reading proofs.

Many of my ideas were initially submitted to criticism in talks at the University of Alberta, the University of Chicago, Mercer University, the University of North Carolina at Chapel Hill, the University of North Carolina at Greensboro, the University of Colorado at Boulder, the University of California at Santa Cruz, and the Massachusetts Institute of Technology. They were also sharpened and enhanced by my work over several summers with three groups of extraordinarily thoughtful elementary and secondary school teachers in connection with summer seminars sponsored by the National Endowment for the Humanities. During the course of preparing this book, I have been supported by a Fellowship for University Teachers from the National Endowment for the Humanities and a University of California President's Research Fellowship in the Humanities. Nearly every page of this manuscript has been improved by the copyediting of Janice Feldstein, and the project might never have been completed without the encouragement and critical wisdom of Alan Thomas. Together with the entire staff of the University of Chicago Press, he restores to the making and manufacture of books the dignity of an art. To all these persons and agencies, as well as to my colleagues and students in the Department of English at the University of California at Santa Barbara who have helped provide such a congenial setting for my teaching and writing, I offer my deepest thanks.

But my largest debt of gratitude is owed to the three members of my immediate family—to my wife, Deborah, who listened to, and helped me clarify, virtually all the thinking that went into this book, and to our two children, Adam and Abigail, who again and again provided models for what in particular I wanted to say about the potential beneficence of experience. Special mention, however, must be made of my daughter, Abigail, who endured, as none of the others, the postponement of too many mutual pleasures as I wrote. In a very special way this is more her book than anyone else's, because it was her patience that helped see it through to its conclusion.

1

Introduction:
In Lieu of a Genealogy of Pragmatism

★

There may be times when what is most needed is, not so much a new discovery or a new idea as a different "slant"; I mean a comparatively slight readjustment in our way of looking at the things and ideas on which attention is already fixed.

Owen Barfield, *Saving the Appearances*

★

This book reflects a prejudice that I associate with the writings of Kenneth Burke. It is a prejudice which holds that if we cannot think against culture, we can at least think across it. To think across culture rather than against it is to suppose that even if we can think in no other terms but those that culture itself provides, we do not have to accept the valuations that culture currently places on them. Our margin of freedom, in this case, derives from two oft-noted but frequently disputed facts. The first is that cultures almost always offer us more than one set of terms in which to do our thinking, which is but another way of saying that cultures, however dominant, are never completely hegemonic. The second is that the terms culture provides for thought are rarely if ever perfectly consistent with themselves; discrepancy, disparity, assymetry, rupture, even contradiction, as poststructuralism has taught us, are inevitable. Either way, spaces open up for a kind of reflection that does not need merely to echo the terms of the environing culture but allows meanings to circulate more freely as the mind moves into the gaps, indeterminacies, instabilities, and crossings thus created.

This book also owes to Burke its way of being theoretical. Unlike much contemporary criticism which, to borrow a distinction from Stanley Fish, seeks to thematize particular critical theories and then apply them in a variety of different textual contexts, my interest has rather to do with the way one theory in particular tends to work and

1

with the sort of insight and appraisal it can furnish in what by any account is a varying inquiry. This is as much as to say that *Thinking Across the American Grain* does not undertake an unfolding discussion of a single subject, nor does it envision the task of criticism as the redescription of what is already known in a vocabulary that is more recherché. Its purpose instead is to draw several of the more prominent and aggressive—and sometimes aggressively competitive—of our contemporary critical rhetorics or discourses into conversation with one another by submitting them to what R. W. B. Lewis has called "a single large illumination."

This kind of study can be deadly if the theory in question takes itself—or allows itself to be taken—too seriously; if it regards itself, to use Emerson's definition of a principle, as anything more than an eye to see with. We clearly live in an age when theory is tempted to claim more for itself, to turn itself into the subject or even the cause of its own seeing. Theory of this sort is always in danger of reifying itself—or, what amounts to the same thing, of treating everything it touches as mere epiphenomena of its own idioms. The theory of which I write, on the other hand, is less interested in essentializing the idiom or style in which it thinks than in deessentializing its putative referents. It holds that "concepts . . . are [simply] things to come back into experience with, things to make us look for differences."[1] This is the theory known as American pragmatism, which is currently undergoing a critical renaissance of sorts.

As I will use the term, pragmatism is considerably more diffuse than the philosophical movement William James inaugurated with the help of some ideas borrowed from Charles Sanders Peirce and then passed on to John Dewey and George Herbert Mead, a movement whose legacy was then reinterpreted for a subsequent generation by Sidney Hook, Morton White, and, to some extent, John Herman Randall, and which is now being kept alive for ours by, among others, Richard J. Bernstein, John McDermott, and Richard Rorty. Not that American philosophical pragmatism wasn't always in the process of breaching its disciplinary boundaries—some of its most vigorous if unacknowledged advocates have included Thorstein Veblen, W.E.B. DuBois, Randolph Bourne, and Burke himself—but it is now just as vitally represented by literary and cultural critics like Richard Poirier and Frank Lentricchia as it is by philosophers like Willard Quine or Hilary Putnam, by social scientists like Clifford Geertz and, before him, C. Wright Mills, as by moral and religious theorists like Jeffrey Stout, Cornel West, and Henry Samuel Levinson.

The intellectual renaissance that pragmatism is currently experiencing seems to have followed almost as a direct response from Geoffrey Hartman's call, in *Criticism in the Wilderness,* for an emigration of native-born ideas from within to complement the much-remarked European immigration of ideas from without. Yet even if American pragmatism is held to represent the most substantial intellectual movement that has been produced in the United States, it would never have been capable of revival if it had not seemed to complement (and in some ways to confirm) rather than contest that body of critical and theoretical thought already transmitted from the Continent. Thus one finds many of the leading figures in the pragmatic movement either anticipating important currents of contemporary European reflection or otherwise articulating with them—Peirce and, later, the Harold Bloom of *Agon,* the new interest in semiotics; James filtered through Frank Lentricchia, the neo-Marxist critique of imperialism; Mead (who was himself preceded in important ways by the sociologist Charles Horton Cooley), the development, via Clifford Geertz, of symbolic anthropology and cultural hermeneutics generally; Burke, many of the habits of mind we now associate with both deconstruction and the new rhetorical criticism; W.E.B. DuBois, mediated in different ways through writers as various as Ralph Ellison, Albert Murray, James Baldwin, and now Cornel West, a new kind of prophetic social criticism allied with religion and sensitive in particular to issues of race and ethnicity; Josiah Royce and his theory of Christianity as a community of interpretation, returning in Stanley Fish's conception of the role of interpretive communities in canon formation and revision; Dewey's interest in the problem of valuation and its relation to the question of taste, resurfacing in Barbara Herrnstein Smith's reexploration of the theory of value and, by way of Pierre Bourdieu, in the question of aesthetic judgment; Richard Rorty, allying himself at once with contemporary European developments in hermeneutics as well as with Derridean "textualism"; Peirce, Dewey, and Mead, serving as crucial influences on the development of Habermas's theory of communicative action, and so on.

Another way to put this would be to say that, with the new materialists, pragmatism asserts that theory is but another name for practice since, as James said, all theory is designed to fit the purpose at hand and "the theoretic truth upon which men [and women] base their practice today is itself a resultant of previous human practice, based in turn upon still . . . previous truth . . . so that we may think of all truth whatever as containing so much human practice funded."[2] With the Marxists, pragmatism believes that the problem is not simply to interpret the world but actually to change it, but unlike the Marxists, as

Frank Lentricchia has noted, pragmatism maintains that we actually begin to change the world the moment we begin to interpret it. With semioticians and poststructuralists generally, pragmatism assumes that the only way we can change the world, much less interpret it, is by learning how to read and then revise the signs by which the world is mediated to us, which makes any act of reading and many acts of writing the essential preconditions for any act of intervention. And finally, with the new ideological critics of gender, race, class, and ethnicity, pragmatism insists that the problem of representation is not only aesthetic but also ethical, not only epistemological but also political.

The new pragmatism of which I speak here and with which I will concern myself in the rest of this book thus bears comparatively little resemblance to the version recently introduced in literary studies that is known chiefly for its predisposition "against theory." On the contrary, the kind of pragmatism to which I refer contends that there is no such thing as a practice without theory; the only relevant question is deciding which theory we shall have: that which claims to immunize practice against theory by pretending that theory has no practical consequences, or that which presumes that the only way we can prevent practice from producing consequences we don't like is by developing better theories about practice.

This kind of pragmatism takes for its principal subject what we might call the workings of theory as such. In this it is perfectly consistent with James's initial desire to develop a method for determining what beliefs discursively amount to and how they become true. But contemporary pragmatic theory has long since given up James's somewhat restricted focus on the nature of knowledge and the meaning of truth and has turned its attention more broadly to issues that are essentially moral and political. The kind of questions it now asks are: what would it mean, in terms of the experience we share with others, if we were to adopt this way of looking at things rather than that? how or what would have to change if our decisions were to take into consideration the views and feelings of those to whom they most matter and/ or those whose views and feelings most matter to us?

If these are questions that cannot be suppressed—Lionel Trilling held them to be the kind of questions that all serious literature asks, for example—they are also questions that cannot be asked, so far as pragmatism is concerned, as though we didn't have some intimation of the range of their possible answers. Pragmatism's break with Cartesianism, as Peirce pointed out, derives from its skepticism about putting all things in doubt, or at least in doubt, as Wilfrid Sellars has said, "*all* at once."[3] But the fact that thought cannot begin without prejudice, or prefiguration, does not mean that it has to end there. Prejudice is always open to correction by the community (or, better, communities) of understanding to which it appeals and from which it derives its authority. Moreover, these are communities whose forms of consensus are not, as Peirce thought they should be, convergent so much as contingent, provisional, changing, disruptive, and perilous.

Hence pragmatism is not only fallibilist but also historicist. The world it affirms is not only a world of many truths rather than one but also a world in which most things are true only at very definite instants. This is a world, as James described radical pluralism, "without a sweeping outline and with little pictorial nobility," a world whose order is only partial and is always being revised in response to what is novel, different, alien, incongruous, other. Because experience in such a world is unstable, precarious, and open, thinking must often occur, to invoke Burke's figure, "on the bias" and may even find the possibility and implications of such thinking thrust forward as one of its central subjects.

That is clearly the case here. This book, to say it one more time, is about pragmatism as a way of thinking aslant. I have approached this issue from two directions. The first has to do with the way pragmatism, as a framework for thinking, operates in some of its major intellectual representatives, from its least-familiar precursor, Henry James, Senior, to its best-known successor, Richard Rorty. The second has to do with the way pragmatism, as a method of reflection, interacts with and responds to various issues of contemporary critical moment, from the rebirth of ideology, the spread of interdisciplinarity, and the development of the "new historicism" to the attenuation of the Protestant and Enlightenment heritages in American literary culture and the erosion of public discourse. These two different approaches to pragmatism reflect my double interest in recuperating certain of the meanings of the pragmatic tradition that may have been temporarily lost to us, or, in any event, have undergone important modification since their initial formulation, and in demonstrating how some of these meanings continue to elucidate, and sometimes to allay, contemporary conceptual and methodological perturbations not only within the academy but also frequently outside.

*

Of all the contemporary perturbations on which pragmatic insights may shed some light and for which they may even furnish a modest corrective, none is more significant than the question of "culture" and the related issue of "canons." Here, one might say, pragmatism tries to convert downward not only by challenging the notion that cultures constitute the accumulated symbolic wealth of past experience, but also by questioning the nostrum that canons comprise a set of works in which that wealth is represented and displayed for the sake of contemplation, cultivation, even self-confirmation. Culture as the amassed moral capital of the ages whose formal, institutionalized veneration often pays yet further "symbolic dividends" to professional intellectuals, or at least yields "narcissistic gratifications"; canons perceived as a repository of monuments to the gratuitous achievement of a kind of "purposiveness without purpose"—all this is replaced in pragmatism by a view of culture "as a sort of more or less inexhaustible toolbox," canons as so many sets of directions that show you what can be built with its assistance, or, in other words, that display how the toolbox can be used.

Pragmatism thus gives way to what might be described as a "non-fetishistic relationship to authors and texts" that construes their importance less in relation to the issues they have settled, resolved, in effect closed, than in relation to the questions they continue to keep alive and insistent. This is why the widening of the canon by opening it to more and different authors is only the first step, albeit an absolutely necessary one, in changing the canon and thus altering the way culture represents its own resources to itself. Until new texts and new authors are brought into functional relations with established ones— relations, in other words, that demonstrate how those new authors and texts increase, or at least extend, the power of the symbolic capital already accumulated by predecessors who have delineated what else can be constructed, remedied, or revised with their assistance—culture doesn't really change; it merely grows fat about the middle, or, what amounts to the same thing, ingests what it doesn't yet know how to digest. Thus pragmatism is prepared to say that while there may be no way of dissociating cultures from canons, there is a world of difference between thinking of canons as treasuries to be protected and hoarded and as savings to be invested, portfolios to be managed and risked.

If in this context the economic idiom proves offensive, the effect is clearly intentional. But its offensiveness, in this context, is less a result of the disparity between its tenor and its vehicle than of the fact that it was designed to produce such an effect by someone who is not, in fact, an American or even in any explicit sense a pragmatist. The author of the passages quoted in the last two paragraphs could easily have been, say, William James who with all his talk about "cash values" and truth as "something that pays," that saves "labor," established the precedent for pragmatism's reversion to the language of the countinghouse and the marketplace to discuss serious intellectual issues. Just as easily, it could also have been Kenneth Burke who kept up this, to many, rebarbative practice with his frequent references to "symbolic mergers," "investment," "corrective discounting," and the like. As it happens, however, these passages are cited from the writings of someone who, though sympathetic with their work, is only distantly related to the American philosophical pragmatists and bears no great love for the cultural ethos of American late-market capitalism. I am referring to the French sociologist Pierre Bourdieu.[4]

My view of pragmatism, then, should seem unexceptional to all but those I tend to think of, bending only slightly the meaning of Friedrich Schleiermacher's apt phrase, as its "cultured despisers."[5] These are people who, quite often without the least prejudice against it, are nonetheless convinced that pragmatism's modest critical renaissance is merely a local affair with minimum intellectual interest beyond the rather narrow confines of academic life in the United States; that by bracketing the discussion of first and last things, pragmatism has given up the title to philosophy altogether—and thus its chance to participate in a conversation that includes such contemporaries as Levinas, Derrida, Gadamer, Lyotard, and Habermas—and has simply become another way of getting intellectual work done; and that, as a result, pragmatism has little to contribute to what many people think of as the fundamental problem of our time, the problem of "The Other."[6]

Enough has been said already, I hope, to challenge the claim that the pragmatic renaissance is simply a provincial matter. If Habermas's indebtedness to Peirce, Mead, and Dewey, or Bourdieu's to James, or Denis Donoghue's to Kenneth Burke did not settle the issue, then surely the convertibility already alluded to, of pragmatist motifs into postmodernist preoccupations, does. One of the more important projects for intellectual historians in our time is to trace the intersecting trajectories of American pragmatic thought and the whole poststructuralist revolution, and one of the subtexts of my own discourse is that over the next decade or two pragmatism may well prove to be the most intellectually resilient American response to the quicksands and carapaces of cultural postmodernism.

As for the charge that pragmatism is just another way of thinking about issues that are not "ultimates," or of thinking about them in a "nonultimate" way, this assertion is at once correct and also misleading. While pragmatism is very decidedly a method for performing intellectual work in a world without absolutes, this is not the same thing as saying that it is a mode of reflection that rules out the possibility of thinking about ultimates. Dewey deals with such matters explicitly in at least three different books—in *Experience and Nature,* in *Art as Experience,* and in his far less successful *A Common Faith*—and James provided them with their greatest psychological interpretation in *The Varieties of Religious Experience.* But the real point is not whether pragmatism has ever attended to such issues but whether it encourages any distinctive way of construing them. I think that it does. Pragmatism holds that our moral and religious ideas are validated by a process of reflection that is essentially no different from the one we employ for the rest of our beliefs. The intellectual test we put to them, by instrumentalities however conscious or subconscious, has to do with whether or not they place us in better, meaning more effectual, touch with the rest of our experience; with whether or not they conform to, or at least generally confirm, the rest of our practices. Such reasoning is not in itself, of course, theological or metaphysical; it merely affords a way of accommodating such questions without prejudging whether they are necessarily more important or more consequential than other kinds of questions. To many people in the modern world religious or theological questions are more important; to many others they are not. The only point that pragmatism wants to make—but it is a point essential to the question of its relation to such matters—is that we go about determining their meaning and authority in the way we decide the meaning and authority of any other kinds of ideas: by assessing their congruence with the rest of the assumptions we make about the real.

To this degree, then, pragmatism is a way of doing intellectual work that doesn't rule out any kind of reflection other than the desire, curiously typical of so many intellectuals in our time, to rationalize one's own diffidence by adopting positions so overly determined, so ideologically seamless, as to permit, and even to encourage, the suspension of all speculation about the consequences of those ideas. In the name of theories that too often conflate rather than correlate idea and action, that tend to confuse if not identify ideology and power (thinking of injustice is not righting a wrong, being self-reliant doesn't turn one automatically into a market capitalist) these intellectuals manage in effect, and paradoxically, to dissociate them. When criticism is viewed as "war by other means," you rarely get more than a "revolution without tears," which is to say no revolution at all but merely the intellectual simulation of one that is designed to let everyone off the hook but those who are demonized by such strategems. The real casualties in these academic guerrilla operations, which are as recurrent a tactic of the right as of the left, are our students, who are further susceptible to the illusion, encouraged by so much of the popular or mass culture of our time, that social and intellectual change can be purchased quickly and on the cheap.

The final issue is whether pragmatism can be said to reserve any place for "The Other," to exhibit any sense of "otherness." I am persuaded that it does in at least three interrelated ways. The first derives from its internal principle of self-correction. By encouraging the submission of all positions, all theories, to the revisionary scrutiny of their own interpretive communities, pragmatism concedes that all knowledge is both social and open to criticism. If the evidence for the truth of any proposition is always far from complete and if all of our most stable convictions about matters of fact are, as James said in his 1897 definition of "radical empiricism," simply "hypotheses liable to modification in the course of future experience," the only way to test their relative soundness is by reference to the opinions of other parties who have both an interested, and sometimes not so interested, opinion as to the outcome of such issues.[7]

Second, by directing attention away from beginnings, causes, first principles, a priori reasons, fixed categories, closed systems, and historical necessities, and toward consequences, results, effects, fruits, and implications, pragmatism accentuates the singularity and concreteness—to put it more exactly, the alterity—of facts, details, particulars, individuals, exceptions, mutations, idiosyncracies, discrepancies, discontinuities. Pragmatism acknowledges that it may be more comforting to be a lumper, a "Platonist," what William James termed a *rationalist,* who sees homologies everywhere, but it is more diverting to be a splitter, an "Aristotelian," or in James's nomenclature a *radical empiricist,* whose heart is always moved by the perception of the distinctive. Ancient habits, these, which have never been more alive than in the discourse of the present which aspires to be postmodern, or at any rate up-to-date. Lumpers tend to talk the language of "complicity" and to adopt an accusatory tone, in fact, a whole language of insinuation, that is reminiscent of nothing so much as the discourse of espionage agents and the secret police. Splitters often revert by contrast to a quasi-religious language of dark mystery—their talk is replete with semigeological metaphors about fissures, ruptures, and faults—and adopt modes of address more appropriate to the relationship between priest and initiate.

Third, by insisting that thought is sedimented with symbols, that feeling is semiotically inflected, pragmatism assumes that the only way to come to terms with the so-called Other is by coming to terms with the forms of its constituted "otherness." In this reformulation of their relationship, "The Other" is to be understood not simply as the opposite of the self but also as, at the very least, a kind of construct of the self, a construct, one might say, of, whatever else it is, the self's own imagined alterity. At any given historical moment when such a distinction is in play, this not only makes "The Other" integral to the self's own constitution—the self knows itself in part only by constructing something "other" over against which to define itself—but confirms the fact that internal to the self is a potentiality for, even a predisposition toward, "otherness" that frequently encourages the self to define itself in opposition to whatever is presumed to exist outside of and over against it.

But this way of putting the distinction is not entirely satisfactory, perpetuating as it does the illusion that these categories are not only ideally stable but also, with respect to one another, inherently benign. Such, of course, is far from the case. As any colonialized people can attest, this construction inevitably casts "The Other" in a role that is both complementary and subordinate to most of those who designate them as such, and potentially deprives those so designated of the possibility of using their marginalization to resist such practices and, by recasting the construction from their own side, to reverse some of their more invidious effects. Bell Hooks gets what is problematic about this construction exactly right, politically as well as epistemologically, when she notes the erasure accomplished, whether knowingly or not, by "this speech about the 'other'":

No need to hear your voice when I can talk about you better than you can speak about yourself. No need to hear your voice. Only tell me about our pain. I want to know your story. And then I will tell it back to you in a new way. Tell it back to you in such a way that it has become mine, my own. Re-writing you I write myself anew. I am still author, authority. I am still colonizer, the speaking subject and you are now at the center of my talk.[8]

The only alternative to this perpetuation of colonial rule through the institution of a categorical scheme initially designed to overcome it is to see that "the work of knowing," as Richard Poirier calls it, enables travel along its axis in both directions and that it leads toward an object that can be identified with neither of its poles, neither subject nor object, neither "self" nor "other."[9] What is to be discovered by means of its use, so pragmatism contends, is a discursive arena of communicative exchange and interactive influence and modification that can only be found in the transit between such points and can only be known by means of its resistance to capture or representation—they often come to the same thing—by any of their presiding terms.

To put this more simply, pragmatism holds that if "otherness" is always in part a fabrication, a kind of "fiction," the only way of coming to terms with what it masks as well as refracts from beyond the self is by perceiving it from the perspective of an "otherness" potentially ingredient within the self, an alterity that is always susceptible to deeper alienation and strangeness as well as to greater familiarization. If "The Other" reveals itself, paradoxically, only to the eyes of a self that is already incipiently "other," or, as Bakhtin describes it, "exotopic," that "otherness" does not, whether for Mead or for the C. Wright Mills of *Sociology and Pragmatism,* constitute a meaning that is either, in any but a very complicated sense, determinate or self-confirming.

But this is only another way of remarking, with Geertz as well as with Bakhtin, that there is no seeing wholly "from the native's point of view" and there probably shouldn't be. If there were, as Bakhtin notes, nothing would be gained by doing so—beyond, that is, the possible subordination of one people's perspective to another people's politics—but the exchange of one frame of reference for that of another. Unless there is, as Hooks maintains, reciprocal modification of each category by its opposite, of "self" by "other" and of "other" by "self," there can be no increase in self-knowledge, no challenge to prior conceptions, no opportunity for misunderstanding, no risk of personal confusion and disruption, no possibilities that meaning will be deformed, no danger that understandings will prove incommensurable. Unfortunately, things aren't that simple.

★

They aren't that simple because so much of modern and postmodern discourse about what is presumed to be "foreign," "remote," "strange," "unusual," "aberrant," or "opposite" is often a way of projecting onto others, and almost inevitably socially marginalized others, what we most fear or desire, despise or despair of achieving, in ourselves. "Going primitive," to amend a recent title only slightly, is in many cases merely a way of postponing the difficulties and hazards of growing up.[10] In psychological jargon, the forms that the categorical differentiation of the social imagination into "self" and "other" most often take in modern discourse might be described as a reaction formation to the loss or absence of qualities or values once imagined to have been fundamental to our shared humanity but now understood either as inimical to, or unattainable in, our maturity. Their fantasized unavailability is essentially appeased, or rather displaced, through a curious tactic of idealization in which they are metamorphosed into forms like "innocence," "simplicity," "spontaneity," "irrationality," "sensuality," "polymorphous perversity," "aggressiveness," "savagery," "barbarism," "beastiality," "archaicism," or whatever. The purpose of this tactic is to distance us from such qualities sufficiently so that, in a symbolic sense at least, they can be both noncontaminating and self-flattering at the same time.[11]

This is an old story, perhaps, but one that has been engrafted onto our modernity (or postmodernity, if you prefer) in a particular way. Its distinctiveness lies in the paradoxical character of its psychology, and the clue to what is paradoxical in its psychology lies in what another recent book on "disillusionment and the social origins of psychoanalysis" calls "the ability to mourn."[12] This is an ability that "going primitive" so often forestalls and that pragmatism, like psychoanalysis, tries to encourage. Both encourage it by developing therapies—in Freud's case psychological and "analytic," in James's and Dewey's intellectual and critical—that are essentially so many valedictions permitting mourning. The self, as they see it, is constantly compelled to recreate itself in the image of some past that it fears (and occasionally simultaneously hopes) has been lost to it, and then to repress or sublimate that fact by pretending that this past can still remain present and available to the self when it is imaginatively reified as some form of cultural alterity.

Mourning is the process by which the self can—and must—shed itself of such narcissistic attachments in order to become free to recreate itself instead out of whatever elements of the social or public world are still sedimented historically in its own psychic life. To engage in the process of becoming a mature self, then, is neither for psychoanalysis nor for pragmatism to give up the past altogether; it is merely to abandon the attempt to compensate for the continual disintegration of its unity and coherence by absolutizing some version of it as a suitable model for the construction of selfhood. In short, psychological maturity depends on sacrificing the security of defining the self in terms of some common set of symbols that once organized, or at least were presumed to organize, much of communal life for the sake of trying to refashion oneself out of the new forms of subjectivity and sociality that emerge from the relaxation of its constraints.

This is as much as to argue that if pragmatism and psychoanalysis share a surprisingly similar view of mental and emotional health, it is because in the broadest historical sense they possess what might be thought of as a remarkably parallel genealogy. Each is the product of a process of spiritual disinheritance from the "common cultures" of Judaism and Christianity—a process that began as early as the age of exploration and discovery in the early modern period; that was furthered by the development of physical science in the seventeenth cen-

tury and the new spirit of enlightenment and philosophical criticism
in the eighteenth century; that was propelled forward even more rapidly by the social, political, and economic revolutions of the nineteenth century; and that in the deep inward turn of the twentieth has
now seemingly found its culmination in what Philip Rieff calls the
"triumph of the therapeutic."[13] While this process of disinheritance
was, and had to be, replicated in the lives of their particular founders—
for Freud this involved a strong rejection of the liberal Judaism of *fin
de siècle* Vienna, for James and Dewey a considerably less radical break
with the cultural Protestantism of Victorian New England—psychoanalysis and pragmatism represent anything but a simple acceptance of
or capitulation to it. Both were devised instead as attempts to respond
to the loss of a felt sense of cultural as well as personal unity by converting the experience of mourning its disintegration and disappearance into a new opportunity to reconstruct the self out of the activities
that must be brought into play if some other form of personal organization is to take its place.

Homans assumes, as do James and Dewey, that such activities are
primarily devoted to the production and reproduction of meaning and
have their origin in the psychological play of children. One of the signal features of such play, as D. W. Winnicott was among the first to
note, is that it generates a particular kind of space that is required for
its practice. In addition to being a ludic space, it is also a liminal or, in
Homans's coinage, a "transitional space."[14] Located intermediate between the self and the surrounding environment, this space seems to
exist for the sake of allowing the self more or less freely to devise images or models of their relationship without having to test them, without having to pay the consequences in action. Winnicott took this to
be the very space that Freud himself could never quite imagine, much
less describe, the space reserved for the experience of things cultural.[15]

As Winnicott defined it, this "transitional space" is created by the
child's need to find some symbolic substitute for the loss of its mother.
Such substitutes are found in "transitional objects" the child creates
out of its fantasy life, symbolic objects intended to help the child negotiate the separation from its mother without losing complete contact with her. The creation of the "transitional object" makes possible
the initiation of a passage from dependence toward autonomy through
the intervention of a symbolic surrogate that can, as it were, convert the mother's anticipated and feared withdrawal (or absence) into a
simulated form of her presence. Without such surrogates, Winnicott
reasoned, the self cannot develop sufficient ego strength to form its
own identity. With their help, on the other hand, the child can begin
to reshape its identity in relation to a symbolic form that is neither

exactly an image of its mother—or, rather, of the child's image of her presence—nor an image of something altogether different from her remembered image. The transitional object actually becomes a symbol of what it bridges: the distance between mother and child, which in other terms is the distance between society and the self. The symbol or transitional object effects this bridge by converting an emblem of the child's feared loss of its connection *with* the world into a sign of its increasing powers of relatively autonomous self-creation *in* and *of* that world.

The only problem with this model, as Homans so perceptively observes, is that Winnicott didn't carry it far enough; didn't see that the model also describes the same psychological process by which, through fantasy, adults also negotiate the relations between their freedom and their dependence. In both instances, symbolic intervention provides the key, and the door it unlocks opens into an area no less real for being marginal, a world composed wholly of meanings that link self and world through the activity of a kind of play that is inherently aesthetic. The chief difference between the transitional space the child occupies and the one that adults inhabit is one of scale. Where the symbolism of the child's public world is bounded by the image of the mother, the symbolism of the adult's is bounded by the whole social, and particularly the historical, surround.

To put this more strongly, if Freud and Winnicott together perceived that the work of mourning, both personally and historically, produces as its most significant result a space for the creation, interpretation, and enjoyment of meanings, neither of them understood, as the later James and the later Dewey each realized, that this cultural territory is also the site of the adult self's most consequential labors. Winnicott couldn't see this because he identified such play primarily with the fantasy activity of children; Freud because he found such play, and the narrative activity that so often accompanies it, taking forms he considered not only illusory but also, as in myth and religion, potentially delusional. If Winnicott couldn't quite abandon the Freudian habit of reading all adult experience as a repetition of, rather than an analogy with, the experience of children, Freud couldn't quite manage to rid himself of the scientific habit of viewing all imaginative experience as symptomatic.[16]

★

Pragmatism, it must be said, suffers from no such difficulties. Pragmatism can avoid them because it is inclined to find much of the cure for psychological misery in what Freud could rarely think of as anything but part of the disease—however brilliantly adept he became, through the interpretation of dreams, in diagnosing its forms of pathology. Pragmatism assumes that we can never get beyond stories, narrative, illusions, because the "analytic" or critical instrumentalities through which we break their spell are no less figurative than the material of which they are composed and the strategies by which they sometimes hold us so destructively in their thrall.

Kenneth Burke described this more pragmatic view of psychoanalysis as a form of secular conversion downward that produces a kind of "exorcism by misnomer."[17] The target of this process of secular conversion is the "system of pieties" that the patient has erected on "the altar of [his or her] wretchedness," a system that must be dissolved before the distress can be alleviated.[18] The psychoanalytic technique is to confront the patient's pietistic system, or grammar of motives, with a rationalization so impious as to seem sacrilegious, so offensive as to enable the patient to achieve, in the famous Burkean formula, "perspective by incongruity." For this, only a radically profane, which is to say "scientific," rationalization will do, one which is so terminologically at variance with the patient's own vestigially "religious" explanation of the problem that it can aesthetically, as it were, defamiliarize it. The "painful influences" of an essentially sacred "network of appropriateness"—"the thoroughness of the outlying structure thus tending to maintain the integrity of the basic psychosis"—are exorcized "by appeal to the prestige of the new scientific orientation."[19] But Burke would be quick to add that if the "scientific" pretensions of psychoanalytic discourse are crucial to the success of its methods, the only results those methods ever yield are fundamentally fictive. What the patient receives for his or her pains is simply an alternative narrative of his or her difficulties and a different hermeneutic, or theory of reading, for determining their chances of resolution.

On this view of the psychoanalytic transaction, we remain the creatures, as well as the subjects, of narratives, fables, stories, tales, but we can redraw the coordinates of our dependence and autonomy by trying to rewrite them. The more we learn to rewrite our own and other people's stories, the more we achieve what C. G. Jung called "individuation" but Homans defines rather differently as "the desire 'to become who one is.'"[20] This is a desire that in pragmatic terms reinstalls us in the space reserved for cultural experience not simply as descendants but also as contributors. While such cultural activity is often undertaken alone, it is anything but private, solitary, or solipsistic.[21] If becoming a self involves absorbing a cultural inheritance and also appropriating one, these are activities that, far from dissociating the self from its historical and social surround, actually enable the self to extend its experience of the sociohistorical environment in forms that are no longer infantile. Such extension occurs when the self no longer needs to use cultural interpretation and criticism to revalorize its own self-image but can use them instead to strengthen its relations with all those social others, both in the past and in the present, who have achieved their own different balance between solidarity and independence by working through the same (or similar) symbolic materials.

While Freud might not have disagreed with this last observation, he was inclined to accept one and only one narrative version of the process by which it occurs and the terms by which it can be described. This was, of course, his famous metapsychology, a narrative whose "scientific" nature simultaneously guaranteed its infinite openness to modifications in detail and its equally absolute resistance to any challenges to its basic structure. The metapsychology was for Freud a story that was not only true but also incontestable. By contrast, pragmatism has maintained the position—though not without, as in Burke, considerable shifting from one foot to the other—that it is healthier to keep looking for, and listening to, and making up new stories than it is to insist that all of our experience—and perhaps everyone else's to boot—must be encompassed within the structures and tensions of one single story. In part this expresses no more than the difference between wanting—as the positivist in Freud desired—to be right, and hoping—as the artist in William and Henry James was willing to settle for—to be interested and perhaps even interesting, or at least not boorish.

The quest for certitude is probably inevitable so long as the ordering of experience remains so hazardous an enterprise. The capacity for curiosity nonetheless remains a virtue so long as our own experiential orderings can be enhanced when brought into interpretable relations with the narrative and conceptual shapings of others. Though the confidence that certainty inspires may not be altogether inimical to the ripeness that curiosity requires, the moral stances to which they conduce are scarcely the same. In the last analysis, it may simply come down to a question of what one thinks the world of experience affords. One can be right only in a world in which certainty is a guarantee rather than merely a goad. One can be interesting only in a world where diversity is not merely a distraction, in which difference is not regarded as a deformity.

*

All of the chapters in this book are designed in one way or another to substantiate this point. Chapter 2 attempts to set the terms of the following discussion by diagnosing the critical impasse created by the new ideologization of American cultural criticism and by showing how pragmatic reflection can chart at least one of the ways out of it. In addition, this chapter seeks to demonstrate that William James's value to the pragmatic movement lies not only in the initial impetus he gave to it but also in his ability to foresee and encourage so many of the different lines of inquiry it has subsequently pursued. Chapter 3 is based on my feeling that the development of American pragmatism cannot be fully understood without an appreciation of Henry James, Senior's contribution to its origins: when his contribution to its origins becomes more widely accepted he will seem less like a cultural eccentric or sport and more like a cultural visionary. It is also my belief that as the elder James emerges from the long shadow that Ralph Waldo Emerson has cast at the commencement of the pragmatist tradition in America, it will also become clearer that American pragmatism possesses roots in Calvinism as well as in transcendentalism and that it is not without—as William James first declared, then Dewey insisted, and lately Sidney Hook has reminded us—a sense of the tragic.

Chapter 4 seeks to argue that if all cultures of criticism are not cultures of democracy, this does not rule out the fact that the only kind of culture fully consistent with democracy is a culture of criticism. This is a point that deserves to be restated because it has become intellectually fashionable in recent years to maintain that a critical culture that is democratic is essentially a contradition in terms. This conviction strikes me as belonging to the same order of confusion as the belief that currently identifies the idea of independence, as in independent thinking, with the ideology of individualism. Chapter 5 assesses some of the problems faced by a culture of democracy in our time and shows how Richard Rorty's project for the renovation of intellectual method attempts to address them. While I find myself, to my surprise, growing increasingly suspicious of, or at any rate uncomfortable with, some of the directions in which Rorty's pragmatism has led his liberalism, it is necessary to acknowledge that no one in our time has done more to help revive pragmatist thought than Rorty himself, and my own work is deeply indebted to him.

Chapter 6 begins a somewhat different line of inquiry by examining the legacies of two of the most influential spiritual traditions in the United States, American Protestantism and the American Enlightenment, and the "pragmatist turn" their relations have produced in the literature of the last two centuries. While this book makes no pretense to historicize its treatment of the theory that is its subject, this chapter offers one version of what such a treatment might look like. Chapter 7 takes for its subject what many believe to be the most promising as well as the most problematic development in American literary and cultural studies of the last quarter century. As a way of reinscribing the political within the aesthetic, the social within the representations of the subjective, the "new historicism" looks to some like just another classier version of formalism, to others like an apology for cultural reductionism, to still others like a social pragmatics of symbolic exchange. The determination as to which essentially it is seems on my reading to lie in what it ultimately makes of the concept of ideology and how it engages questions not only of power and containment but also of creativity and self-criticism.

Chapter 8 takes up an analysis of the nature and dimensions of the interdisciplinary impulse in contemporary literary studies and seeks to show how interdisciplinarity can be perceived as the pragmatic antidote to disciplinary essentialism. This perception involves an acknowledgment that the epistemological attempt to determine whether interdisciplinarity opens or closes the mind may be as unsatisfactory as the political attempt to sort out responses to interdisciplinarity along an axis that runs from the reactionary to the radical. Outside the academy as well as within, the real differences seem to run in another direction altogether. Chapter 9 then circles back to some of the issues initially raised in the first two chapters by surveying the prospects for the development of a kind of critical discourse that possesses public accessibility and resonance in the face of the twin dangers of academic pluralization and symbolic solipsism. In this final chapter it is assumed explicitly, in the others somewhat more implicitly, that cultural criticism in America is always—if not only—a conversation about, as well as a conflict with, what political sociologists, intellectual historians, literary critics, public philosophers, moral theologians, and other students of our culture now call "American civil religion." If this helps to explain why so much of the best cultural criticism in America is devoted to the question about, as Aretha Franklin puts it so memorably, "Who's zoomin' who?" it also accounts for why so much cultural criticism in America has trouble avoiding a hieratic tone. The great temptation for the American cultural critic is to stand and deliver. The essential challenge is to develop a voice that is attentive, answerable, and, as much as possible, unassimilable.

PART ONE

PRAGMATIC REPOSSESSIONS

2

Beyond Transcendence or Beyond Ideology?
American Cultural Criticism and William James

★

Our nouns and adjectives are all humanized heirlooms, and in the theories we build them into, the inner order and arrangement is wholly dictated by human considerations, intellectual consistency being one of them. . . . We plunge forward into the field of fresh experience with the beliefs our ancestors and we have made already; these determine what we notice; what we notice determines what we do; what we do again determines what we experience; so from one thing to another, altho the stubborn fact remain that there *is* a sensible flux, what is *true of it* seems from first to last to be largely a matter of our own creation.

William James

★

If one were looking for a way to describe the present era in contemporary American literary and cultural studies, one could scarcely do better than associate it not, as in Daniel Bell's phrase, with the "end of ideology" but rather with its rebirth. Almost everywhere one turns these days, one finds people exploring cultural mindsets that are presumed to define the conceptual and emotional frames within which readers like writers, historical actors like historical interpreters, determine what constitutes meaning. Nor is this analysis of ideology the preoccupation of any particular school of interpretation or specialty alone. Concern with ideology is no more exclusively the preserve of neo-Marxists than of Derrideans, of Renaissance scholars than of gender critics. Instead it serves to focus the work of most contemporary thinkers who seek to relate the products of individual consciousness to more collective forms of mentality and the systems of power that help determine their significance and effectuality.

Contemporary interest in ideology, however, has not developed without certain problems of its own. One of them, though comparatively minor, is related to slippage in the term itself. In current American scholarship, for example (I won't try to speak for European or

Third World), ideology refers to everything from ideas in the service of power to complex semiotic systems that, as Clifford Geertz has proposed, are designed to provide maps of the political world that simultaneously demarcate its boundaries and furnish directions about how to move around within it. About the only thing these definitions share in common is the view that ideology is often disguised or concealed in the operations of cultural life, that its concealment follows as a direct result of the fact that ideological form is inevitably synecdochical, and that by substituting parts for wholes ideologies seek to legitimate or delegitimate various forms of social privilege.

A more serious problem derives from the difficulties that this "ideologization" of so much American scholarship creates for the possibilities of cultural criticism itself. If culture amounts to nothing more than a set of ideological formations that wholly permeate the semiological worlds that constitute it, as many of its modern students imply, then in what sense is it possible to achieve sufficient perspective on such formations to bring those worlds under critical scrutiny, much less to propose ways of revising them? In the writing of many contemporary American scholars (and, I might add, many of the more interesting ones)—Philip Fisher, Myra Jehlen, Sacvan Bercovitch, Jane Tompkins, Jonathan Arac, Walter Benn Michaels—this question is essentially rhetorical. Ideology not only conditions meaning in culture; it also constitutes virtually the whole of it. And it virtually constitutes the whole of cultural meaning by furnishing all of the terms by which culture might otherwise be challenged and surmounted from within. Walter Benn Michaels puts it this way: "Although transcending your origins in order to evaluate them has been the opening move in cultural criticism at least since Jeremiah, it is surely a mistake to take this move at face value: not so much because you can't really transcend your culture but because, if you could, you wouldn't have any terms of evaluation left—except, perhaps, theological ones." [1] Therefore, as Myra Jehlen argues, critics must move toward a position that is "beyond transcendence" by moving back in the direction of those cultural— which is to say ideological—prejudices of gender, class, and race that make us the socially specific creatures that we, like our subjects, are. [2] Jehlen's immediate reference is to those realms of unmediated spirit or eternal verity that were purportedly sought, or predictably defended, by the classic—and virtually all male—writers of the American Renaissance. But her phrase actually extends to any critical attempt to seek methodological refuge in some theoretical standpoint transcendent to experience itself.

★

One can begin to appreciate the importance of establishing a position for criticism "beyond transcendence" only when one realizes how deeply inscribed within our modern cultural practices is the quest for a critical perspective that is transcendent. Indeed, one could argue that one of the chief intellectual practices of the West, at least since the end of the Middle Ages, has been to establish, defend, and exploit such culturally transcendent critical perspectives now that they are, so to speak, no longer given with, or in the terms of, culture's own self-description. Thus the greatest cultural heroes and heroines, or, conversely, the greatest cultural achievements, inevitably become those who, or which, are taken to represent values seemingly immune to the changing discourses in which they are defined—Erasmus, say, at the beginning of the early modern period, Milton in the Puritan era, Newton in the age of Enlightenment, Wordsworth in the romantic age, and so on.

Not surprisingly, this quest for a normative perspective outside of culture from which and by means of which to criticize the products created within it has, again from the Renaissance onward, proceeded hand-in-glove with the search for the grounds of what might be described as a unitary humanism, the term "humanist" no longer reserved exclusively for those who have undertaken such a quest themselves but eventually extended to apply more broadly to all those who have been appointed the consolidators or conservators of whatever discoveries this quest has yielded in the past. From this point of view, the "humanities," as we now call them, represent above all else those texts in which these putative discoveries about our common human nature have been made and are now represented, the concept "humanism" standing in the broad sense for the philosophy or vision of experience they all somehow mutually embody or reinforce.

As I have argued elsewhere, these assumptions became critically articulate in the modern period in the work of a variety of American intellectuals from Lionel Trilling to Reinhold Niebuhr, from Hannah Arendt and Mary McCarthy to T. S. Eliot.[3] The crux of their humanism rested on the belief that if it is not possible to withdraw from culture altogether, it is at least possible to achieve a perspective virtually invulnerable to its presiding assumptions. Such perspectives, it was held—whether as in the case of Niebuhr they derive from the self's existential ability to stand outside itself, or as for Trilling they result from what Freud described as our residue of biological urgency, or as for Arendt they spring from what the Romans called our "humanitas," that is, our thirst for a freedom so absolute that, as Cicero said, one cannot be coerced in one's associations with other human beings and things, even by beauty, even by truth—such a perspective, the argu-

ment went, places one beyond the reach of culture's control by permitting one to scrutinize it from a perspective independent of its official
versions, or at least beyond the coercion of the various specializations
through which it is interpreted and comprehended. Moreover, these
intellectuals believed that through the exercise of such rigorous self-
scrutiny and uncoerced, which is to say, imaginative desire, culture is
not only purged of its false overlay of socially sanctioned meaning but
is actually regenerated as a practicable alternative to the inherited or-
thodoxies it was created to replace.

This understanding of humanism—and of the belief in cultural
transcendence on which it rested—has now, of course, been placed
under severe critical censure by virtually all of those methodologies
that we associate with poststructuralism. While the terms of censure
may vary with the method employed, the burden of the critique remains the same. All those humanistic standpoints formerly assumed
to exist "beyond culture," as Lionel Trilling phrased it in the title of his
book of 1965, are now conceded by contemporary intellectuals living
on an axis between, say, Frankfurt and Berkeley to be mere creatures
of it, and creatures that have no other purpose than to subordinate one
form of mentality to another. Like the chief cultural supports of this
critical transcendentalism—the correspondence view of truth, the
copy theory of knowledge, and the mimetic conception of art—the
temptation to seek methodological refuge in some theory, or theoretical standpoint, transcendent to experience itself has now been revealed
to be a form of self-deception or delusion—though from the point of
view of most poststructuralists it is a politically useful one. By privi-
leging such semisacred abstractions as Reason, Objectivity, Science,
History, Democracy, the West, Material Conditions, the State, the
Feminine, Blackness, the Third World, Communism, Individualism,
Market Capitalism, or whatever, all forms of cultural transcendentalism, so ideological and other poststructuralist critics contend, have
simply served as disguised expressions of the will to power.

★

This diagnosis has by now become one of the familiar features of
poststructuralist criticism in general. Suspicious of all conceptual attempts to hypostasize cultural alterity, the new ideological criticism
seeks to redirect attention to those racial, economic, and sexual factors
that are more material to aesthetic as well as social and political production. But as Edward Said has pointed out, this "Manichean theo-
logizing of 'the Other'" is by no means restricted to criticism that is
prestructuralist.[4] Rhetorical recourse to "transhuman authority," to-

gether with an often telltale reliance on varieties of indeterminacy, paradox, undecidability, the unthinkable, silence, the abyss of meaning, and nothingness is no less a feature of the contemporary criticism that foregrounds logocentricity and the disciplinary state than it is of that which privileges the single, separate, or what is otherwise known in America, thanks to Quentin Anderson, as "the imperial self." [5]

According to Said, this critical deference to the metaphysics of cultural otherness reflects a residual religious nostalgia that inflects even the most militant modernist and postmodernist methodologies, and has converted many of them, no matter what their professed allegiances, into another variant of what can still nonetheless be described as "religious criticism." [6] By "religious criticism" Said, of course, means a good deal more than criticism that operates within the intellectual shelter of some traditional orthodoxy; he means all reflection that, he thinks, shares with most other religious discourses an interest in premature closure, in metanarrative, and in pious subservience to what William James called "the transempirical."

Said sets over against this a criticism that is worldly, iconoclastic, and "secular." Antithetical to all "organized dogma," this criticism would be not only resistant to all forms of totalization but also suspicious of all institutionalizations of "professionalism"—in short, a criticism that is concerned to advance what Said calls "noncoercive knowledge produced in the interests of human freedom" by remaining disbelieving, cosmopolitan, and, above all, "oppositional." [7] Oppositional or secular criticism, as he envisions it, seeks to challenge and, where possible, to deconstruct all the forms in which literary study, whether intentionally or not, has collaborated in the maintenance of cultural, which in the modern West is to say, religiohumanistic piety; and along with others like Jonathan Culler, Said associates the possibility for such oppositional thinking with a criticism that is not only intransigently adversarial but also emphatically comparative. [8] Indeed, Said and Culler both come very close to identifying secular or oppositional criticism with the field or specialization of comparative literature itself, and they define comparative literary study, by which they really mean comparative cultural criticism, as essentially a critique of religion, or, rather, a critique of the potential forms of the collusion, perhaps even conspiracy, between organized religion and the critical defense of the Western literary tradition that, so they hold, is implied by the titles of such widely known books as *The Genesis of Secrecy, The Great Code, Deconstruction and Theology,* and *Violence and the Sacred.*

Whether oppositional alterity is anything we can in fact think and thus practice—or even conceive and thus enact by thinking its opposite (since, as Derrida would say, "thinking . . . the opposite, . . . is still in complicity with the classical alternatives")—ideological critics like Jehlen would most likely put it differently.[9] While sharing Said's suspicion that all forms of "religious criticism" are ethically atavistic and intellectually bankrupt, they would dispute his hope to establish a new basis for criticism in relation to "its difference," as he says, "from other cultural activities and from systems of thought and method."[10] The argument is based on the grounds that the processes by which any cultural form produces and reproduces meaning—through the development of mental sets that privilege certain semiotic sign systems for recognizing meaning and ignore, suppress, or efface others—is largely hidden even from itself. Thus all texts, the more radical ideological critics would argue, even secular critical texts, are at best representations, at worst symptoms, of the processes by which all cultures, like all languages, mask the effects of the ideas they promote.

*

In American literary and cultural studies, there can be little doubt that Sacvan Bercovitch is among the most sophisticated and persuasive, as well as influential, advocates of ideological criticism. One of the features of Bercovitch's writing that makes it so attractive is his willingness to lay his ideological cards on the table, to declare "the principles" of his own "ideological dependence." Bercovitch holds certain "truths" about ideology "to be self-evident: that there is no escape from ideology; that so long as human beings remain political animals they will always be bounded in some degree by consensus; and that so long as they are symbol-making animals they will always seek in some way to persuade themselves (and others) that their symbology is the last, best hope of mankind."[11] These are altogether sensible principles that have been embraced by everyone from Richard Hofstadter, C. Vann Woodward, and Bernard Bailyn to Thomas Bender and David Hollinger, from Constance Rourke and Henry Nash Smith to Leo Marx and Daniel Aaron. Difficulties arise only because of the lengths to which Bercovitch has been increasingly prepared to carry them. For not only does he associate ideology with hegemony and history with self-fashioning; he also maintains that the interlinked system of ideas, symbols, and beliefs comprising ideology and controlling processes of historicization constitutes the chief means "by which a culture—any culture—seeks to justify and perpetuate itself."[12] So conceived, ideology is not only conservative but also coercive. What distinguishes it from other symbolic or semiotic systems with which it might be compared (art, religion, science, everyday gossip) is how it absorbs all the elements of cultural conflict within itself, converting the "rituals of diversity," as Bercovitch says, into "a rite of cultural assent." [13]

Bercovitch's most powerful expression of this view is still to be found in his well-known work, *The American Jeremiad*. A brilliant revisionist study of the rhetorical form that Perry Miller first isolated, a sermonic form that Puritan clergy employed on election days and other civic occasions to remind a backsliding people of their covenantal obligations to build a Holy Commonwealth in the New World, Bercovitch argues that Miller misinterpreted the function of the jeremiad. Far from defining the moral and spiritual costs of running this theological "errand into the wilderness," as Miller believed, and thus acquainting the faithful of New England with the exorbitant religious price of cultural accommodation, the jeremiadic declarations of seventeenth-century transgression, through their ritual repetitions of remonstrance, kept alive a sense of the sacrality of the original errand thus being betrayed; and by surviving a succession of historical transformations, these litanies of iniquity were, by the nineteenth century, to become the chief literary vehicle for the expression of the central American faith, or what Bercovitch calls simply "the American ideology." [14]

As the earliest form of cultural criticism in America, Bercovitch argues that the jeremiad became the principal instrument of socialization, the most potent discursive formula for developing national consensus. And even where the myth that lay at the heart of this consensus generated its detractors, as during the period known as the "American Renaissance," the ritualized rhetoric of the jeremiad still provided American authors like Melville, Hawthorne, or Stowe, who were inclined to rebel against aspects of that myth, not merely with the terms but also with the form by which to transcend it from within.

It therefore very nearly goes without saying that the efforts of writers like Emerson, Thoreau, Melville, and Whitman to transcend ideology by defining a position resistant, if not immune, to it were essentially futile. As Bercovitch remarks with perfect consistency but questionable reasoning, when the American Jeremiahs of the nineteenth and twentieth centuries thunder against their culture, they thunder in vain. The whole of their intellectual and literary revolt simply amounts to a rejection of America as it is—commercial for Emerson, materialist for Thoreau, racist and spiritually hypocritical for Melville, historically divided and emotionally stunted for Hawthorne, socially alienated and physically unloving for Whitman—for the sake of creating in their art a vision of America as it ought to be— the commonplace converted into the sublime for Emerson, a middle landscape for Thoreau, the boundless realm of spiritual quest for Melville, a new era of sexual and spiritual frankness between human beings for Hawthorne, an Open Road for Whitman. But in any case, they remain coiled within the very "American ideology" they would escape.

More recently, Bercovitch has found the monolithic sound of this last phrase both misleading and inaccurate, conceding that "the American ideology" is more like a rhetorical battleground of competing and often antagonistic outlooks than a symbolic synthesis. But he still insists that it retains sufficient coherence to reflect the interests and conceptual forms of the American middle class as it has evolved during three centuries of historical contradiction and discontinuity, and that it has thereby achieved "a hegemony unequaled elsewhere in the modern world." [15] Thus for all of his admirable circumspection about its univocality, Bercovitch is still prepared at times to accord "the American ideology" the power to convert all overt forms of cultural dissent into covert forms of cultural consensus and to reduce all expressions of political radicalism to the gestures of a reactionary politics:

It undertakes above all, as a condition of its nurture, to absorb the spirit of protest for social ends; and according to a number of recent critics, it has accomplished this most effectively through its rhetoric of dissent. In this view, our classic texts re-present the strategies of a triumphant middle-class hegemony. Far from subverting the status quo, their diagnostic and prophetic modes attest to the capacities of the dominant culture to co-opt alternative forms to the point of making basic change seem virtually unthinkable, except as apocalypse. This is not at all to minimize their protest. The point is not that our classic writers had no quarrel with America, but that they seem to have had nothing but that to quarrel about. Having adopted the culture's controlling metaphor—"America" as synonym for human possibility—and having made this tenet of consensus the ground of radical dissent, they redefined radicalism itself as an affirmation of cultural values. [16]

Bercovitch's intentions are not to close off interpretation but to open it up by "recognizing," as he puts it, "the limitations of ideology"; yet on his own account there is nowhere beyond ideology from which to do so. Thus his own critique is no more capable of surviving the demolition of his argument than, by his reckoning, is Melville's or Emerson's. Like them, he, too, is imprisoned within the ideology of America, but only because he has supposed, or rather, postulated, that its nineteenth-century critics invested the word "America" with precisely the same sense of human possibility as did the purported targets of their revisionism.

To state this differently, there is something of an ex post facto character about many of Bercovitch's arguments. Less archaeological or genetic than genealogical, they are based on the possibility of undertaking *after the fact* a reconstruction of the formal conditions that must have been present *in advance* for any meaning, text, or institution to have been produced with the specificity it achieves at the moment of its historical appearance. The aim of these arguments, like the aim of the new historicism, with which Bercovitch's criticism possesses close affinities, is to recover the ideological within the aesthetic, but their effect is just the opposite. By reducing all questions of social and political hegemony to questions of rhetoric or ritual, he merely succeeds, or so it seems to me, in reaestheticizing ideology.[17]

But this is not the only difficulty with Bercovitch's position. For one thing, he, like other ideological critics, confounds the notion of ideology, or political templates for changing reality, with the concept of world view, or metaphysical templates for describing reality. Therefore, he is left without any way of explaining how, as Leo Marx has suggested, a world view like progressivism, which envisions American history as a record of continuous progress, could produce such different modern ideologies as, on the one hand, contemporary neoconservatism, which is committed to some variant of market capitalism, and, on the other, contemporary democratic socialism, which is committed to some form of collective solidarity.[18]

For another, by everywhere assuming, though nowhere demonstrating, that the central fact of American history from colony to nation has been the steady growth of the middle class, and by insisting that this class has consolidated its power in the United States chiefly through its rhetorical ability to define itself ideologically in terms of the sacred symbol of "America" itself, he very nearly winds up retreading an argument for American exceptionalism. This is accomplished by confusing the claim that all rhetorics of "redemptive" (meaning soteriological) American themes strengthen the hegemony of the middle class with the claim that, in the same way and to the same degree, the hegemony of the middle class is strengthened by any rhetorics redemptive of the thematics of America as such.

Last but not least, Bercovitch overlooks or discounts the counter-ideological, or at least potententially subversive, cultural impulses of this "redemptive rhetoric" in America by situating its origins in the seventeenth century, with the paradoxical effects of the Puritan jeremiad, rather than a century or more earlier, with the early-modern development of what deserves to be called, after Walt Whitman, "New World metaphysics."[19] By locating the origins of America's culturally redemptive rhetoric in the self-contradictory oppositions of jeremiadic declension, Bercovitch glosses the fact that from its earliest European expressions—in everything from Christopher Columbus's "Letter to Lord Sanchez . . . on his First Voyage," Amerigo Vespucci's *Mundus Novus*, and Peter Martyr's *Decades of the New World* to Thomas Hariot's *Brief and True Report of the New-found Land of Virginia*, Sir Walter Raleigh's *The Discovery of Guiana*, Shakespeare's *The Tempest*, and Francis Bacon's *The New Atlantis*—the term "America" has always served the political interests of both cultural consensus and cultural dissensus.

In this sense, as Bercovitch would agree, "America" was invented before it was discovered or discovered, as Edmundo O'Gorman has shown, in large part as a result of its "invention," and its symbolic invention was determined in no small measure by the Renaissance need to define a set of spiritual possibilities that constituted a genuine alternative to those that had become exhausted in Europe principally for Western men. The rhetorical history of America thus begins not with the history of the betrayal of its symbolic definition in the colonial and postcolonial eras but rather with the history of America's symbolic invention in the precolonial era. Furthermore, this history turns out to be a complex and contradictory record not only of how Europeans (and European ideologies) first imagined America and how America (or the symbolic versions of it) eventually altered the imaginations and the ideologies of Europeans, but also of how the symbol's "sacred" meanings have never wholly lost their culturally adversarial tenor even when they have lent themselves to co-option by the vehicles of cultural or ideological dominance—indeed, even when they were produced at the expense of effacing the existence of "America's" native inhabitants. How else explain the almost palpable sense of moral, not just conceptual, dissonance to which Bercovitch's own rhetoric can appeal, especially when it reveals discrepancies between professions of belief—with which the sacred symbol of America was, and still is, associated—and the social, political, and ethical practices it has tacitly as well as expressly promoted?

But these various objections ultimately boil down to one which derives from the philosophical prejudice built into a position like that of Bercovitch and other ideological critics: that cultural texts are unable to engage in processes of reflection on the values that generate them without at the same time being subsumed by those values. Walter Benn Michaels expresses a typical example of this view in *The Gold Standard and the Logic of Naturalism* when he notes the futility of attempting to determine what it meant for Theodore Dreiser to approve or disapprove of consumer culture by observing that "it seems wrong to think of the culture you live in as the object of your affections: you don't like it or dislike it, you exist in it, and the things you like and dislike exist in it too." [20]

In addition to presupposing that culture is monolithic and essentially seamless, that it encompasses the whole of experience and is at every point consistent within itself, this view tends to conflate culture with ideology without furnishing any precise reasons as to how or when they are the same. Thus Michaels first argues that "Even Bartleby-like refusals of the world remain inextricably linked to it— what could count as a more powerful exercise of the right to freedom of contract than Bartleby's successful refusal to enter into any contracts? Preferring not to, he embodies . . . the purest of commitments to laissez-faire, the freedom in contract to do as one likes." But then he turns around and admits that such reasoning may be completely fallacious if, as Brook Thomas suggests, "Bartleby's persistent 'I would prefer not to' undermines the contractual ideology that dominated nineteenth century law." [21]

One question that is left hanging here—and that hangs over much ideological criticism—is how to decide between such alternatives. By what principle of interpretation, or in view of what material or textual evidence, does one determine that ideology does, or does not, encompass a given case? A second concerns the precise relationship between cultural form and ideological function. Not a little ideological criticism presumes that the effects of certain practices are inevitably predefined, at which point, as Gerald Graff notes, ideology becomes reduced to "a preestablished calculus of subversive and repressive traits," whereupon "any textual leaning toward individualism, naturalization, totalization, unified subjectivity, universalism, Cartesian dualism, narrative closure, the specular gaze, and determinate textual meaning can be designated as repressive, panoptic, and normalizing." [22] Or, to switch to the American cultural register, any reference to Nature, self-reliance, spiritual antinomianism, the innocent eye, the tragic vision, the frontier, pragmatic thinking, the machine in the garden, worlds elsewhere, experience, liberalism, or otherness itself invokes what Bercovitch is otherwise fond of calling, in *The Puritan Origins of the American Self,* "the myth of America." [23]

What gets lost in this blanket application of ideological categories to social practices is any sense either that ideologies function in different ways in different circumstances—the gospel message of antebellum southern evangelicalism to "preach liberty to the captives" meant one thing to white Christians and another to black[24]—or that they are sometimes divided within and against themselves. Kenneth Burke reminded us as long ago as 1931 that whatever else it is, an ideology is simply "an aggregate of beliefs sufficiently at odds with one another to justify opposite kinds of conduct."[25] But in addition to things lost in the wholesale application of ideological categories to social practices, there are also things that can be dangerously confused. One of them is the relationship between ideology and hegemony. This is the relationship between what we might call the more or less articulate and formal meanings, values, and convictions by which a dominant group defines and extends its authority and power over other groups and the whole repertoire of practices and predispositions by which such meanings become experienced, as Raymond Williams stated, as whole lived realities. A second is the difference between resemblances, parallels, analogies, and other structures of typification, on the one side, and homologies, or correspondences in origin and development as opposed to appearance and function, on the other.[26]

Clearly, for example, the rhetoric of market capitalism in the antebellum period and its association with the concept of political freedom meant one thing to the American slave, Frederick Douglass, and quite another to white slaveholders like Colonel Edward Lloyd, Hugh Auld, and Edward Covey. To Douglass, the ideological linkage between capitalism and liberty quickened his resolve to escape by enabling him for the first time to envisage what it might mean to lay claim to the rights of his own labor. To his southern owners, on the other hand, the same rhetorical association further legitimated their practices as slaveholders by enabling them to view the "peculiar institution" as extending their rights as free people to hold property.

Or, to take another example, if Herman Melville and the Young Americans of the 1830s and 1840s were both responsive to the antebellum challenge to create a culture commensurate with America's democratic possibilities, they responded to that challenge in significantly different ways. What the Young Americans wanted was simply a literature that would capture the spirit of Jacksonian nationalism. What Melville produced in *Moby-Dick* was a text that in drawing out the tragic dimensions of his democratic and capitalist materials, while inverting the theological myth of historical entitlement to which they provided ideological support, sought to reassociate the idea of "America" or the "New World" with a realm of experience that (as he dramatizes in "The Pacific") transcends all his culture's historically and culturally available God-terms, including itself.

These examples obviously would not satisfy Bercovitch. While conceding that free-market values energized Douglass's desire to escape the slave system, Bercovitch maintains that on a deeper level those same values inevitably manipulated and constrained him, virtually reenslaved him, by restricting Douglass's definition of freedom to the terms of "self-possessive individualism" provided by the ideology of antebellum northern culture.[27] And Bercovitch would no doubt go on to argue that, so long as Melville's desire to overcome the God-terms provided by his culture still derived from the critique he made of those same God-terms, his quest never succeeded in escaping the ideological system in relation to which it defined itself. But by this point ideological criticism risks becoming wholly circular and virtually tautological. What is worse, this ideological self-reflexivity is almost inevitably achieved, as Milan Kundera amply demonstrated in *The Unbearable Lightness of Being,* at the price of rendering everything that it would encompass but cannot quite subsume simultaneously trivial and meaningless, weightless and banal.

Just how much so can be gauged by placing over against the ideology of "self-possessive individualism" that so many of the "new Americanists" who take their lead from Bercovitch's work see as absolutely dominant in nineteenth-century American experience the poetry of someone like Emily Dickinson.[28] "Self-possessive individualism" is, of course, the phrase C. B. McPherson used to connect forcibly the Enlightenment's affirmation of human freedom with the unrestrained self-interest later sanctioned by apologists for nineteenth-century free-market capitalism. This linkage between eighteenth-century individualism and the rapaciousness of nineteenth-century free enterprise has now become the club with which the intellectual left continues to beat what remains of the corpse of American liberalism, but it has been forged at the expense of a certain amount of historical distortion and suppression. McPherson's account of the origin and outcome of liberalism, as James Kloppenberg has noted, simply glosses the eighteenth-century countertradition to Hobbes's pessimism. This is the tradition that associated the notion of individual liberty not with individual license but rather with natural religion and civic responsibility.[29] Representing the other side of Locke—the side that McPherson didn't write about—this countertradition joins the experience of freedom with the exercise of social responsibility, a fusion that for a moment at the end of the eighteenth century held out the prospect of adjusting the quest for individual independence to the needs of the community. While this historical moment was short-lived, it nonetheless demonstrated that liberalism's belief in the autonomy of the self did not have to give way to the irresponsible individualism that turned the nineteenth-century marketplace into what Henry James called "the great grope of wealth" and that converted democracy into little more than a blueprint for inequality.

One of the more striking commentaries on this tradition is provided by Emily Dickinson's poems on death. Indeed, it could be argued that if American literature provides no more dramatic literary
representation of this trope of possessive individualism, nowhere is the
trope itself turned more spectacularly against cultural consensus and
toward cultural dissensus. These are poems in which the self constituted through Dickinson's speech not only envisions her own demise
but also has the audacity to preside over this occasion for the sake of
showing how, against all the Victorian Christian conventions of con-
trition that death is supposed to inspire, she remains undaunted and
thus will not defer. This process of ideological resistance is powerfully
rendered in a poem like "I heard a fly buzz when I died," where the
poet reports on the moment of her own extinction. Such a moment is
supposed to mark the end of the self's autonomy, its agentic capacity,
but Dickinson is bent on showing how instead it only heightens hers
to the very end when, to echo Robert Frost, the last "Put out the light"
is uttered. The reader is constantly compelled throughout this poem,
and others like it, to take the speaker's point of view. Yet the insistence
on that point of view conveys an impression that is subversive of, even
an outrage against, the traditional religious view of death. Here death
is accorded significance by the speaker not because, as conventional
wisdom dictates, it serves as the possible prelude to new life but only
because, as the speaker's behavior implies, it does something for and
to the self—or, rather, because it allows the self to keep doing something for itself. In other words, the experience of death is far more
important to the speaker because it is hers than because it is supposed
to have certain ideological consequences. Hence she refuses to give
death the last word even as she imagines death turning her words back
into silence, or, as the poem calls it, back toward "stillness," the "stillness between the heaves of storm." Rather than expressing the disintegration of the self in death, or the preparation of the self for ultimately
overcoming death, "I heard a fly buzz when I died" represents the
masked but insistent hubris of a self that dares to use the imagination
of death itself to assert her queenly rights.

But what have Dickinson's queenly rights to do with the predominantly, if not exclusively, male ideology of self-possessive individualism in mid-nineteenth-century America? Merely this: they represent
her co-option of it for the sake of resisting the victimization it brings
to women. Her queenly rights, which she will here snatch from the
clutches of death itself, represent her attempt, really her demand, to
retain a measure of individual sovereignty, even the sovereignty of
loss, in a world of power. It could, of course, be maintained that this is

the gesture of most of Dickinson's major poetry, but whether it is or not, this gesture, which amounts to the counterstatement in all her poems on death and despair, has a particular salience here. It shows again and again how the ideology of self-possessive individualism is, or at least can become, self-contradictory; how it can be used at one and the same time not only to capitulate to male power, whether personal or supernal, but also to spurn it. Even where ideology is omnipresent, then, it need not be construed as necessarily omnipotent.

*

Among American intellectuals, if not modern intellectuals, one of the very first to understand this fact within the terms of this present discussion was, so far as I know, William James. That is, James was the first American thinker to argue that while ideology, or something very much like it, colors the whole of our conceptual life as human beings, it does not—or at least does not need to—determine all the ways we can reflect on this process. There is no little irony in the fact that some of James's richest reflections on this process occur in an essay entitled "Humanism and Truth." On James's reading, humanism should have taught us that experience comes to us initially in the form of questions that are then digested or assimilated through reference to fundamental categories wrought so long ago into the structure of human consciousness that at least within specific cultural traditions they seem practically irreversible. This apparent irreversibility in turn not only allows the categories themselves to dictate "the general frame within which answers must fall" but also "gives the detail of the answers in the shapes most congruous with all our present needs."[30] We thus encounter experience culturally, James argued, as "now so enveloped in predicates historically worked out that we can think of it as little more than an *Other*, or a *That*" . . . to which we respond "by ways of thinking . . . we call 'true' in proportion as they facilitate our mental or physical activities and bring us outer power and inner peace."[31]

To the humanist this meant, or should mean, James deduced, that reality is "an accumulation of our own intellectual inventions" (or interpretations) and truth therefore a function of the relation between our notions and our needs.[32] But James differentiated his own position from that of many contemporary ideological critics—Bercovitch among them—by insisting that our needs do not thereby inevitably imprison us within our notions. For James reasoned that even if we cannot determine whether these inventions or interpretations of ours, these ideological "Others" or "Thats," possess any absolute or real structure—or if they have any, whether that "structure resembles any

of our predicated whats"—we can, James concluded, assisted by the
critical imagination, determine the difference it makes to think so, or
the alterations in experience that would be necessary if we thought
otherwise.[33]

This is the task that James assigned to the much-maligned theory of
critical inquiry he termed pragmatism. Better described a generation
later by Dewey as "the discipline of severe thought," pragmatism was
devised as a procedure for liberating, in Foucault's words, "the power
of truth" from "the truth of power." James and Dewey both believed,
in other words, that if truth, as we would now say in this ideological
age, is always related to some system of power, humanists can still
emancipate it "from the forms of hegemony, social, economic, and
cultural, within which it operates at the present time."[34] Such emancipation is possible because power is never stable and therefore can never
be monolithic. Dependent not on a fixed source of sovereignty from
which its "descendant forms," as Foucault called them, emanate and
contain all forms of potential resistance, power results from a "moving
substrate of force relations which, by virtue of their inequality," are
constantly creating openings for conflict, contestation, transgression,
subversion, and even appropriation.

Resistances . . . can only exist in the strategic field of power relations. but this
does not mean that they are only a reaction or rebound, forming with respect
to the basic domination an underside that is in the end always passive, doomed
to perpetual defeat. . . . The points, knots, or focuses of resistance are spread
over time and space at varying densities.[35]

To return this to the Jamesian language of subjects and predicates, the
challenge is to develop critical strategies for determining what our encounters with experience as an ideological predicate do to us and what
our repredicating of experience as a form of conceptual alterity does
to it.

It could therefore be said that pragmatism affords the possibility of
doing cultural criticism from a perspective that is not only "beyond
transcendence," as Jehlen conceives it, but also "beyond ideology," as
Bercovitch describes it. Such a perspective is located beyond ideology
and transcendence alike not because it can escape their superventions
but only because it can resist their simplifications. As James noted as
early as 1876, pragmatism may be no more than "the habit of always
seeing an alternative, of not taking the usual for granted, of making
conventionalities fluid again, of imagining foreign states of mind";[36]
but it is a habit capable of cultivation precisely because the dominance
of all social systems, the hegemony of all ideologies, is, as Raymond

Williams maintained, inevitably selective. Since no social system can exhaust what Edward Said calls "the essential unmasterable presence that constitutes a large part of historical and social situations," there is always potential space left over for what Williams described as "alternative acts and alternative intentions which are not yet articulated as a social institution or even [a] project."[37]

This is the space that pragmatic criticism likes to explore—Said's no less than James's, Poirier's, Bernstein's, or West's; Rorty's no less than Dewey's, McDermott's, Cavell's, Smith's, or Lentricchia's—by reconceiving texts not only as, in deconstructionist terms, undecidable objects, or as, in variants of Marxist criticism, ideological templates, but also as sites of effective action, as scenes of forceful statement— "with consequences," as Said writes, "that criticism should make it its business to reveal."[38] From this it should be clear that while pragmatic criticism advocates no particular policies, it does possess a specifiable politics. It is a politics distinguished by the democratic preference for rendering differences conversable so that the conflicts they produce, instead of being destructive of human community, can become potentially creative of it; can broaden and thicken public culture rather than depleting it.

This is a politics that can still be called humanistic, then, not because it is based on some unitary image of the human, or because it assumes that any conception of humanity must be grounded in a structure of things impervious to the contingencies of experience itself. It is humanistic for two other reasons: first, because it views all attempts to make cultural discourse monologistic or univocal as forms of totalism, potentially even of totalitarianism; and, second, because in the realm of critical and theoretical practice it measures all forms of totalism, and especially of totalitarianism, against a distinctly dialogical and moral gauge: "any theory [indeed, every theory] must be measured by its capacity, not to demolish its opponents, but to expropriate what is valid and insightful in its strongest critics."[39]

For certain of pragmatism's friends, not to say its enemies, such exhortations may raise more problems than they resolve. What exactly is meant by "expropriation"? What renders a criticism "valid" or, for that matter, "insightful"? By what standard is the strength of a criticism determined, and who gets to decide? Such questions disclose what some think of as the Achilles heel of pragmatism, or at least of William James's version of it, because they essentially permit only one answer.[40] It is the theorist alone who rules on such matters, the theorist being redefined in James's reformulation as a kind of intellectual statesman who is adept not only at differentiating among contested positions but also, where possible, at mediating their disagreements, or where impossible, at noting their differences. Whichever the case, the theorist is always, and necessarily, in sufficient command of the situation to be able to discriminate alternatives, which is to say that the one kind of criticism the pragmatist cannot expropriate is a criticism of his or her own moral position as theorist, as discriminating intellect. In other words, Foucault's critique of the subject can't really touch the pragmatist because the effect of the pragmatist move, whatever its intention, is not to disconfirm the subject but to reconfirm it.

James's response would be to say that Foucault's critique of the subject doesn't really touch Foucault either. How could it without dismantling Foucault's critique of everything else? But James would go on to say that this way of posing alternatives, however modish, is too Manichean. The real issue for James would be whether Foucault, or those who think like him, are susceptible to any critique, to any corrective discounting at all. Pragmatism does not pretend to be without prejudice; it merely holds that all prejudices are subject to revision if we can learn how to replace the foundationalist "quest for certainty," whether ontological or ideological, with a more provisional relation to our convictions and a more quizzical attitude toward where they may carry us and what sorts of criticism they can sustain. The latter alternative is possible only because we live amidst the predications of more than one ideology at a time, and the predications of no one of these ideologies can subsume all the rest. The grain of cultural experience is thus interwoven and cross-hatched in ways that make it possible for the predications of which it is composed not only to confront but also, as it were, to address one another. Pragmatism is simply one method for advancing the discussion among them, a discussion that is not restricted to consensus but can sustain real conflicts so long as they remain within the limits of the conversable.

I realize that there are serious problems with this view of culture. It is perfectly possible that widening and deepening the terms of cultural dialogue won't necessarily change anyone's mind, much less alter the structures of power. Moreover, the modern corporate state typically cultivates varying points of view not for the sake of engaging real differences but only for the sake of dissipating their force. But history, it would seem, provides us with no other choice but to get on with the conversation, and democracy, such as it is, furnishes us with no better model for the exchange of feelings and ideas. The fate of everyone human these days is becoming more and more interdependent on people and groups whose contrary tastes and temperaments they can neither alter nor avoid. Thus to change only slightly the most famous line of W. H. Auden's "September 1, 1939," it is not that "We must love one another," but that we must listen to and try to understand one another, "or die." A good place to begin is with the shrewdest insights of our toughest critics, or, more precisely, with the counterarguments, whether express or implied, of those "whose attitudes and actions in relation to our [own] beliefs" have the largest consequences.[41] Admittedly, it is not always easy to determine such matters. This is why it is necessary to add, against ideologists of every stripe, that criticism will always remain less like, in the narrow sense, a science and more like, in the broad sense, an art.

3

Henry James, Senior:
Pragmatism's Forgotten Precursor

★

The recognition of the direction of fulfillment is the death of the self,
And the death of the self is the beginning of selfhood.
All else is surrogate of hope and destitution of spirit.

Robert Penn Warren, *Brother to Dragons*

★

On May 30, 1850, Edwards Amasa Park of Andover Theological Seminary preached an important sermon in Boston's Brattle Street Meeting House before the Convention of the Congregational Ministers of Massachusetts. His title was "The Theology of the Intellect and that of the Feelings." Though this subject may have been suggested to him two years before, when his theological colleague from Hartford, the more famous Horace Bushnell, made use of a similar distinction in an address also delivered at Andover on the relation between "Dogma and Spirit," Park's title reflected an opposition which had found its chief expression in the American tradition a century earlier in the writings of Jonathan Edwards and which went all the way back in the European tradition through the theologies of Friedrich Schleiermacher and Martin Luther to the Bible itself. Park was hardly insensible of the importance and magnitude of this legacy, but his chief purpose was less to establish or defend the distinction between these two kinds of theology than to interpret its consequences, to show how each kind of theology needed the other to do full justice to the nature and substance of the Christian claim of faith.

The theology of the intellect, with its preference for evidence over opinion, reason over intuition, precision over intensity, harmony over conflict, the literary over the figural, and the general over the specific, was far better suited for dogmatics than for preaching, for dialectics than for confession, for speculation than for narrative. The theology of the feelings, on the other hand, with its opposite tendency to sub-

40

ordinate consistency to assertiveness, logic to feeling, certitude to sensitivity, the discursive to the poetic, and the concrete to the universal, was far more appropriate to the tract than the treatise, the homily than the catechism, the history than the disputation. Park's point was that neither type of theology is sufficient without the other, just as a confusion of either with its complement might destroy the integrity of both:

> It is this crossing of one kind of theology into the province of another kind . . . which mars either the eloquence or else the doctrine of the pulpit. The massive speculations of the metaphysician sink down into his expressions of feeling and make him appear coldhearted, while the enthusiasm of the impulsive divine ascends and effervesces into his reasoning and causes him both to *appear,* and to *be*...hot-headed.[1]

Park wanted a recognition of the claims of both kinds of theology so that he might effect a reconciliation between the intellectual and pietistic elements not only within himself but also within the body of the Christian faith of his time, between the Evangelicals who made so much of the heart and what might be loosely called the Unitarians who put such store in the head, between popular revivalists and Harvard intellectuals. Park himself was a member of neither radical party. It was the older orthodoxy of New England that he wanted to repossess, only softened and made more sensible by an anthropology which acknowledged that human beings are at once sentient and rational.

There is no way of knowing whether the elder Henry James ever read Park's sermon—had he done so, he would have undoubtedly regarded it as an expression of what he was fond of calling the "old theology" rather than the "new"—but there can be scarcely any question at all about the relevance of its presiding distinction to his own life and work. For the writings of the elder James—a series of books which, if one includes the unfinished manuscript published posthumously by his eldest son William comes to well over a dozen volumes[2]—are clearly inscribed with the same kind of confusion that Park had noted in his sermon: massive metaphysical speculations that often cast a leaden shadow over an unusually spirited and expressive speaker, thus giving rise to that contradictory set of impressions which Park evokes with the phrases "cold-hearted" and "hot-headed."

In truth, however, something very nearly the opposite was the case with the elder James. If his heart suffered from anything, it was not from an absence of feeling but rather from an excess of it, whereas his speculations and judgments often appeared intemperate or impulsive only because he viewed his ideas, however universal their scope or implication, as living realities, felt possibilities. James's problem was that he was clearly a theologian of feeling compelled to express his religious faith in what most systematic thinkers would regard as a jerry-rigged theology of intellect. Continually tempted, really seduced, into conveying what T. S. Eliot once called "the logic of feelings" in "the logic of concepts," James's medium frequently constituted a downright obstacle to, if not parody of, his message. Hence the well-worn quip that Charles Eliot Norton ascribed to William Dean Howells to the effect that James not only wrote *The Secret of Swedenborg* but also "kept it."[3]

★

This remark has often been irresponsibly converted into a justification for dismissing James as a mere eccentric when Howells himself, as it happens, could not. Even if Howells was temperamentally indisposed to take an active interest in what James found so compelling about the ideas of the seventeenth-century mystic Emmanuel Swedenborg, he had still absorbed enough of a respect for Swedenborg's ethics from his own father to respond favorably to the richest kernel of truth James found in him. This was, of course, what James called the "divine natural humanity" to which, in Swedenborg's estimation, all human beings are heir, and which, in the new dispensation, so James argued, would destroy all those superficial social and political distinctions by which governments had falsely divided one human being from another.

Strange as this conviction may sound to contemporary ears, it converged almost precisely with the underlying assumptions of that progressive faith that united all the "men of good hope" of that era. These included, along with Howells himself and Emerson before him, people like Edward Bellamy, Henry George, and Henry Demarest Lloyd, men whose political religion had a way of turning very quickly into a broad-based religion of humanity roughly parallel in its convictions to the views of writers as diverse as Mazzini, Victor Hugo, and James himself. Daniel Aaron has defined the profile of this "secular religion" as follows:

The religion of progressivism conceived of the mediator between God and man not as an individual Christ but as a universalized Christ, Christ as a symbol of humanity itself. It broke with the orthodox Protestant assumption that "God's redemptive operation," to quote Gronlund, is "confined to the isolated individual bosom" and refused to make religion a private affair between one man and his God. For the progressives, God appeared to man through men and revealed himself in human history and institutions. Men were damned or saved collectively. They entered into communion with God when they shed their selfish personalities and united with one another in a confederation of love. According to this religion, social evil was not confirmed by individual criminal acts but by what the elder Henry James called "our organized inclemency of man to man." And in turn, social good could not be attained through individual acts of charity but through the organized clemency of man to man.[4]

Except for omitting the claim that religion possesses a tragic side which entails the death of the old egoistic self to make way for the rebirth of a new social self, this summary of the faith of the progressives could also stand as a fairly accurate, brief statement of the theology of the elder James. If he differed with the later progressives, just as he had with the earlier transcendentalists, over the question of the reality and governance of evil, his view of salvation was still as egalitarian as those of the first and as infused with a spirit of optimism—albeit a very much more tempered one—as that of the second. As William James summarized his father's conception of the world, it flowed from two basic perceptions:

In the first place, he felt that the individual man, as such, is nothing, but owes all he is and has to the race nature he inherits, and to the society into which he is born. And, secondly, he scorned to admit, even as a possibility, that the great and loving Creator, who has all the being and the power, and has brought us as far as *this,* should not bring us *through,* and *out,* into the most triumphant harmony.[5]

Yet few people then or now have perceived the depth of James's relationship to either the transcendentalists or to progressives, or, for that matter, to any other major group of thinkers and writers in the American tradition, including his two sons and the form of thinking and mode of inquiry known as pragmatism which, in their very different ways, they each had such a hand in developing. Instead, the impression which with certain notable exceptions has continued to prevail is the one most vividly conveyed by E. L. Godkin, of an interesting and, in his own terms, formidable eccentric with no very clear intellectual outline who was alienated from, and disavowed by, the only sect or group, in this case the Swedenborgians, to whose cause he professed any allegiance at all:

Henry James, the elder, was a person of delightful eccentricity, and a humorist of the first water. When in his grotesque moods, he maintained that, to a right-minded man, a crowded Cambridge horse-car "was the nearest approach to heaven upon earth!" What was the precise nature of his philosophy, I never fully understood, but he professed to be a Swedenborgian, and carried on a correspondence full of droll incidents with anxious inquirers, in various parts of the country. Asking him one day about one of these, he replied instantly, "Oh, a devil of a woman!" to my great astonishment, as I was not then thoroughly familiar with his ways. One of his most amusing experiences was that the other Swedenborgians repudiated all religious connection with him, so that the sect to which he belonged, and of which he was the head, may be said to have consisted of himself alone.[6]

Oddly enough, this witticism did not prevent Godkin from closing his recollection with the observation that James "was a writer of extraordinary vigor and picturesqueness, and I suppose there was not in his day a more formidable master of English style."[7]

This almost parenthetical remark by someone who was closely associated with James Russell Lowell and Charles Eliot Norton in the founding and editing of the Nation and destined to become one of America's most liberal and distinguished journalists—he was also a resident of Cambridge, Massachusetts from 1875 to 1881 and a frequent dinner guest at the James's—is no mean compliment. Yet it only deepens the mystery of obscurity to which James fell victim almost immediately after his death and from which he has never fully recovered, despite the efforts of such scholars as Austin Warren, Ralph Barton Perry, F. O. Matthiessen, Frederick Harold Young, Leon Edel, Quentin Anderson, R.W.B. Lewis, Richard Poirier, Jean Strouse, and others.[8] Clearly, part of the reason derives from James's turn toward theology at a time when this mode of reflection was rapidly going out of fashion among those more progressive thinkers with whom he wanted to communicate. For all the originality and prescience of many of his insights, James's stubborn insistence on casting his ideas in a framework of thought both esoteric and untraditional frequently made his views sound too vague and recondite to his contemporaries.

Then, too, James lived in an age growing rapidly impatient with thinkers like himself—Josiah Royce was to suffer a similar fate—who refused to permit their interest in and sympathy for concrete problems from obscuring their still more fervent vision of what transcends and resolves them. Though James was as absorbed with the individual and the concrete as the next person—indeed, his son, Henry, observed at one point in Notes of a Son and Brother that there was in his father, for all his love of the abstract, not the least embarrassment of the actual about him—he remained steadfast in his belief that the key to all particular issues lay in reconstituting our conception of the whole. A philosophical monist by inclination, though not always by practice, James suffered a fate of incomprehension not dissimilar from the one that befell those two other metaphysical visionaries of the age, Herman Melville and Walt Whitman.

There were also, it is true, other, more personal reasons for the disappearance of the elder James's work from public view, reasons having to do with both the remarkable development of certain members of his family and a specific but rarely noticed element of his style as thinker and writer. To begin with, James's work was quickly and extensively overshadowed by the writings of his two more gifted and famous sons. "Henry, Junior," as he was known by the family, had already published six books before his father finished his most mature work, *Society the Redeemed Form of Man* (1879), and by the time the elder James died three years later, his novelist son had added even more titles to this list. William's productive outflow of books and essays did not commence in earnest until 1890, with the publication of the two volumes of his brilliant and still undervalued *The Principles of Psychology,* but he had already begun teaching at Harvard in 1872, had established his pioneering laboratory in psychology and initiated his labors on the massive *Principles* by 1876, and had acquired many of his most durable convictions by 1884, when he edited his father's last work in progress entitled "Spiritual Creation" and published it, together with an "Autobiographical Sketch" and an introduction of his own, as *The Literary Remains of the Late Henry James.*

If the elder James had lived long enough to witness the full measure of it, this astonishing achievement of his two sons, which so thoroughly eclipsed his own, would neither have alarmed nor displeased him. For one thing, it constituted an eloquent vindication of the principles by which he had sought to educate them, or, more accurately, by which he had permitted them the freedom to educate themselves. For another, central to his thinking, as we shall see in due course, was an abhorrence of the emotion of envy. This hatred of envy may have come rather easily to a man who, soon after he reached his majority, came into a fortune large enough to save him from the trouble of having to earn a living for the rest of his life, but it was also of a piece with his conviction that the most despicable thing about human beings is their predisposition to an overwrought sense of self, the most admirable their capacity to subordinate their own interests to those of other human beings. In addition—and this leads to the second reason that James's work sunk so rapidly out of sight—there was about virtually all of his writing an elusive, almost ineffable, quality that resisted any sort of systematic intellectual exposition. To put the matter as simply as possible, it was not that James didn't mean every word that he wrote; only that, by his own admission, he could never quite express exactly what he meant.

One can lay part of the blame for his ineffectuality as a writer on the deficiencies of his chosen medium—as Emerson had realized almost a generation before, theology was no longer the intellectual idiom in which an influential number of the members of the educated classes chose to do their most serious thinking—and the limitations of his own verbal gifts. But it was not that James couldn't marshal words to do the bidding of his mind. The real problem was that he lacked conviction that his mind could fully encompass and express his truth. With at least one part of himself, James knew that his truth was deeper than his philosophy, perhaps deeper than any philosophy, and that the only way to bridge this gap was with the elasticity of his own religious sensibility, the personal authority of his own faith. But this amounted to believing that, and thus writing as though, his theories were secondary to his truths and that, as William had said of those same "truths" after the elder James's death, they could not be separated from his life. One was therefore left with a writer whose integrity of being was more evident than the integrity of his ideas. Or as his son Henry put it in his own autobiography, "His tone . . . always so effectually looks out, and the living parts of him so singularly hung together, that one may fairly say his philosophy *was* his tone." [9]

In any case, the reason why his books failed either to attract or to hold any very large audience is clear enough. Being more of an expression of sentiment than of science, of convinced feeling than of clear-headed reasoning, his writing was difficult to place. Systematic theology written in the moralistic tone of the familiar essay is not quite what he produced or aimed at, but it was what much of his writing sounded like, and the results were almost foreordained. As one who according to his children was better at living the truth he wanted to express than at expressing the truth he lived, James did not quite seem to fit anywhere and so was dismissed by some of his contemporaries and neglected by most of the rest.

Yet to anyone who actually takes the time to read him carefully, it becomes clear that the elder James appeared, and continues to appear, out of step with his time only because in certain ways he lived, to be sure, at an odd angle, so far in advance of it. His strong association with the progressives who came after him, with their belief in a reformation of society based on the social rebirth of the individual, is one sign of this. But a much more telling indication of James's prescience, even of his moral and theological prescience, is revealed by his perception of the kind of criticism to which this same secularized religion of the progressives would become vulnerable—as when their visionary dream of society gave way to a kind of benevolent social idealism that was then exposed two generations later by a group of thinkers following the lead of Reinhold Niebuhr and other so-called neoorthodox theologians as but another mask of egoistic self-approbation.

In this James was at one with all the great Christian critics of Christianity, believing that human beings are most culpable precisely when they deem themselves most virtuous, that the greatest "spiritual evil," as James put it for himself, is always committed in the shadow of the highest religious ideals, in short, that moralism is an expression of self-love. But James was also convinced that what in the twentieth century would come to be known in Protestant circles as the neoorthodox critique of theological liberalism—for that is what this perception amounts to—must be complemented by a neoliberal critique of theological neoorthodoxy, or at least of its doctrine of God and its view of creation.

That is, James shared with the process theologians of the present, who take their inspiration from the work of Alfred North Whitehead, and with their pragmatist precursors in philosophy, like his son, William, or, later, John Dewey, an aversion to any conception of the Deity that stressed the neo-Reformation themes popularized in the first half of the twentieth century by theologians such as Karl Barth and the Niebuhr brothers. Their view of a God who is "wholly other," unchanging, and impassible but for that single moment in history when, in the person of his son Jesus Christ, he is said to have undertaken a divine rescue operation to save a species of creatures who now bear almost no moral trace of the image in which they were made and who are absolutely undeserving of this unmerited act of grace—this conception was anathema to the liberal, indeed, the pragmatic side of Henry, Senior's theology. His reasoning was that if God is not closer to human beings than they are to themselves and, consequently, if he does not in some sense need them as much as they need him—in fact, if God did not take his stripes with the rest of us—then the religion of the Incarnation made no sense and he wanted no part of it.

But this rejection of the Reformed—or, as James experienced it, the High Presbyterian—image of God possessed various consequences for one's conception of life as well. As William James would spend much of his philosophical energy attempting to explain in pragmatist terms, life lived in the face of such a theological rejection becomes intelligible only in terms of the trope of process, nature becomes illustrative of change, and history displays, or at least can display, some measure of creative progress. Otherwise, to paraphrase one of James's more colorful figures, the Deity is reduced to some immense duck who continues to emit the same unchanged and unimproved quack that he first uttered on the day he was born!

The elder James was actually more theologically sanguine. At only small risk to the great Antiochean tradition of Christology from which he consciously or unconsciously drew, James conceived of God as the perfect man, as what is divine in our natural humanity when that humanity achieves its full realization, and he made no bones about what this amounts to in terms of traditional Christian conceptions of divinity. As he put it with characteristic verve and belligerence in the advertisement to what, paradoxically, is one of his more thickly metaphysical volumes:

I find myself incapable, for my part, of honoring the pretension of any deity to my allegiance, who insists upon standing eternally aloof from my own nature, and by that fact confesses himself personally incommensurate and unsympathetic with my basest, most sensuous, and controlling personal necessities. It is an easy enough thing to find a holiday God who is all too selfish to be touched by the infirmities of his own creatures—a God, for example, who has naught to do but receive assiduous court for a work of creation done myriads of ages ago, and which is reputed to have cost him in the doing neither pains nor patience, neither affection nor thought, but simply the utterance of a dramatic word; and who is willing, accordingly, to accept our decorous Sunday homage in ample quittance of obligations so unconsciously incurred on our part, so lightly rendered and so penuriously sanctioned on his. Every sect, every nature, every family almost, offers some pet idol of this description to your worship. But I am free to confess that I have long outgrown this loutish conception of deity. I can no longer bring myself to adore a characteristic activity in the God of my worship, which falls below the secular average of human character. In fact, what I crave with all my heart and understanding— what my very flesh and bones cry out for—is no longer a Sunday but a weekday divinity, a working God, grim with the dust and sweat of our most carnal appetites and passions, and bent, not for an instant upon inflating our worthless pietistic righteousness, but upon the patient, toilsome, thorough cleansing of our physical and moral existence from the odious defilement it has contracted, until we each and all present at last in body and mind the deathless effigy of his own uncreated loveliness.[10]

This inversion, almost deflation, of theological expectations— God's omnipotence revealed in his capacity for dependence, his sublimnity in his appetite for the ordinary, his reality in his realism—was not exactly peculiar to James alone—Emerson proved himself a master of such inversions in "The Divinity School Address"—but he was almost alone among his contemporaries in finding it so central to Christianity. It was consistent with what, in *Christianity the Logic of Creation*, he found so distinctive about the doctrine of the Incarnation itself. Creation required a divine incarnation, James reasoned against the traditional Christian explanation, not because human beings would recognize the truth in no other way—clothed, as it were, in the incarnate form of their own humanity—but because when God took upon himself the abject form of another human being, he reversed all of humanity's expectations about the incarnate form in which the divine life should manifest itself.

Even more startling was James's answer to the question of who the divine man, the incarnate one, really is. He is none other, as James said in "A Scientific Statement of the Christian Doctrine of the Lord, or Divine Man," than the artist or aesthetic person. James did not restrict the definition of the artist to those who pursue specific vocations such as painting, music, or sculpture, but extended it to all persons who, whatever their specific vocation, fulfill it by following the inspiration of their own individual genius, the inward compulsions of their own nature, quite apart from any sense of physical necessity or social responsibility. This was not to argue that artistic creation is inconsistent with duty or necessity or even that it is incompatible with promoting one's physical and social well-being. It was merely to state that when the Artist turns such interests into the animating principles of his or her work, he or she sinks to the level of the artisan or craftsman. Where the first obeys only his or her own internal taste or attraction, the second is controlled strictly by physical necessities or social obligations. "The artisan," James claims, "seeks to gain a livelihood or secure an honorable name. He works for bread, or for fame, or for both together. The Artist abhors these ends, and works only to show forth that immortal beauty whose presence constitutes his [or her] inmost soul." [11]

It is worth speculating whether this distinction between the artist and the artisan would have appeared so natural to James—a century later Dewey was eager to soften it in *Art as Experience*—if, instead of deriving his living from the beneficence of a comfortable inheritance, he had been compelled to get it, to borrow one of most arresting images for the industry of God, by the "sweat of [his] brow." But if the distinction carried with it certain implications to which James may have been insensitive, it also registered an insight almost nowhere else appreciated in nineteenth-century Protestant reflection and only infrequently acknowledged in nineteenth-century aesthetic thought. This was the realization that in subordinating "the service of nature and society" to "the obedience of their own private attractions," true Artists overcome—actually dismantle—the traditional cultural hierarchy of functions and forms. In other words, the Artist is not tethered to any particular technical vocation, be it painter, musician, poet, or sculptor, or obliged to subscribe to a set of inherited generic conventions.

The humblest theatre of action furnishes him a platform. I pay my waiter so much a day for putting my dinner on the table. But he performs his function in a way so entirely *sui generis,* with so exquisite an attention to beauty in all the details of the service, with so symmetrical an arrangement of the dishes, and so even an adjustment of everything to its place, and to the hand that needs it, as to shed an almost epic dignity upon the repast, and convert one's habitual "grace before meat" into a spontaneous tribute, instinct with a divine recognition.

The charm in this case is not that the dinner is all before me, where the man is bound by his wages to place it. This every waiter I have had has done just as punctually as this man, which attests that in doing it, he is not thinking either of earning his wages or doing his duty toward me, but only of satisfying his own conception of beauty with the resources before him. The consequence is that the pecuniary relation between us emerges in a higher one. He is no longer the menial, but my equal or superior, so that I have felt, when enter- taining doctors of divinity and law, and discoursing about divine mysteries, that a living epistle was circulating behind our backs, and quietly ministering to our wants, far more apocalyptic to an enlightened eye than any yet con- tained in books.[12]

By discovering the Artist in the work of the waiter, James is here not only dissolving the relationship between art and life but also resi- tuating the operations of spirit in the materials of the mundane. Any activity can be invested with "the divine life," as James uses the phrase, so long as it is the work of one who, like the Artist, "acts of himself, or finds the object of his action always *within* his own subjectivity." This is what James calls "the only adequate image of God in nature," the signature of the "Divine Man."[13]

★

In this radical aestheticization of the Christian meaning of incarnation and redemption, James creates the impression that he was very nearly determined to throw over the entire theological inheritance of Calvin- ism. But this would be a misrepresentation. For however much his idealization of the artist and the practice of art reflects the earlier con- cerns of romantic philosophers and artists and foreshadows the way in which his son, Henry, in particular, would redefine, in the title of John Dewey's most important book, "art as experience," the elder James was not prepared to relinquish the entire Protestant legacy of the past. While he anticipated various theological and, more important, philo- sophical developments of the future, he was also concerned to preserve and transmit central strains of the Calvinist tradition—so much so, in fact, that he often struck many of his liberated contemporaries as a holdover from some earlier age of faith.

It is no accident, for example, that comparatively early in his career James confided in a letter to Emerson a belief, recently revived by certain evangelical Christian scholars, that "Jonathan Edwards *redivivus* in true blue" would still make the best reconciler and critic of the kind of philosophy that has grown up since the middle of the eighteenth century.[14] However, James was never committed to repossessing the Calvinist legacy so much as humanizing it. What he wished to preserve was what was still usable, religiously and culturally, in its formulations. This amounted to retaining its sense of how God is glorified in the dependence of his creatures, stressing its belief in the inevitability and universality of evil, and reemphasizing its conviction of the need for deliverance and new life—but not at the expense of allowing the doctrine of God's sovereignty, as Calvinism called it, from obscuring the fact of God's immanence. James was not willing to sacrifice a sense of God's accessibility for the sake of maintaining a sense of his aseity.

These convictions necessarily involved some basic modifications of the traditional Calvinist scheme of salvation—the philosopher Ralph Barton Perry later went so far as to describe it as a complete inversion. Where Calvinism traditionally assumed, for example, that human beings fall collectively, as a result of the natural moral imperfection of human nature as such, and then are saved only as God elects certain individuals who through faith have exhibited their readiness to receive what they cannot earn or secure for themselves, James postulated, to the contrary, that human beings fall individually, precisely as a result of believing themselves personally meritorious of divine solicitude, and then are saved only when they relinquish their pride in themselves and learn to identify their own lives with the collective nature and destiny of their fellow and sister human beings.[15]

This was probably the most profound of James's revisions of cherished Calvinist assumptions but scarcely the most notorious. The most notorious of his proposals for a renovation of the orthodox Protestant scheme of salvation—though one in which he unknowingly received tacit support from certain of his contemporaries[16]—was probably his positive or affirmative interpretation of the Fall. According to the view he put forward so emphatically in *The Nature of Evil* and several of his other books, the Fall was the result of neither some accident or unintentional mistake on God's part, as certain liberal Unitarians proposed, nor of some primal act of disobedience on the part of human beings, as traditional Calvinists were want to claim. It was rather a necessary and wholly salutary step in God's beneficent plan for human redemption. In awakening Adam from his state of sensuous slumber to a knowledge of good and evil, Eve had merely precipitated in him the development of that moral conscience identical with conscious selfhood, or, as James termed it, "proprium," which he considered the requisite stepping-stone to salvation. Without a moral understanding of the conscious sense of themselves, human beings could not discover what a spiritual liability that sense was, or how they could obtain new life not through repentance merely but only by committing what James called "moral suicide, or inward death to self in all its forms." [17]

Yet this, in turn, implied another departure from traditional formulas of regeneration. Moral suicide was prepared for, and then undertaken, "not by learning" but "only," as James suggested in a letter to one of his favorite female correspondents, "by *unlearning*." [18] The actual process of rebirth, whereby the self is delivered into full awareness of its divine sociality, could only be conceived, to quote from the same letter, as a kind of "demolition" or "undoing": as a process of decreation leading to that moment of spiritual awakening when the self discovers "his object a *life* within him, and no longer a *law* without him." [19] Human redemption still implied reunion with God, but the spatial conception of this transaction had changed. Human beings are no longer lifted up and out of themselves into communion with a deity who exists, as it were, above and beyond them, but are rather lifted out of themselves and into a relation with the neighbor, the social other, for communion with a deity who exists nowhere more completely than in the universally human. Furthermore, on this view the nature of the atonement changes. Jesus Christ is no longer construed as a substitutionary victim compelled to satisfy the affront made to God's own sense of honor by his creatures' original act of disobedience, nor is he conceived as a propitiatory sacrifice intended to mitigate the punishment human beings rightly deserve for having betrayed the demands of a just God. Jesus is conceived rather as a representative figure who demonstrated that the only way to achieve reunion with the Creator is by dying to self and becoming one with humankind.

The result of all this theological revisioning was a new conception of the purpose of creation and a severely restricted view of the role of the church and of organized religion in general. The elder James could still say with Jonathan Edwards that man's dependence is God's glory, but only after having dissociated the word "dependence" from all connotations of the word "subservience" and then by resituating the realm of God's most creative activity in the center of the human soul itself.

In James's vision of things, God is glorified in the act of completely emptying himself into the being of another, in the act of giving up all special claims to himself. He relinquishes the opportunity of remaining what human beings recognize as God for the sake of realizing himself in the universal humanity of his creatures. Thus Incarnation becomes the chief aim of creation itself.

In this scheme of things the church's role is radically reduced to what James called, in *Substance and Shadow,* a wholly purgative rather than a nutritive function. At best, organized religion is no more than a way station on the road to salvation, an institution whose sole purpose is to awaken in its followers a sense of death rather than life, "to reveal to them the dearth of life they have in themselves as morally and finitely constituted, in order to prepare them for that fullness of life they shall find in each other as socially constituted." [20] James could thus conclude, and not without a certain measure of biblical precedent, that "the sinner . . . and not the sin is as yet God's best achievement in human nature: when this achievement becomes somewhat universalized by society itself coming to the consciousness of its shortcomings, we shall at last have a righteousness and a health and wealth which shall never pass away, which shall be for the first time on earth Divine and permanent." [21]

This last observation may serve as a way of gauging part of James's relationship to his age. Coming to maturity just as the transcendental era was becoming ascendant in its small sphere of American cultural experience, James could hardly avoid participating in what F. O. Matthiessen, following William Ellery Canning, termed "the moral argument against Calvinism." [22] Yet what differentiates James from Emerson, and especially from the company of humanitarian optimists and perfectionists that Emerson had trailing after him, is that while willing to dispense with many of the outmoded and (to him) repellent formulations of Calvinism, he was not willing to dispense with all the substance underneath. Even if James detested the "new Divinity men" just as much as any good transcendentalist did—probably not realizing the degree to which he shared common cause with them on several crucial issues—James was never out to found a new religion but only to pump fresh life into an old one. And in this, it might be observed, his relation both to Calvinism and to his age bore a strong resemblance to that of another native New Yorker, the novelist Herman Melville. Each man rebelled violently against what they perceived as the rigid and rigidifying letter of New England Calvinism, but both retained a vital respect for the spirit underlying some of it. Yet this ambivalence was more than their countrymen could easily comprehend. Melville's novels were quickly relegated to the status of children's books or travel narratives, while James's volumes, when they were read at all, were typically regarded merely as footnotes to Swedenborg and mysticism generally. In Melville's case, this oversight has, of course, been handsomely rectified; in James's, it has yet even to be widely noticed.

But the affinities between James and Melville do not stop with the fate that befell their immediate reputations. If both writers suffered neglect because of their ambivalent feelings toward the unconscious metaphysic that their culture was attempting to cast off, so in almost equal measure both found their chief spiritual resource in the new irregular metaphysic that their age was attempting to put in its place. For what do all of James's books represent, from *Moralism and Christianity* to *Society the Redeemed Form of Man,* if not an exhaustive—and, at times, exhausting—attempt to recuperate that democratic conception of the Deity which Melville articulated in the second of his "Knights and Squires" chapters in *Moby-Dick:* of "the great God absolute! The centre and circumference of all democracy!," as Melville called him, whose "omnipresence" is "our divine equality"? This is clearly not to suggest that James derived from Melville himself any of his own ideas about "the just spirit of Equality" who, as the novelist went on to say, "hast spread one royal mantle of humanity over all my kind!" It is simply to reiterate that the sole object of James's entire lifework, like the implicit aim of Melville's passage, was to fuse Christianity and democracy into what might be called a revisioned and revisionary religion of "the kingly commons," and that this religion of "the kingly commons," even if Melville's faith in it was never secure, required a displacement of the old Calvinistic sense of the God above by a more democratic and egalitarian sense of the God within and without.

In this, it need hardly be added, James and Melville were scarcely alone. One sees intimations and foreshadowings of this marked shift in theological emphasis as early as William Ellery Channing, and by the time one reaches Emerson one finds it realized in a form that would later typify much of the progressive social and political thought of the nineteenth century. But where Emerson subordinated the community to the individual and then raised the individual to a level coequal with God, James and Melville held onto the older and wider perception that the individual finds his completion only in relation to others. Divinity was thus discoverable neither in the Oversoul, nor in the infinitude of the private man, but rather, if anywhere, in that "abounding dignity," as Melville referred to it, which is potentially common to the humanity of all persons.

James's traffic with egalitarian ideas was a long one. Owing much to the temper of the times when he first began writing—the late 1840s and early 1850s was the era of Brook Farm, the *Harbinger* magazine, increased abolitionist agitation, Fourierist and Owenite experiments—together with the loosely political cast of his own mind—after all, he described the unreconstructed Calvinist God as a political tyrant and rejected his rule as a form of social despotism—James was much vexed with questions of human freedom and, particularly, of equality. Not that he could understand either issue independent of his emerging theology. Socialism was to be preferred to civilization because, as he stated in an address in 1849, when understood from what he called, in a letter to Emerson, "the highest point of view," it was able to render, as civilization could not, a kind of unconscious service to the divine life in human beings. Something like this same argument found its way into his writing a year later when he described the uses of democracy as largely, and not incidentally, propaedeutic: "to prepare the way," as he puts it, "by a disorganization of the political life of men, for their perfect society or fellowship." [23]

But the full extent of James's democratic sentiments cannot be measured until the outbreak of the Civil War when he was asked only three months later to deliver the Independence Day Address for the residents of Newport, Rhode Island. The subject of his talk was "The Social Significance of Our Institutions" and his inevitable text the Declaration of Independence. James wasted little time in moving directly into its great statement about equality which, as he pointed out, did not assert that human beings are born equal but only that they were created equal. This then enabled him to argue that all individuals are worthy of each other's respect not because of their personal differences, which are, of course, plentiful and obvious, but chiefly because of their common needs, wants, and affections. But James's real aim was to turn the Declaration's reaffirmation of human solidarity back on the question of what was at stake in the War between the States.

Assuming that the Civil War was precipitated by a dispute over slavery, James refused to believe the eruption of hostilities was an accident. There was enough of a Presbyterian in James, or at any rate a predestinarian, to believe that this conflict had to have a cause and that its cause could be no other than the expanding social consciousness of the race, that is, an increased sense of the breadth and depth of human unity. Viewed in this light, the war possessed a religious purpose that transcended the abyss of suffering it caused on both sides, and James minced no words about its meaning. Any institution, or party, or participant opposed to the increasing realization of this sense of solidarity for which the war was fought not only constituted an offense to God but also worked to diminish the life of all human beings everywhere.

★

James came to this fusion of Christian and democratic principles by a route that was uniquely his own. Apart from such negative factors as his rebellion against the oppressive Presbyterianism of his father and then, later, his encounter with a mixture of biblical conservatism and strict Reformed confessionalism as a student at Princeton Theological Seminary, James seems to have been influenced most explicitly by three interrelated currents of thought. The first derived from the writings of Robert Sandeman, a Scottish cleric strongly influenced by the reform movement initiated by his father-in-law, the Reverend Joseph Glas. This was a movement that, in addition to recovering certain apostolic practices such as the kiss of peace and the weekly celebration of the Eucharist as a common meal or love feast, sought to reemphasize the Reformation doctrine of justification by faith rather than works and to democratize church administration not only by making the offices of bishop, pastor, and elder elective rather than appointive but also by abolishing all qualifications to such offices on the basis of education or lay occupation. However, Sandeman carried several of these reformist impulses much further. Opposed to the works–righteousness basis of every form of moralism, he was even more adamantly insistent than his father-in-law that justification has nothing to do with good works, with meritorious behavior, and is based solely on the gracious and completely unmerited operations of faith. He also laid particularly strong emphasis on the democratic solidarity of primitive Christianity.

James was responsive to both the antinomian and the egalitarian dimensions of Sandeman's ideas, and in 1838 he brought out an edition of Sandeman's 1757 *Letters on Theron and Aspasio,* introducing it with an unsigned two-page preface. But Sandeman's influence on James's later thought was comparatively slight when compared with the more massive impact of the writings of Emmanuel Swedenborg and Charles Fourier. Of the two, James's exposure to Swedenborg was clearly the more consequential, even if its occurrence was more accidental.

James's initial introduction to the writings of Swedenborg probably occurred as the result of an article published in the *Monthly Magazine* in 1841 by a young English physician named J. J. Garth Wilkinson. Wilkinson was a recent convert to Swedenborgianism who in later years, as Swedenborg's editor, translator, and interpreter, was to become one of James's closest intellectual friends and the namesake of his third child. But his deeper introduction to Swedenborg didn't take place for another five years and turned out to be more fortuitous still. Precipitated by an emotional and spiritual crisis that had already been going on for some time, Swedenborg's writings actually enabled James to surmount it. The circumstances attending that crisis, and the part which Swedenborg's writings played in helping to resolve it, are among the better-known facts of the James family history. What is less well known is that the crisis itself was strangely reexperienced, in forms appropriate to their own lives, by three of James's children, William, Alice, and Henry, Junior, who subsequently inscribed it as a paradigmatic event in the particular history each of them wrote about themselves.[24]

The elder James's spiritual crisis commenced during one of the family's extended periods of residence in England when James was comfortably settled, along with his wife, Mary, and their first two children, William and Henry, in a small house near the Great Park of Windsor. In the intervening years between his withdrawal from Princeton Theological Seminary and his establishment in England, James had continued to work away in leisured independence on various metaphysical questions that had vexed him almost from the time of late adolescence—the reconciliation of science and religion, the question of nature's meaning and unity, the purpose of creation as revealed by a mystical and symbolic interpretation of the Book of Genesis. James had begun to suspect that he was on the brink of some major, new theological discoveries, but all he possessed to show for his efforts was the mountainous pile of manuscripts on his desk. Still, he had excellent reasons to feel pleased with himself just then. His health was good, his circumstances were congenial, his family was coming along grandly, and he was excited about his work.

But then late one afternoon in May of 1844, his composure and sense of well-being completely, and for no apparent reason, abandoned him. As he lingered by himself at the dinner table enjoying the glowing coals in the grate, which seemed to reflect back to him his sense of self-contentment, he suddenly and inexplicably found himself confronting an invisible, almost inconceivable terror. It was as though some deathly presence were squatting at the other end of the table, "raying out from his fetid personality influences fatal to life." In the space of a few seconds James found himself reduced "from a state of firm vigorous joyful manhood to one of almost helpless infancy."[25] It was all he could do to keep from bolting out of the room, and when he finally did quit his chair to seek the protective comfort of his wife's presence, his sense of self had been utterly shattered. As he interpreted it many years later:

It was impossible for me . . . to hold this audacious faith in selfhood any longer. When I sat down to dinner on that memorable chilly afternoon in Windsor, I held it serene and unweakened by the faintest breath of doubt. Before I rose from the table it had inwardly shrivelled to a cinder. One moment I devoutly thanked god for the inappreciable boon of selfhood; the next that inappreciable boon seemed to me the one thing damnable on earth, seemed a literary nest of hell within my own entrails.[26]

James's collapse was no doubt owing partly to physical and spiritual exhaustion which left him vulnerable to a severe attack of depression. But he was later to insist that it was actually the result of something else, something that could only be understood as part of God's plan for his life and that provided direct evidence of his own spiritual regeneration. Intelligence concerning these last matters came quite by accident, as a result of James's wholly fortuitous meeting with a certain Mrs. Chichester who lived in the neighborhood of one of the water cures that James had frequented over the last two years in an effort to work himself out of his depression. When Mrs. Chichester learned of the circumstances of his collapse, she informed him that he was probably suffering from the experience of what she termed a "vastation." This was the name Swedenborg gave to a preliminary stage in the process of spiritual redemption, a stage which if rightly appreciated and cultivated could lead through awakening, purgation, and illumination to that rebirth of the individual in all his or her "Divine Natural Humanity" which for Swedenborg was the sole purpose and destiny of Creation itself. James reported that he needed to hear little more. Despite medical warnings about overtaxing himself, he rushed to London to purchase several of the master's volumes—he actually bought *Divine Wisdom* and *Love and Divine Providence*—and once he had opened them found himself enthralled:

I read from the first with palpitating interest. My heart divined, even before my intelligence was prepared to do justice to the books, the unequalled amount of truth to be found in them. . . . Imagine a subject of some petty despotism condemned to die, and with—what is more and worse—a sentiment of death pervading all his consciousness, lifted by a sudden miracle into felt harmony with universal man, and filled to the brim with the sentiment of indestructible life instead, and you will have a true picture of my emancipated condition.[27]

Almost before James had put these two volumes down, disputes were to arise over whether or not the Swedenborg he claims to have read bore any relation to the original. Thirty years of correspondence and close personal friendship could not convince Wilkinson that James and Swedenborg shared any other term in common but the notion of the "Divine Natural Humanity," though this remained a concept that from Wilkinson's orthodox point of view James didn't understand either. As Wilkinson remonstrated in a revealing letter written soon after his receipt of a copy of *Society the Redeemed Form of Man,*

Swedenborg's Divine Nature is Jehovah triumphant in Jesus Christ over his infirm humanity, and over all the hells which had access to it: transforming his natural into the Divine Nature. Swedenborg goes to this end, and to the consequences of a new and everlasting Church proceeding from this Divine Nature. Your Divine Natural, unless I misunderstand you, is diffused in all men, giving, or to give, them infinitude of some kind, and abolishing heavens and hells as mere preparations for the Godhead of Humanity. . . . And at last, the Christ Himself seems to disappear into Humanity, as God has disappeared into Christ; and Man is all in all.[28]

Wilkinson was shrewder than he knew, though for him the real danger was not so much the deification of human beings as the degradation of the church. What, in any case, Wilkinson could not accept was James's willingness to undercut the importance of the church as the New Jerusalem for the sake of identifying the Incarnation with humanity itself. But this, of course, is exactly what James intended. He was opposed to Christocentrism in theology for the same reason that he abhorred ecclesiasticism among Christians—not only because they both encouraged sectarianism and were therefore destructive of that sense of human solidarity that for him was the ground of all religious experience, but also because their inevitable claims to special favor, and their consequent promotion of distinctions between believer and nonbeliever, or elect and inelect, or the saved and the damned, served to encourage precisely that form of self-righteousness that, again for James, was the root of all evil.

It should come as no surprise that James found confirmation of these views in the final thinker who influenced him decisively during these early years. This was the social theorist, reformer, and utopian Charles Fourier. James had started reading Fourier while he was still recovering from his collapse in 1844, but he was quickly to find himself among a large and disparate company. By 1846 the Fourierist enthusiasm had swollen from a small group of disciples converted by Albert Brisbane four years earlier—George Ripley, Horace Greeley, and Parke Goodwin becoming the most famous American exponents—to a movement with approximately 200,000 followers. The popularity of Fourierism, however, was anything but an isolated phenomenon. Closely related in spirit to the idealist ethos of such sister phenomena as the Free Soil movement, the Owenite experiments, transcendentalism, and abolitionism, members of one group frequently belonged to, or were sympathetic with, several of the others. All partook of that reformist spirit, often strongly millennial in character, which swept across the northern part of the United States in the years following Jackson's presidency and which called for some great renovation in the social fabric of the nation.

Fourier was important because he offered a scientific blueprint for such a renovation. What he produced was a transcendental social science that served as a perfect complement to the spiritual science James had already acquired from Swedenborg. If Swedenborg had provided James with a way of understanding how the emerging social sentiment of the era, the new feeling of human fellowship, could be interpreted as evidence of God's redeeming and transforming work in the world, Fourier furnished a concrete outline of the way this new social sentiment might be actualized in the social order.

The only trouble with Fourier's recommendations for social reform is that they were based on the assumption of human innocence. Evil was due not to anything inherent in human nature itself, Fourier maintained, but solely to the restrictions that society had placed on it. Redesign society in such a way that those restrictions are removed, Fourier argued, and human beings, in their newly recovered spontaneity, will again be able to act in behalf of the good. James was prepared to be convinced, at least with part of himself. This was the iconoclastic side of himself that delighted in the role of the social nonconformist. "Make society do its duty to the individual," James declared in such a mood, "and the individual will be sure to do his duties to his society." [29] But with the other half of himself, the side that found the very thought of selfhood so problematic, James knew that this wouldn't do. The redemption of the individual, as of society, required something more profound than a readjustment of the social order; it required a rebirth and regeneration of the individual him- or herself as a social being.

*

James's repudiation of the idea of human innocence and his deepening appreciation of the extent of human culpability and interdependence can be discerned in his changing relations with two of his more famous correspondents and literary friends, Ralph Waldo Emerson and

Thomas Carlyle. James first met Emerson in the early spring of 1842 after James had attended one of Emerson's lectures in New York and invited him to call. James was immediately attracted to Emerson because of the spiritual heroism so evident in the older man's religious quest. Emerson struck James in much the same way that Hawthorne struck Melville: as one prepared to seek out the very reality of things with no regard for anything but the truth. Yet at the same time James was aware from the very beginning that Emerson's search was shadowed by the very things it glossed, and he spent much of their relationship trying to determine what they were.

At first James was merely troubled by the difficulty of drawing Emerson out, of dissociating the speaker who charmed with his words and uplifted by his example from the man who thought and questioned and felt. Emerson impressed him from first to last as a kind of divine presence who was so serenely composed within himself, and so magnanimous and tender in his relations with others, that it was all but impossible to get to, much less to get at, the sentient self underneath. James wanted to be instructed as well as inspired, to be challenged and also enlightened, to share Emerson's puzzlement along with his illumination, and on this score Emerson could not—or would not—help him. Emerson seemed temperamentally incapable of explanation, much less dispute, while James not only thrived on such things but also could not live without them.

As the years wore on, however, and the relations between them began, at least after the middle of the century, to cool, the problem ceased being merely temperamental and took on a moral dimension. Emerson was not only elusive but also evasive; he seemed blind, perhaps even willfully so, to the ethical ambiguity of his entire project. Unable to appreciate that the kind of self-consciousness he was always preaching was potentially evil as well as good, Emerson was always promoting as a cure for the human condition what James took to be part of the disease.

But the real question was whether Emerson's blindness on this point—his refusal to take into his purview any evidence supplied by consciousnesses other than his own—was not itself symptomatic. Was not Emerson's sublime indifference to any arguments that might challenge his position, and thus complicate his optimism, itself an expression of that very egotism whose evil was so pervasive elsewhere? If it were, James could not bring himself to hold Emerson personally accountable for it. Finding Emerson, as he put it in an unfinished essay entitled "Spiritual Creation," "fundamentally treacherous to civilization, without being at all aware himself of the fact," James excused this deficiency in his older friend as an aspect of his monumental moral innocence:

He appeared to me utterly unconscious of himself as either good or evil. He had no conscience, in fact, and lived by perception, which is an altogether lower or less spiritual faculty. The more universalized a man is by genius or natural birth, the less is he spiritually individualized, making up in breadth of endowment what he lacks in depth.[30]

This enabled Emerson to convey a sense of the infinite in the human precisely because he was so, at least self-consciously, selfless. But that selflessness in him, however inspiring, was a natural not an acquired gift and thus had little, finally, to do with the anthropological adventure to which the elder James imagined that the rest of humankind is committed. His son, William, noted the same distinction but described it in his own more pragmatic terms:

My father was a theologian of the "twice-born" type, an out-and-out Lutheran, who believed that the moral law existed solely to fill us with loathing for the idea of our own merits, and to make us turn to God's grace as our only opportunity. But God's grace, in Mr. James's system, was not for the individual in isolation: the sphere of redemption was *Society*. In a Society organized divinely our *natures* will not be altered, but our spontaneities, because they will then work harmoniously, will all work innocently, and the Kingdom of heaven will have come. With these ideas, Mr. James was both fascinated and baffled by his friend Emerson. The personal graces of the man seemed to prefigure the coming millennium, but the resolute individualism of his thought, and the way in which his imagination rested on superior personages, and on heroic anecdotes about them, as if these were creation's ultimates, set my father's philosophy at defiance. For him no man was superior to another in the final plan. Emerson would listen, I fancy, as if charmed, to James's talk of the "divine natural Humanity," but he would never *subscribe;* and this, from one whose native gifts were so suggestive of that same Humanity, was disappointing. Emerson, in short, was a "once-born" man; he lived in moral distinctions, and recognized no need of a redemptive process.[31]

The same could surely not be said for James's other friend. James first met Carlyle in 1843 and then resumed their acquaintance during another visit to England in 1855. Carlyle supplied precisely what Emerson seemed to lack: a mind that had reasons for everything and a crotchety skepticism about the sincerity of all human motives which could never be satisfied with anything but a second spiritual birth. Carlyle fed James's love for argument and contentiousness but went beyond them to a cynicism so pervasive and relentless that it hardly left room for anything else. James had to admire and respect Carlyle for the trenchancy of his social criticism, for his deadly aim in unmasking every form of human folly, but he could not follow Carlyle when the latter used his eye for human weakness to support his pessimism about the whole human race. On occasion James was able to assume a light attitude of amused disapproval toward Carlyle, as when he referred to him in a letter to Emerson as "the same old sausage, fizzing and sputtering in his own grease." [32] But he was also capable of drawing very accurate aim himself, as when he noted in the "Personal Recollections" he published after Carlyle's death the way Carlyle's cynicism could turn splenetic:

His own intellectual life consisted so much in bemoaning the vices of his race, or drew such inspiration from despair, that he could not help regarding a man with contempt the instant he found him reconciled to the course of history. Pity is the highest style of intercourse he allowed himself with his kind. . . . "Poor John Sterling," he used always to say; "poor John Mill, poor Frederick Maurice, poor Neuberg, poor Arthur Helps, poor little Browning, poor little Lewes" and so on; as if the temple of his friendship were a hospital, and all its inmates scrofulous or paralytic. [33]

James could enjoy Carlyle's declamations but not his wholesale condemnation. Though he himself frequently used the abstract as a kind of club to beat the actual over the head, he could still never forget, as Ralph Barton Perry has said, "the Man in men." [34] Nor, for that matter, could he overlook the element of good amid all the ill. James was fundamentally reconciled to the divine Providence which guides human affairs in a way that Carlyle clearly was not, and this made all the difference. However pointed and stinging his criticism of his fellows, and however frontal and slashing his assaults on various ideas, James's invective was never cruel or sardonic. For all of his noisy thunder and bombast, there was always a generous dose of the quixotic knight-errant about him, one who, whether he knows it or not, inevitably ennobles both himself and his windmills by tilting at them with such gusto.

This was reason enough for many people to cultivate James's friendship, his society, despite their lack of sympathy with or interest in his ideas. There was an elemental humanity in him very like the substance he kept imputing to his fellow mortals. Even when he baited Bronson Alcott for being "an egg half hatched . . . [with] the shells . . . yet sticking about [his] head," [35] or railed against a conception of the Deity as absolute, irrelative, and unconditionally perfect, on the grounds that "any mother who suckles her babe upon her own breast, any bitch in fact who litters her periodical brood of pups, presents to my imagination a vastly nearer and sweeter Divine charm," [36] there was a brightness, a color, a robust vigor to his polemics which, however unfortunate his tendency to use figures of speech disparaging to women, tempered censure with concern, judgment with humor. "To exalt humble and abase proud things was ever the darling sport of his conversation," his son William reported, "which, when he was in the *abasing* mood, often startled the good people of Boston, who did not know him well enough to see the endlessly genial and humane intuition from which the whole mood flowed." [37] Yet genial and humane the intuition was, because James seemed to embody in himself what he imputed to his God: a sense of insufficiency rather than self-sufficiency that sprang from his intuitive grasp of the fact that human beings, like God, are incapable of realizing themselves except in others.

★

It was this singular unity of sensibility in their father—what Henry, Junior, described as "a passion peculiarly his own" by which he "kept together his stream of thought, however transcendent, and the stream of life, however humanized" [38]—that so impressed his two sons when they looked back upon his life and that partially accounts for the surprisingly strong impact he was to have on them both long after he was dead. Indeed, it would not be too much to say that, while James made little impression on his contemporaries in either the world of letters or the religious community (the two, of course, being throughout much of the nineteenth century something of the same), he still left an enormous and as yet insufficiently appreciated imprint on American culture. That imprint came most directly by way of the influence of his two eldest sons who subsequently divided between them so much of the intellectual and spiritual heritage of the nineteenth century that was passed on to the twentieth. But thanks to the labors of Leon Edel, Ruth Yeazell, and Jean Strouse, we can no longer overlook the contribution Henry, Senior's daughter Alice made to this process. [39] For if Alice James never managed to develop a new way of thinking that, like pragmatism, encompasses the ineffable and the mysterious within rather than beyond experience precisely where it meets the needs of the heart, she nonetheless defined in her remarkable *Diary* what in moral terms this new mode of reflection, developed in their different ways by her two older brothers, amounted to.

Alice's *Diary* portrays the pragmatist outlook as a strategy for finding one's bearings in the face of "the common lot of pain and sorrow" where, as she puts it, "the only thing which survives is the resistance we bring to life and not the strain life brings to us." [40] This was Alice sounding like William, the William who could take questionable ad-

vantage of her life of infirmity by drawing, as she must have sus-
pected, certain of his richest insights in his paper on "The Hidden
Self" from her own history of affliction.[41] But Alice could also span
what has too often felt like a gulf in American cultural history by
sounding instead exactly like her brother Henry:

> How it fills one with wonder to see people old eno' to have stored experience
> never apparently suspecting that of all the arts the art of living is the most
> exquisite and rewarding and that it is not brought to perfection by walling in
> disabilities, ceaseless plaints of the machinery of life and the especial tasks
> fallen to their lot. The paralytic on his couch can have if he wants them wider
> experiences than Stanley slaughtering savages, the two roomed cottage may
> enclose an infinitely richer, sweeter domestic harmony than the palace; and the
> peaceful cotton-spinner win victories beside which those of the reverberating
> general are dust and ashes—let us not waste then the sacred fire and wear away
> the tissues in the vulgar pursuit of what others have and we have not; admit-
> ting defeat isn't the way to conquer and from every failure imperishable expe-
> rience survives.[42]

How much of the legacy of pragmatism seems to be here, interestingly enough in intonations as reminiscent of Emerson as of brother
Henry! The notion of living as an art to which we bring aesthetic expectations that can only be measured by a moral standard; the sense
that the near and the common are as richly endowed with spiritual
possibility as the distant and the exotic; the conviction that some of
life's highest rewards come from the enriching of experience and not
from its displacement or translation into something else like posses-
sions or power; the belief that the goods of life survive nowhere else
but in the imagination and the memory, which need no transempirical
support to be maintained, as William said in a famous formulation, but
possess in their own right, as every American author from Nathaniel
Hawthorne to William Faulkner and Toni Morrison has dramatized,
"a concatenated or continuous structure"[43]—this could serve as at least
a partial description of the whole pragmatist tradition in American letters.[44]

But if the tone here is one that Henry, Junior, shares with Emerson
and Alice shared with both, the underlying inspiration for this passage
comes from Alice's absorption of the conversation of her father. Not
that Alice didn't "wonder at Father's fulminations against what seemed
so extinct"; they may have seemed like "ugly things" in her youth, but
what struck her as an adult was their undreamt-of "vitality."[45] And
nothing quickened her sense of repulsion more vigorously than the
spectacle of a religion "imposed from without" whose virtue was
"taught, not as a measure of self respect but as a means of propitiating

a repulsive, vainglorious, grasping deity."[46] In place of a religion that was "the spontaneous inspiration of an aspiring soul," she regrettably found available for her own comfort, and in terms that almost exactly echo her father's, something like the direct opposite:

A God with fixed and rigid outlines to be worshipped within a prescribed and strictly formal ritual, not a Deity that shapes himself from moment to moment to the need of the votary whose bosom glows with the living, ever clearer knowledge of divine things. A faith propped up by a resounding rhetoric descended from the ages, and by the vain repetitions of men; not a faith which is the sacred secret of every soul within which it springs impregnable, whose communion is the common joys and sorrows, the simple sights and sounds, and whose ritual shrouds itself from vulgar speculation in the individual mystery.[47]

If the elder James could not have registered this spiritual complaint more affectingly, it is important to understand exactly what is being expressed. Alice is not merely decrying the terms in which contemporary religion offers an object for human worship; she is also converting downward that faith in what constitutes human solidarity which her father passed on not only to her but also, to be sure in quite different ways, to her two more famous siblings.

★

This is a large claim and may on first hearing sound exaggerated. After all, did not William differentiate himself from his father quite explicitly when he pointed out, in his introduction to *The Literary Remains,* that the elder James was a philosophical and theological monist who would brook no compromise with ethical and philosophical pluralists like himself? And did not Henry then confess in his turn, in a letter acknowledging receipt of this volume, that despite all his love and admiration for his father's person, he could never make head nor tail of his ideas? Indeed, did not Henry admit that when his exposure to his father's system of reflection was most intense, he was "converted" to "a total otherness of contemplation"?[48] The answer is obvious, but there is equally persuasive counterevidence on the other side of this issue, beginning with the letter William wrote to his father four days before his death. This is the letter in which he conceded that no matter how different their expressions of it, he derived virtually the whole of his intellectual life from the elder James.[49] Or, again, one could cite the comment that Henry, Junior, made thirty years later in *Notes of a Son and Brother,* where he suggests that none of the children could really escape being affected by "Father's Ideas," as Henry, Senior's wife called them, just because their "quality of intellectual passion," their "force of cogitation and aspiration" constituted so large a part of the "daily medium" and contributed to "the explanation both of a thousand surface incoherences and a thousand felt felicities." [50]

Yet the question of influence cannot be resolved through personal testimony of this kind. The process of its occurrence is always more subtle and direct. The elder James himself described its more probable form of operation among the members of his household when he observed, in a letter to Emerson, "that a vital truth can never be transferred from one mind to another, because life alone appreciates it. The most one can do for another is to plant the rude formula of such truth in his memory, leaving his own spiritual chemistry to set free the germs whenever the demands of his life exact it." [51] The rude formulas of their father's truth, his ideas, clearly made comparatively little impression on William and Henry (though more on William than on Henry), either when those ideas were first uttered in their presence or years later when both men tried to remember them. It was the germs of "vital truth" that got transmitted, but these were not set free until their own individual lives demanded it, and they were then developed only as the "spiritual chemistry" of their differing natures permitted it. Henry, Junior's trust in moments of vision and his equally strong interest in the sensuous or felt qualities of thought, no less than his intense absorption with the sin of self-culture and his moral emphasis on the virtue of self-denial and the horror of self-withholding; William's fascination with the psychology of healthy- and morbid-mindedness and his emphasis on spiritual processes of change and growth, no less than his firm insistence on having a say about the deepest reasons of the universe and his criticism of the blindness human beings practice on one another—all show the unmistakable influence of their father, even though both men could find support for their views in other sources as well.

But evidence of a paternal legacy is even more striking if one examines some of the values that William and Henry share in common. Consider, for example, the emphasis they both place on the virtue of intellectual sympathy. An expression of that sense of solidarity that their father took to be the divine form of human beings, their respect for the integrity (not to be confused with solipsism) of selfhood surfaces in Henry in his obsession with the unique perspective of the individual consciousness. Beyond this, it can be seen as well in his belief that the only way to appreciate so distinctive an expression of such a consciousness as is represented, for example, by a work of art is by imaginative penetration to the heart of the pattern of the whole, as the novelist remarked in his famous analogy of the Persian rug, before

attempting to define its controlling figure. In William this same emphasis is reflected in his belief that the only way to comprehend another person's ideas is by placing yourself at the center of his or her
philosophical vision, where you can then understand all the different
observations that flow from it. "But keep outside," he warned in *A
Pluralistic Universe,* "use your post-mortem method, try to build the
philosophy up out of the single phrases, taking first one and then another and seeking to make them fit, and of course you fail. You crawl
over the thing like a myopic ant over a building, tumbling into every
microscopic crack or fissure, finding nothing but inconsistencies, and
never suspecting that a centre exists." [52] What are such sentiments as
these but an extension of their father's belief that the virtue of trying
to put yourself in the position of another owes its authority to divine
precept and example, an example that the elder James perfectly emu-
lated himself, according to his novelist son, "there being no human
predicament he couldn't by a sympathy more *like* direct experience
than any I have ever known enter into"?[53]

This was closely related to the stress each placed on the sacredness
of life itself in all its individual expressions, a belief that evoked, supported, and confirmed their equally brilliant gifts not only for personal
observation but also for psychological insight. If it is often remarked
that Henry, Junior, was the creator of a new kind of psychological realism in American fiction, it is too often forgotten that William's masterpiece, and the work from which all his later volumes flowed, was
his two-volume *Principles of Psychology.* But again, what was this but
an appropriation, according to their own lights, of their father's conviction that life in all its interior processes as well as outward forms is
resident with a meaning that encompasses it and that must be ferreted
out if human beings are to savor its full significance? The elder James
"fairly fed" on such matters because he thereby conceived himself to
be trafficking with the incarnate purposes of God himself. His two
sons, like his daughter, clearly possessed reasons less explicitly theological for attending to such processes, but they all still took no fewer
pains to evoke the appropriately religious emotions of awe and wonder
when, through careful observation, they found themselves in the presence of their mysterious force and power.

Most notable of such affinities, however, is the fact that all three
children took to heart their father's view of the universe as unfinished.
Creation was to them as to him an ongoing process whose purpose is
ultimately to dissolve, as William said of his father's system, the divine
in the universally human. This is not to argue that they echoed the
elder James's confidence that the outcome of this process is religiously

assured or that what is sacred in its operations can be successfully isolated and acknowledged for its own sake. It is sufficient to say that they shared his belief that every step of the way is momentous and that each human soul mirrors in its own spiritual odyssey the central actions of a more universal drama whose meanings are to be found only in the felt sense of it. This was essentially to identify the principle of the sacred in experience with the drama of experience itself and then to define the drama of experience in relation to the kind of consciousness to which it gives rise and by which it can be appreciated. Henry, Junior, captured exactly this more religiously *diffused* as opposed to, in his father's case, religious *suffused* sense of experience when, in "The Art of Fiction," he wrote:

Experience is never limited, and it is never complete; it is an immense sensibility, a kind of huge spider-web of the finest silken threads suspended in the chamber of consciousness, and catching every air-borne particle in its tissue. It is the very atmosphere of the mind; and when the mind is imaginative— much more when it happens to be that of a man of genius—it takes to itself the faintest hints of life, it converts the very pulses of the air into revelations."[54]

This view of experience compelled each of the children, like their father, to develop a method, and the necessary sentiment to go along with it, for interpreting experience to itself. If that method and that sentiment are what we now call pragmatism, it should now be obvious why, whether as a theory of inquiry or as an attitude toward its outcome, pragmatism would have been inconceivable without the contribution of Henry James, Senior. This is, of course, to view pragmatism as something more than a philosophical perspective and something different from a technique for measuring consequences. It is to regard it as, in the broadest sense, a metaphysical outlook, by which I mean, as William said so beautifully, "a mode of feeling the whole push, and seeing the whole drift of life forced on one by one's total character and experience, and on the whole *preferred*—there is no other truthful word—as one's best working attitude." [55]

William came closest to defining what that outlook amounted to in his notion of "radical empiricism." Radical empiricism conceives of life as an interwoven, interdependent structure that can only be grasped in its fullness by being grasped in its relations, its transitions, its tendencies, its fluidities. A view already germinating in his father's theory of creation that became, in effect, the lesson life enforced in Alice's *Diary* and that life unfolded in Henry's fiction, radical empiricism always contained a double thrust. As William first formulated it in *The Will to Believe,* it amounted to the fallibilist conviction that our

most stable convictions are no more than "hypotheses liable to modification in the course of future experience."[56] When James later expanded his understanding of this outlook in his *Essays in Radical Empiricism,* however, it took on a more ontological character by combining
a refusal to admit "into its constructions any element that is *not* directly
experienced" with an insistence that its constructions always include
within themselves "any element that *is* directly experienced." In summary this amounted to saying that "the relations that connect experiences must themselves be experienced relations, and any kind of relation experienced must be accounted as 'real' as anything else in the
system."[57] Yet what was this view of life, of reality, as process but the
unarticulated ground, however attenuated, on which the elder James
rejected every other idea of creation but one that wholly implicated the
deity itself not only in its incompleteness but also in its imperfections?

Such an observation does not amount to saying that either of his
sons or his daughter was a disciple of their father. Neither William,
nor Henry, nor Alice took his or her father's ideas at face value and
simply expressed them in another medium. What they were receptive
to instead was the element of "vital truth" underneath, an element that
they then appropriated according to their own taste and genius. The
point is that such "vital truths"—and not the ideas which are but rude
formulas for them—is what a culture is made of, and to this extent we
can say that, for all their superficial differences, the elder James and his
three remarkable children belonged to the same one.

But this, in turn, suggests the necessity of a fresh reassessment of
Henry, Senior's whole relation to the American tradition and particularly to the ongoing current of pragmatic reflection within it. Where
until now he has been typically regarded as an American eccentric, an
anachronistic throwback to an earlier age of theology he had already
outlived, the elder James deserves to be reconsidered as one of the two
major precursors—Emerson obviously being the other—of the pragmatic "vision" or, again to borrow from William, the "way of just
seeing the total push and pressure of the cosmos" that his children variously developed.[58] In addition to forcing the advocates of Calvinism,
or what was left of it, to measure the meanings of their faith—or what
William James described more accurately in pragmatic terms as their
"more or less dumb sense of what life honestly and deeply means"[59]—
by the standard of ordinary human experience, the elder James forced
the new advocates of experience to remember what Calvinism once
taught about the need for being twice-born. To both he issued a call
which, despite various efforts by the likes of Robert Bellah for the cov-
enental tradition and Richard Rorty for the pragmatist, they have still

to heed. It was a call for a new form of social solidarity, a new kind of human community, in which there is no moral responsibility more compelling than to remain a human being speaking to other human beings about what is inherently sacred and salutary about the spontaneous, universal, and potentially diverse sense of humanity they share as their natural birthright.

What James did not go on to affirm, at least in terms acceptable to the late twentieth century, is how truly various that sense of humanity can and must be, particularly when women are not conceived, as the elder James was predisposed to conceive them, as soft, angelic, domestic, and, in Emily Dickinson's extension of the stereotype, "dimity" creatures whose chief purpose in life is construed to be little more than the care, support, and nurture of men. Nothing so risks James's captivity by his age—indeed, nothing so nearly enfeebles his system—as the truncated and patronizing view of women that, as it happens, his ideas by no means obliged him to hold and in many respects encouraged him to reject. But that is another story altogether. Here it is only necessary to remark that if the elder James was able to break the religious idea of the human free of all (or at least most) theologically hypostasized versions of it, it would take others, and among them his two sons, to show how the idea of a shared and universal humanity could still do justice to what could yet be viewed as potentially sacred about the diversity of its expressions.

4

John Dewey and the Culture of Democracy

★

The theme is nothing, the life is everything.

Henry David Thoreau

. . . the task of democracy is forever that of the creation of a freer and more humane experience in which all share and to which all contribute.

John Dewey

★

Despite the recent work of philosophers like Richard Rorty, Richard J. Bernstein, and John McDermott, or, for that matter, Sidney Hook, John Herman Randall, and Morton White from an older generation, it would scarcely be an exaggeration to say that John Dewey is presently the most misunderstood major thinker in America today; he is surely the most unappreciated.[1] And even where there exists a disposition to take his achievement seriously, there still remains considerable confusion as to the precise nature of its basis. Unlike Rorty, Bernstein, and McDermott, for example, who perceive his contributions to have ranged from the areas of philosophical method and social criticism to cultural theory and metaphysics, Dewey is still misapprehended for the most part either as an educational philosopher with a penchant for democracy or as a moral philosopher almost naïvely committed to the application of scientific methods to the solution of social problems. Either way, Dewey becomes a kind of cultural apologist for the progressive mentality of a particular era, and his intellectual accomplishments are taken to be as dated as its own political preoccupations and historical obsessions.

This assessment is not only unfair; it is seriously inaccurate. As a case in point, democracy played a crucial role in Dewey's reflections about education—and, in turn, the issue of education occupied an important position in his thinking about social questions—not because he took the school to be the central democratic institution in society, but because he was convinced that education constitutes the foremost institutional responsibility in a democracy. Dewey's thoughts on education, then, simply stemmed from his convictions about the work that any free society must make institutionally primary, and that work, he believed, should be concerned with the release and development of the potential of every one of its members. Thus Dewey insisted that the test of any social institution—government, business, art, religion, *or* education—should be "the extent to which they educate every individual into the full stature of his [or her] possibility."[2] Education, in other words, was for Dewey but another name for the moral work of culture in its broadest social sense.

Or, again, Dewey's commitment to the methods of science, notwithstanding some occasionally incautious and simplistic or contradictory remarks, derived scarcely at all from his slavish acceptance of the results of scientific inquiry and technological progress—Dewey, in fact, called time and again for a moral evaluation of the achievements of scientific progress using the pragmatic tests of science itself—but rather from his conviction that the scientific method of hypothesis, experimentation, and confirmation represented the only epistemologically feasible intellectual procedure in a world no longer founded on the rock of ontological essentialism, or what we now more fashionably call "logocentricism." The scientific method, as Dewey very loosely conceived it, was simply the only way left to think to any useful purpose in a mental universe where neither philosophy, nor theology, nor any other mode of insight possesses privileged access to the real, and where, as a consequence, the function of inquiry can no longer remain the discovery of life's essence, or the nature of Nature, but must be reconceived as the attempt to put us in more significant and constructive touch with the actual elements of experience as such. "Because science starts with questions and inquiries, it is fatal to all social system-making and programs of fixed ends. . . . Scientific method would teach us to break up, to inquire definitely and with particularity, to seek solutions in terms of . . . concrete problems as they arise."[3]

What seems in both cases to account for the range and depth of the misconceptions from which Dewey and his work have suffered is the intellectual failure of many to attend to the theoretical premises from which his more mature reflections proceeded and the critically radical ends to which they led. It is too easily and too often forgotten, for example, that Dewey launched his later work as a philosopher with a book that called not only for reconstruction *in* philosophy but also for

a reconstruction *of* philosophy. Dewey argued for a displacement of
the method of empirical verification by a method of pragmatic valida-
tion and also urged his colleagues to repudiate the view that philosophy is concerned with the establishment of eternal verities in favor of
the notion that philosophy is in the business of assessing values. Philosophy, Dewey maintained, should no longer try to stabilize experience by determining its absolute forms but should seek to augment
experience by exploring its capacities for richer fulfillment. In other
words, if the possibilities of modern critical inquiry originated in an
act of metaphysical deconstruction, it could fulfill itself only through
an act of aesthetic reconceptualization. Just as the "quest for certainty"
had to be repudiated for modern philosophy to inaugurate its work, so
the redefinition of experience as a form of art and the reformulation
of the purpose of art as life's continuous revaluation of itself—and thus
as the formal realization of its own possibilities—were necessary for
modern philosophy to pursue it constructively.

In exchanging the metaphysical "quest for certainty" for the aesthetic reconception of enhancement, Dewey was assisted by his emphatically historicist and simultaneously social conviction that given
forms of philosophy, as Hegel had originally taught him, develop in
response to the pressures and problems of the communal life around
them, and that these philosophical forms change, whenever they do
change, only because, for whatever reasons, men and women subsequently decide to experience that life differently. It is certainly no secret that Dewey associated the most significant changes in the life of
his own time with the development and advances of scientific understanding, but he by no means restricted the scope or significance of
these changes to the achievements of science itself. Science had
wrought a profound, and so far as Dewey was concerned, irreversible
alteration in the life of the present age chiefly because it had entirely
transformed our relation to the whole of experience. Far from merely
redefining some of the constituents of experience, the developments of
modern science had effectively destroyed many of our former Western
hierarchies of conceptual as well as social privilege and, at the same
time, opened up new modes of both individual and collective association and participation. Thus, for Dewey, the most significant results
of scientific progress had far less to do with the conquest of Nature, or
even with the development of techniques for the management of society, than with what he took to be the democratization of experience
itself.

But if the democratization of experience constituted the greatest single development in the life of his own era and set it apart from all others, its meaning, so far as Dewey was concerned—not only socially and politically but also epistemologically, morally, and metaphysically—had yet to be fully thought through and critically appropriated. This, in a word, is the intellectual task that Dewey set for himself. The challenge, however, was formidable. The task was not simply to delineate, or even to redefine, the philosophical implications of democracy itself. It was not even to reconceive—though it would inevitably entail—the reconception of philosophy as a critical mode of cultural discourse instrumental to—indeed, indispensable for—the actualization of democracy in the community. The task could only be fulfilled by a reconceptualization of the idea of culture itself in its democratic form, and for Dewey this necessitated a different valuation of the role of the aesthetic in creating this new culture and a major reconception of the role of critical inquiry, really cultural criticism, in furthering it.

*

In many American intellectual circles, the idea of democracy is currently in bad odor. Discredited on the left by its association with the moral compromises and then political collapse of postwar liberalism, it has been trivialized on the right by its ideological expropriation as the basis of free-enterprise capitalism and an arrogant and selfish individualism. As the justification and major propellant of economic expansionism and imperialistic adventurism in the late nineteenth and early twentieth centuries, Dewey took exception to this form of democratic individualism as both intellectually as well as morally bankrupt. At the same time, however, he believed that some form of individualism is absolutely indispensable to democracy. If the deficiencies of what he referred to as the "old individualism" derived from its focus on the exclusive needs of personal existence, the aim of a "new individualism," he felt, should be to meet the needs of social or corporate existence. To be more precise, Dewey held that individualism must be restructured around the principle that the moral development of each separate self in a democracy is in a profound and specifiable sense dependent upon the collective contribution of all other selves.

Dewey stated this principle formulaically in *The Public and Its Problems* as the task of converting the Great Society into the Great Community and then went on to define the life of the Great Community as one whose ideal goal is the wedding of "free social inquiry" to "the art of full and moving Communion." The idea of communion in this construction is no mere afterthought. In terms of its ingredients—communication, participation, sharing—it expresses the very essence of Dewey's notion of democracy and colored his interpretation of all three of the classic elements of the democratic creed:

Fraternity, liberty and equality isolated from communal life are hopeless abstractions. Their separate assertion leads to mushy sentimentalism or else to extravagant and fanatical violence which in the end defeats its own aims. . . . In its just connection with communal experience, fraternity is another name for the consciously appreciated goods which accrue from an association in which all share, and which give direction to the conduct of each. Liberty is that secure release and fulfillment of personal potential which takes place only in rich and manifold association with others: the power to be an individualized self making a distinctive contribution and enjoying in its own way the fruits of association. Equality denotes the unhampered share which each individual member of the community has in the consequences of associated action.[4]

Regarded as an idea, then, democracy for Dewey is no alternative to other concepts of associated life but rather the form which that life should take when it expresses itself in cultural terms.

Yet despite the best efforts of political thinkers like Michael Walzer, Sheldon Wolin, and Christopher Lasch, there continues to remain in America an extreme reluctance to think through the kinds of cultural implications that Dewey associated with democracy, much less to construe the term the way Dewey did, as implying the form of a particular culture. The notion that democracy can be identified with a particular form of culture, much less a culture that, if not fully realized in America is still far from being merely stillborn, has not been seriously entertained in a theoretical way by any work in American cultural or intellectual history since Ralph Henry Gabriel's now dated and seriously deficient *The Course of American Democratic Thought* and F. O. Matthiessen's magisterial but, in this connection at least, still oddly neglected *American Renaissance,* though Henry Nash Smith and Larzer Ziff more recently revised, challenged, and extended some of Matthiessen's insights in *Democracy and the Novel* and *Literary Democracy,* respectively, and in *Uncertain Victory* James Kloppenberg has more recently still attempted to place Dewey's politics in a broader Atlantic cultural tradition of late nineneeth- and earlier twentieth-century social democracy and progressivism. Despite Dewey's long preoccupation with the subject, the only thinkers who have systematically tried to explore the link between the concept of a specific culture of democracy and the name of John Dewey are, since the generation comprised of Irwin Edman, John Herman Randall, and Sidney Hook, other philosophers themselves like, in a limited sense, Richard Rorty and Rich-

ard Bernstein and, in a somewhat more extended sense, John Mc-
Dermott, Cornel West, and now Robert B. Westbrook.[5]

Though Dewey remained skeptical about dissociating the idea of
democracy from the social structures that expressed it and the legal
arrangements that protected and nourished it, he was nonetheless anything but reticent to discuss its essence variously and, at times, ad nau-
seam. One of his better-known formulations is to be found in *The
Public and Its Problems,* where he defines the idea of democracy, from
the point of view of the individual, as the possession of "a responsible
share according to capacity in forming and directing the activities of
the groups to which one belongs and in participating according to
need in the values which the groups sustain."[6] From this Dewey later
extrapolated two criteria for assessing the value of any form of social
life: "the extent [to] which interests of a group are shared by all its
members, and the fullness and freedom with which it interacts with
other groups." These two criteria for democracy encouraged Dewey
to conclude that any "society which makes provision for participation
in its good of all its members on equal terms and which secures flexible
readjustment of its institutions through interaction of the different
forms of social life is in so far democratic."[7]

But Dewey later simplified this idea in an essay composed toward
the end of his career and put the concept of democracy in more philosophic terms by associating it simply with "belief in the ability of human experience to generate the aims and methods by which further
experience will grow in ordered richness." This belief carried with it
an assumption that the process of experience is as important as the
results to which it leads; the corollary of this was that "the special results achieved are of ultimate value only as they are used to enrich and
order the ongoing process [itself]."[8] Thus the function of experience
democratically conceived is educative; conversely, the application of
democratic criteria to education, as Dewey noted elsewhere, implies
"the ideal of a continuous reconstruction or reorganization of experience, of such a nature as to increase its recognized meaning or social
content, and as to increase the capacity of individuals to act as directive
guardians of this reorganization."[9]

The question Dewey faced was how to turn the first conception of
democracy into the second; how to convert the idea of free participation and interaction into the means not only for enhancing experience
but also for producing the aims and methods by which that enhancement could be measured and at the same time extended. The answer
he fashioned was, in a word, cultural: to see democracy not simply as
an idea in need of cultural comprehension but as an idea conducive to

the creation of a particular kind of cultural formation, even a particular kind of culture.

★

Dewey's belief that democracy not only possesses distinctive cultural elements but also contains within itself the possibility of generating a distinctive cultural formation could be construed—indeed, has been construed—in several different ways. One of those ways has been suggested by the social and political theorist George Kateb. Kateb argues vigorously that certain political practices in American democracy, such as electoralism and constitutionalism, have encouraged the development of specific moral qualities. He refers to a disposition to independence in thought and an impatience with collective forms of mindlessness, a desire to democratize all human relations that promote greater equality and a conviction of moral uncertainty, or what he movingly refers to as "a sense that though there are absolute limits [in life], a voluptuous uncertainty as to how to judge and what to think, and what, even, to want, both is a sign of life and is life itself." These admirable moral qualities, he believes, are conducive to the creation of a certain kind of culture.[10] Not surprisingly, Kateb finds this culture best expressed in the sort of individualism that informs the work of such familiar nineteenth-century writers as Emerson, Thoreau, and Whitman.

Yet it is not their egalitarianism that strikes the democratic note for Kateb so much as what Emerson meant by "double consciousness" and Thoreau meant by "doubleness," a complicated quality that does not admit of easy definition. Whitman perhaps came closest to expressing what "double consciousness" or "doubleness" meant for Emerson and for Thoreau when he spoke of it as a creative but skeptical diffidence, or the ability, as he put it in "Song of Myself," to be "Both in and out of the game and watching and wondering at it." In this formulation, "double consciousness" represents neither grasping for certainty nor acquiescing to the flux, but instead seeing everything in all its potential for enlarging experience and seeing experience itself in all its potential for affective appropriation. This ability, as Kateb rightly discerns, entails a mind for which nothing is too strange and implies a cultural ideal in which, as a consequence, everything that exists is a possible resource for poetization, is material for potential creativity.

A second way of construing what Dewey may have meant by the culture of democracy has been suggested by the literary and cultural critic Benjamin DeMott. Where Kateb centers his reflections on the possibility of reviving a new kind of democratic individualism, DeMott focuses his attention on the possibility of developing a new kind of social imagination among individuals within a democracy. For DeMott the key to what constitutes the strongest impulse in a culture of democracy is not the freedom that results from an individual's ability to participate in a community of equals but the entailments that such free participation brings with it. As Judge Learned Hand once observed, "the spirit of liberty is the spirit which seeks to understand the minds of other men and women."[11] DeMott concedes that this "spirit" is more of an energy that has actively nourished certain American writers and thinkers than any ideal that they have actually achieved in their literary and intellectual practice, but he goes on to note that without this democratic energy (of which so much American literature and thought is an imperfect expression), it is an open "question whether the nature of the task would be as evident as it is, and whether the perception of need would be as piercing as now and then it still becomes."[12] What selected American artists and intellectuals have held out as a cultural ideal is not only an antiauthoritarian resistance to anything that stunts or subverts the expression of the individual self, but also a marked tendency to sympathize with the victims of such collective oppression, something that in its more positive moods F. Scott Fitzgerald associated with a "willingness of the heart."

Thus for Kateb democracy seems to require an imagination of wary but responsive openness, for DeMott what might be called an imagination of receptive otherness. Kateb construes the culture of democracy as a way of making experience richer, denser, heavier with significance. DeMott views the culture of democracy as a way of making experience more reciprocal, responsible, interactive. Though Dewey was not insensible of the importance of either requirement—either the need to see with an eye that is simultaneously suspicious and surprised, knowing and naïve, or the need to see in part with the eyes of others in order to see at all clearly or fully with one's own—he characteristically turned these requirements in a more critical direction. To put this less obliquely, Dewey conceived democracy not only as conducive to the creation of a culture that was essentially critical but also as in fact conducive to the creation of a special kind of critical culture. For when Dewey asked himself how such a culture is to be constructed and sustained, his answer was through the development of a new mode of cultural inquiry and its attendant forms of creative and critical discourse.

★

Dewey initiated this task in his book of 1925 entitled *Experience and Nature*. Later tempted to retitle it *Nature and Culture,* Dewey thought of this book, as in so many ways it deserves to be read, not only as his central methodological statement but also as his theory of culture. Not that other works like *Reconstruction in Philosophy* and *The Quest for Certainty,* as well as the curiously complementary volume *Art as Experience* and his better-known *Human Nature and Conduct,* didn't contribute significantly to his theory of inquiry and his view of experience; but *Experience and Nature* is where he gave fullest and most balanced expression at once to his "metaphysics," as he called any description of the generic traits of existence, and to what we might term the metaphysics of his method.

Dewey's aim in this book was to create the possibility of a more adequate critique of contemporary values, and he was convinced that the chief obstacle to this critique lay in the traditional tendency to separate nature from experience. Dewey took the position that if nature and experience are conceptually distinct, they are nonetheless empirically continuous rather than disjunctive. Experience, as he put it in a formulation that many of his readers have found subsequently confusing, or at least misleading, occurs within nature and is comprised of nature. By this Dewey means that while nothing can be known outside the realm of experience, the things of which experience is comprised are not identical with experience as such. Such things, in their interactions, are simply the materials out of which experience is made. They become converted into the means or instruments of experience itself only when they are linked with another of the elements of nature, namely, the human mind.[13] Thus Dewey assumes with James that experience refers essentially to modes of doing and undergoing, of acting and suffering, rather than to the things which result from them.

Experience is therefore what James called a "double-barreled word."[14] It refers at one and the same time to events and to their interpretation, or, if one prefers, to processes of occurrence and to processes of inference. But these processes are not distinct even where they are discriminable. Experience is characterized by a fundamental integrity in which there is no a priori distinction between subject and object or action and material. All the classic oppositions of traditional epistemology are overcome in Dewey's empiricism or, more accurately, subordinated to an undifferentiated totality that, as it were, contains them all. And it is from this experienced unity of subject and object, of self and other, Dewey holds, that thought should begin, and not from the "results of a reflection that has already torn into two the subject matter experienced and the operations and states of experiencing." [15]

Dewey has some very shrewd things to say about what happens when thought begins elsewhere. When experience is dissociated from the material that comprises it and the attitudes and aptitudes to which it gives rise, thought then sets out upon "the road that conducts to tools and technologies, to the construction of mechanisms, to the arts that ensue in the wake of the sciences." One could argue that this is precisely the world into which many people believe that Dewey conducted us himself, a world in which intelligence is used as an instrument for the relief of the sense of hazards associated with ordinary experience itself. But even where the benefits of scientific progress are clearly obvious, Dewey does not think they suffice, "because," as he states, "when one neglects the connection of these scientific objects with the affairs of primary experience, the result is a picture of a world of things indifferent to human interests because it is wholly apart from experience." The only alternative is to dissociate the objects of experience from the processes through which they are reached and in which they function, but this merely yields "the absurdity of an experiencing which experiences only itself, states and processes of consciousness, instead of the things of nature." [16]

This conception of an opposition between the experiencing self and the otherness of nature has haunted philosophical reflection ever since the seventeenth century and, from Dewey's point of view, has crippled the power of the intellect by encouraging a false sense of alienation from nature. It has also diminished our sense of reality by relegating to the realm of appearance much of what is found within experience as such. Thus Dewey could write alternately: "The only way to avoid a sharp separation between the mind which is the centre of the processes of experiencing and the natural world which is experienced is to acknowledge that all modes of experiencing are ways in which some genuine traits of nature come to manifest realization." [17] From this Dewey concluded that if it is impossible to dissociate experiences from, so to speak, the experience of them, this is not because experience is necessarily or irreducibly self-reflexive, solipsistic, or self-enclosed, as present-day poststructuralists maintain, but because experience is always overlaid with constructions, conceptions, construals which are the product of former experiences. Yet this layering of experience with interpretations, with meanings, is no accident, according to Dewey; it results from something inherent within, and inherently precarious about, the nature of existence itself.

As Dewey understands it, life is anything but secure, experience anything but predictable:

Man finds himself living in an aleatory world; his existence involves, to put it baldly, a gamble. The world is a scene of risk; it is uncertain, unstable, uncannily unstable. Its dangers are irregular, inconstant, not to be counted upon as to their times and seasons. Although persistent, they are sporadic, episodic. It is darkest just before dawn; pride goes before a fall; the moment of greatest prosperity is the moment most charged with ill-omen, most opportune for the evil eye. . . . Luck is proverbially both good and bad in its distributions. The sacred and the accursed are potentialities of the same situation; and there is no category of things which has not embodied the sacred and accursed: persons, words, places, times, direction in space, stones, winds, animals, stars.[18]

It is no wonder that the gods, as the old saying has it, were born in fear. But Dewey does not take this fear to be a projection onto the universe as a whole, as Feuerbach urged us to believe, of an inborn instinct. He interprets it instead as a response, whether instinctual or learned, to man's interaction with the environment itself. "Man fears," Dewey writes, "because he exists in a fearful, an awful world."[19] Nor has this predicament changed with the centuries of scientific advancement. It is not the facts of existence which have altered during our period of so-called enlightenment, only our methods for obtaining reassurance and comfort. Superstition has given way to a rational sophistication that is often "as irrational and as much at the mercy of words as the superstition it replaces."

Our magical safeguard against the uncertain character of the world is to deny the existence of chance, to mumble universal and necessary law, the ubiquity of cause and effect, the uniformity of nature, universal progress, and the inherent rationality of the universe.[20]

But the basically hazardous character of existence itself remains unchanged, even with the increased measure of prediction and control furnished by science. All that has been effected are the "devices," as Dewey calls them, by which we evade the true reality of our predicament. Life confronts us with an unending structure of uncertainty and uniformity, of irregularity and constancy, of change and perdurance, and our problem is continuously to readjust the relations between them.

In *Art as Experience* Dewey redefines this structure of precariousness and stability in experience—and somewhat softens its harshness—by describing it as an oscillating movement "in which the human organism alternately falls out of step with the march of surrounding things and then recovers unison with it—either through effort or by some happy chance."[21] The point that Dewey makes in *Art as Experience,* with the help of an ostensibly more naturalistic vocabulary, is that the achievement of even a temporary reintegration with the environment never returns the human organism to its prior state. The dissociation and resistance through which the human organism passes before it achieves even minimal readjustment to the conditions surrounding it inevitably add, Dewey argues, something to the human organism that it didn't possess before: ". . . in a growing life, the recovery is never mere return to a prior state, for it is enriched by the state of disparity and resistance through which it has successfully passed." Thus Dewey summarizes: "Life grows when a temporary falling out is a transition to a more extensive balance of the energies of the organism to those of the conditions under which it lives."[22]

*

There can be no gainsaying the fact that Dewey's naturalism is most vulnerable to criticism precisely here. For instead of demonstrating that life develops from this biological matrix and then proceeding to show that its growth is potentially as benign as Dewey's metaphor would have it (where life is at least capable of, if not disposed toward, ever more complex balances of the energies that make it up), he merely posits this notion, or, rather, accepts it as a philosophical given. Yet surely this highly figurative conception of the origin and development of sentient life is far from commonly accepted, and Dewey gives it anything but a commonplace interpretation. Indeed, he finds this construct so useful in a book on art precisely because it enables him to demonstrate just how deeply the aesthetic is rooted in the foundations of experience itself:

The world is full of things that are indifferent or even hostile to life; the very processes by which life is maintained tend to throw it out of gear with its surroundings. Nevertheless, if life continues and if continuing it expands, there is an overcoming of factors of opposition and conflict; there is a transformation of them into the differentiated aspects of a higher powered and more significant life.[23]

Whether this is the metaphysical residue of Dewey's earlier Hegelianism or simply a by-product of his trope, there are difficulties with Dewey's way of expressing himself at this point. If the chief ontological difficulty with this form of naturalism is that it smacks of a new essentialism lifted to the plane of biological mechanics, its chief difficulty aesthetically is that it may lead to yet another version of organicism. Dewey argues, for example, that "that which distinguishes an experience as aesthetic is conversion of resistance and tensions of excitations that in themselves are temptations to diversion, into a movement toward an inclusive and fulfilling close."[24]

Yet at other times Dewey seems to pull back from embracing a simple organicism, with its emphasis on wholeness and unity, when he takes pains to identify aesthetic form not with organic unity at all but with what he calls "a stable, even though moving, equilibrium," a coherence where "changes interlock and sustain one another" through time, achieving a kind of "balanced movement" but no final closures, no ultimate consummations, no absolute conclusions.[25] And in *Experience and Nature* he resists even more strenuously the pull of his own organicist impulses by associating the greatest and most wholly consummate in art not with the completed but with the continuously creative: the mark of all great art, he writes, is not its perfection, whatever that might mean, but its renewed instrumentality for further balanced integrations. In this way, Dewey acknowledges that all our solutions to the problem of experience are provisional, that nothing is finished, that words like "perfection," "wholeness," "completion" are terms that we attach to elements of our experience that are singular not primarily by virtue of what they draw attention to in themselves but because of how they point to, or at least promote, their own self-overcoming, even their own displacement.

But Dewey's biologism does not restrict this capacity for self-surpassing to aesthetic objects. If we can conceive of it as a process that is operative not beyond experience but wholly within it, self-transcendence is here construed as a characteristic of all organic life, and particularly of all the intellectual processes that emerge from it which we call thought. Indeed, Dewey claims that this biological rhythm of alienation from the environment and reintegration with it "not only persists in man but becomes conscious with him; its conditions are the material out of which he forms purposes."[26]

These purposes include aesthetic purposes, but they don't begin there. They begin with the recognition of a separation or break in our previous tie with the environment around us that is registered consciously as an emotion, as a sense of felt need. This emotional experience of disjunction, of rupture, becomes in turn the source of an impulsion to recuperate relations with the environment on a different footing. But this recuperative impulse inevitably encounters resistance that can only be overcome by converting the obstacles that deflect or subvert it into what Dewey calls "favoring agencies." Resistances turn the forward motion of the impulsion back upon itself, into a form of "re-flection," where the "hindering conditions," as Dewey terms them, are reviewed in relation "to what the self possesses as working capital in virtue of prior experiences." [27]

In this encounter between old and new, so to speak, there is more than a mixing or blending of factors. Dewey describes this rhythmic process of rupture and recuperation at one point as "a recreation in which the present impulsion gets form and solidity while the old, the 'stored,' material is literally revived, given new life through having to meet a new situation." [28] At another, thinking of more specifically aesthetic transactions, he speaks of this reflective impulse as converting "mere emotion into interest in objects as conditions of the realization of harmony." [29] But as the terms of this realization become clearer to consciousness, Dewey adds, a further transformation occurs: "the material of reflection is incorporated into objects *as their meaning*" (emphasis mine). [30] Once this latter conversion occurs, something ineradicable is achieved. The expressive self obtains a new awareness of the meaning of the original impulsion, even if its primary intention has been partially frustrated. Obstacles to fulfillment have been converted into sources of insight, leading to an advance, or at least to a deepening, of experience itself: "Blind surge has been changed into purpose; instinctive tendencies are transformed into contrived understanding." [31]

Dewey's ultimate aim in this discussion is to suggest that while the artist is chiefly interested in the phase of this experience that leads to reintegration and reunion, he is by no means indifferent to those aspects of it that are characterized by tension, resistance, disjunction. Indeed, the artist cultivates such elements, as Dewey says a little too glibly, precisely because of their potential to yield the integrations he seeks. But in this, Dewey concedes, the line between the artist and the thinker, between the aesthetic and the discursive, becomes very fine indeed. The difference between them is chiefly one of emphasis. In the continuous rhythmic alternation between disunion and reunion that marks the relationship between what Dewey calls "the live creature" and his or her environment, the thinker makes more of the dissonances and obstacles produced by the break with the environment, the artist more of the possibilities and harmonies born of the desire for reconciliation with the environment.

Yet Dewey was convinced that thinking can itself be described as an art and that its products, like propositions and knowledge, can be conceived as "works" no less artistic than symphonies and statuary: "Every successive state of thinking is a conclusion in which the meaning which has produced it is condensed; and it is no sooner stated than it is a light radiating to other things—unless it be a fog which obscures them." [32]

Here Dewey seems prepared to blur all the distinctions dear to modernism but only in behalf of demonstrating that they are based upon a false premise. What all such distinctions obscure is that art, like science, like thinking itself, is a form of praxis, and thus the only meaningful differentiation to make is not between theory and practice but "between those modes of practice that are not intelligent, not inherently and immediately enjoyable, and those which are full of enjoyed meanings." [33] Only when this perception registers will it finally become obvious, Dewey predicted, that "art—the mode of activities that is charged with meanings capable of immediately enjoyed possession—is the complete culmination of nature, and that 'science' is properly a hand-maiden that conducts natural events to this happy issue." [34] Elsewhere Dewey observed:

The history of human experience is the history of the development of art. The history of science and its distinct emergence from religious, ceremonial and poetic arts is the record of a differentiation *of* arts, not a record of separation *from* art [emphasis mine]. [35]

This belief is, of course, wholly consistent with Dewey's conviction that art is essentially a continuation and refinement of the natural tendencies of natural events, even though, as we shall see, he fully allowed for how, in this conception, new meanings and modes of enjoyment can develop. And it squares perfectly with his aim in *Art as Experience* to reestablish the continuity between the energies of art and the normal processes of everyday life. Works of art constitute what might be called, if we can dissociate the word "art" from its honorific connotations, the fullest possible appreciation of the processes and possibilities of ordinary existence, and thus Dewey defines "the task of aesthetics" as the restoration of "continuity between the refined and intensified forms of experience that are works of art and the everyday events, doings, and sufferings that are universally recognized to constitute experience." [36]

Dewey's conception of the connection between works of art and ordinary experience, and thus of the full extent of the aesthetic task, is only fully grasped in the way he illustrates this observation:

Mountain peaks do not float unsupported; they do not even just rest upon the earth. They *are* the earth in one of its manifest operations. It is the business of those who are concerned with the theory of the earth, geographers and geologists, to make this fact evident in its various implications. The theorist who would deal philosophically with fine art has a like task to accomplish. [37]

Here is where Dewey's organicism, or what is left of it, becomes, as one might say, political and thereby departs markedly from all other

contemporary versions of organicist aesthetics. Dewey's aesthetics refuses all of the comforts of Kant's distinction between the faculties of
knowing, willing, and feeling—which reduces beauty to a purposiveness dissociated "from the representation of an [any] end" and conceives its observation of an object as solely "contemplative," "disinter-
ested," and free from any "representation of its utility"—and all
modern theories of art which have developed from these, most especially the New Critical penchant for defining art, in contradistinction
to science, as a self-referential, autotelic medium whose meanings can
neither be reduced to paraphrase nor rendered apart from its own processes.[38] Not only does Dewey relativize the distinction between the
fine arts and the useful, claiming that "a thing belongs to the sphere of
use when perception of its meaning is incidental to something else;
fine when its other uses are subordinate to its uses in perception";[39] he
assaults the wall that had been built by the early eighteenth century to
segregate art as a whole from the rest of life.[40]

There are only two alternatives as Dewey sees it. Either art represents an addition to nature contributed by something intrinsic to man
alone, the standard term for which is the "creative imagination" (a faculty that Coleridge deemed incomprehensible, and the New Critics
agreed, without the supposition of a Primary Imagination of which
the human or creative imagination is but the secondary expression); or
art constitutes a continuation and extension and potential consummation of tendencies inherent in nature itself. Dewey accepted the second
alternative as the only reasonable intellectual option in a world that
does not concede the need for transempirical support, and he wrote
Art as Experience to prove it. But "prove" may be the wrong word. *Art
as Experience* presents as compelling a case as Dewey could construct
for reconceiving the aesthetic as "the clarified and intensified development of traits that belong to every normally complete experience."[41]
But if this were all that his book accomplished, it would have little
place in a discussion such as this. *Art as Experience* is also an attempt to
show that the aesthetic is not only potential to every experience but
also the destiny of all experience. The aesthetic is that to which experience as such aspires precisely because it is the function of every individual experience to achieve realizations that, quite beyond its own
satisfactions, seek to produce further extensions and enrichments of
experience itself.

★

Dewey's way of demonstrating this aesthetically follows from his biological metaphor for experience as a particular structure of rupture and

recuperation and turns on his discussion of form. Dewey thinks of form in art not as the material out of which art is made but as the fusion or synthesis of the means by which it is integrated. Form in this sense is a dynamic category rather than a static one. Dewey speaks of form as "the operation of forces that carry the experience of an event, object, scene, and situation to its own integral fulfillment." Form is therefore ingredient in every experience seeking completion and not an imposition upon it. Or as Dewey puts it differently, form "marks the matter of an experience that is carried to consummation," and art simply "enacts more deliberately and fully the conditions that effect such a unity."[42] Form and not matter is thus the basis of perception in art, as in all experience, and yet Dewey is by no means a strict aesthetic formalist. To be a formalist would be to suppose that the whole of a work of art, like the whole of an experience, is contained within and is dependent upon its formal elements, and this, for Dewey, is to forget that there are no final consummations in art any more than there are in life generally. All the consummations in art are at once ends in themselves and incitements, instigations, and inspirations to further consummations beyond their own formal confines.

Dewey can therefore link the formal with the novel and the gratuitous by defining art as a perceptual site "where the contingent and ongoing no longer work across purposes with the formal and recurrent but co-mingle in harmony." The word "harmony," however, may convey a misimpression about expressive structures equally distinguished by "unexpected combination, and the consequent revelation of possibilities hitherto unrealized." The unity art represents is one that combines "the generic, recurrent, ordered, established phase of nature with its phase that is incomplete, going on and hence still uncertain, contingent, novel, and particular." And Dewey adds, "the more extensive and repeated are the basic uniformities of nature that give form to art, the 'greater' is the art, provided—and it is this proviso that distinguishes art—they are indistinguishably fused with the wonder of the new and the grace of the gratuitous."[43]

If this leaves one with the problem of explaining how art, then, is in any significant sense different from other natural events, Dewey was willing to accept the challenge. The point he was emphatically interested in defending is that aesthetic experience is no different in kind but only in degree from all other experience. It is the result of an attempt to refine, intensify, and subtilize the satisfactions potential to, but not possible for, nature itself. These satisfactions are at least potential to nature because all natural processes contain within themselves, as essential to their continuation and development, the capacity to convert obstacles or impediments into instruments for further growth. Yet these satisfactions are still not possible for many natural processes because they do not include within this capacity the ability to create new experiences out of meanings derived from earlier experiences. What enables the transformation of the one into the other, according to Dewey, is the agency of the imagination which he understood to be an element in all conscious experience.

Dewey's conception of the imagination, as we have seen, is in many but not all respects conventionally romantic. He generally followed Coleridge in viewing the imagination as esemplastic. Its primary function is to combine various and often discordant elements into new wholes. But at the same time he felt compelled to add that in its most intensified and unexpected forms the imagination produces what he called "the quickened expansion of experience."[44] Thus one might say that Dewey's theory of the imagination is at once romantic and pragmatic. It is romantic insofar as it associates the imagination with processes occurring within the text, and particularly with those associated with the reconciliation of what is diverse and often disjunctive about its material; it is pragmatic to the degree that it identifies the imagination with processes that the text initiates or furthers beyond itself.

Dewey liked to talk about works of art as both products of the imagination and imaginative operations. They are products of the imagination by virtue of the way they replicate in their forms the processes by which meanings from past experience are engrafted onto, and thus become enablements of, the meanings of new experience. They operate imaginatively not simply by evoking a sense of what they express but also by compelling in response a like act of imaginative bridging, absorption, and performance.

What [the work of art does] is to concentrate and enlarge an immediate experience. The formed matter of aesthetic experience directly *expresses,* in other words, the meanings that are imaginatively evoked; it does not, like the material brought into new relations in a machine, merely provide *means* by which purposes over and beyond the existence of the object may be executed. And yet the meanings imaginatively summoned, assembled, and integrated are embodied in material existence that here and now interacts with the self. The work of art is thus a challenge to the performance of a like act of evocation and organization, through imagination, on the part of the one who experiences it. It is not just a stimulus to and means of an overt course of action.[45]

Such activity, Dewey is convinced, is not an end in itself. It exists instead for the sake of human communication. And communication in its turn—and the interaction and participation it makes possible—is to Dewey the highest value imaginable, "a wonder by the side of which transubstantiation pales." [46] The chief instrumentality of communication is language, or what we would mean by discourse, but in this conception language exists not for the sake of expression alone but for the sake of the community it makes possible among those who become parties to it. Dewey was therefore convinced that language is active and effective in a double sense. Not only does it release and amplify the "energies that enter into it, conferring upon them the added quality of meaning"; in so doing it establishes a relationship in which "the activity," as Dewey called it, of all parties to the discourse "is modified and regulated." [47] Communication thus provides Dewey with the most important model for what he means by democracy, which he defined most simply as "conjoint, communicated experience." [48] Hence to see, finally, how art could become for Dewey constitutive of a new form of culture, we must determine what he meant by democracy as a cultural form. And to determine what Dewey meant by democracy as a cultural form, we must perceive how he associated the form of democracy with a new mode of intellectual inquiry and its attendant forms of creative and critical discourse.

★

Dewey assumed that the subject matter of this new mode of intellectual inquiry would be cultural values, anything purportedly possessing intrinsic qualities or significance. Of such qualities or significance themselves, Dewey was convinced that little can be said; values simply represent those attributes of things that cause us to notice and enjoy them, to treat them as objects of desire. In a world where experience is wholly immanental, values are thus another name for prejudices. But while Dewey was convinced that we can never talk directly about values or prejudices as such, he was also certain that they comprise virtually the only subject that we ever really do discuss. Values constitute virtually the whole of the substance of discourse because we are always converting them from mere objects of desire into images of the desirable. However, the moment we do this, values cease to supply symbols of appreciation only and become sources of appraisal as well. What was formerly a prejudice undergoes metamorphosis into a prescription. In this process, values no longer remain another one of the immediacies of experience and become instead a mediational form within experience.

The translation of values from one mode of existence to the other is effected through thought. In this more considered or thought-ful sense, as, that is, images of espousal as well as objects of enjoyment, values or prejudices arise in response to difficulties, perplexities, conundrums. Something is sensed to be "the matter," to be "wrong," and values thereupon offer themselves as devices for resolving it. In this defensive or functional view of value formation, values take on the character of critical solutions to cultural problems. They become sources of power as well as of pleasure and are thus rendered discussable. Whatever we cannot say about them as instances of pleasure, we can say about them as forms of purposive activity. To this kind of talk Dewey applied the generic term *criticism,* adding that philosophy is simply this critical function become aware of itself "as intelligent inquiry into the conditions and consequences of a value object." [49]

For Dewey, to redefine philosophy as a critique of cultural values or prejudices was to assume that one of the chief offices of the cultural inquiry it sponsors is a form of intellectual disrobing. The purpose of this intellectual disrobing is to examine the garments of cultural sense-making we call values to see what the wearing of them does to us and what happens to them when we put them on. Dewey did not, of course, believe that anyone can actually shed the garments of culture entirely and hence recover in experience the pristine condition of living without them, but he did contend that by imaginative reconstruction and intelligent analysis of the situations from which they arise and the results in which they issue, we can repossess what he described, in a language that anticipates the interpretive moves of much recent hermeneutic theory, as a kind of secondary naïveté or cultivated innocence. As I have noted elsewhere, Dewey referred to this critical procedure as "the discipline of severe thought" but insisted that its crucial intellectual meaning lay not only in its importance as an end in and of itself but also in its role as our chief implement for furthering culture as a whole. [50] Only by emancipating and expanding the meanings of which experience is capable, Dewey maintained, can culture advance; and only by critically assessing the valuations of which cultural experience is composed can the meanings potential to it, but not yet effectively realized within it, be successfully liberated. Such liberation is what Dewey meant by social reform in its deepest sense.

★

It is worth noting that Dewey did not suppose that the responsibility for social and cultural reform, as here defined, falls solely on the shoulders of philosophers, or, more broadly, of cultural critics alone; or, rather, as we have previously observed, he did not draw the arbitrary line that once very nearly strangled philosophy and criticism alike by differentiating and then separating the critical arts from their imaginative siblings. On the contrary, in Dewey's conception of them, both

criticism and art, both the scientific disciplines of severe thought and
the imaginative, are equally evaluative. That is to say, both are charged
with the task of interpreting and assessing all the expressions of any
culture's valuational life—beliefs, customs, institutions, feelings—
"with respect to the good."[51] By "good," however, Dewey did not
have some preexistent ideal in mind. Since philosophy as he understood it—criticism as we might understand it—possesses no private
store of knowledge, no privileged models of truth, it enjoys no special
insight into morality. Just like the arts of imaginative discourse—and,
again, it should be noted that up to a point Dewey refused to differentiate between art and ideation, between the representative forms of the
imagination and of the intellect—criticism or philosophy seeks nothing more than the perpetuation and enhancement of the goods already
found in existence or potential to it.

At this point, however, at least in *Experience and Nature,* Dewey was
prepared to sever critical discourse from what he thought of as "the
freer office" of artistic discourse, by giving the former the more specialized task of appraising values in their conceptual and not merely
their felt relation both as to where they have come from and where
they can go, or, in other words, in light of what they're good for, how
they matter. Not that Dewey didn't believe that art is critical as well as,
to use his rather awkward word for it, "consummatory"; only that its
criticism, as he maintained in *Experience and Nature,* is performed precisely as a result of its consummations. Art criticizes not by direct
statement but only through indirect projection. It does so, as Dewey
later phrased it in *Art as Experience,* by holding up to the imagination
possible outcomes of merely potential experiences, experiences
which, in their contrast with actual conditions and their probable consequences, nonetheless constitute, he believed, the most searching
evaluation of the latter that can be made.

Dewey therefore was convinced "that art is more moral than moralities." Moralities merely consecrate the status quo, reinforce the established order. Art, by contrast, challenges the status quo and desta-
bilizes the established order by "keeping alive the sense of purposes
that outrun evidence and of meanings that transcend indurated
habit."[52] In other words, the moral function of art is identical with its
critical function: "to remove prejudice, do away with the scales that
keep the eye from seeing, tear away the veils due to want and custom,
perfect the power to perceive."[53]

In *Experience and Nature* Dewey seemed to feel that this is not
enough, that the moral criticism performed by works of art will always remain incomplete and in that sense fail to fulfill the goal of all
criticism to institute and perpetuate "more enduring and extensive val-

ues," unless and until it can be made intellectually self-conscious of both its roots in past experience and its bearing upon future experience.[54] Expressed in different terms, Dewey seemed to be saying that art needs to be completed by criticism, and a criticism that is distinctively historical and philosophical at the same time. But in *Art as Experience* Dewey shifted his position by arguing that art *is* criticism, that the reflective and the critical are absorbed within, or at least compatible with, the imaginative. Taking a more Shelleyan view and giving that perspective what is perhaps its most emphatic modern restatement, Dewey insisted that the imaginative faculty encompasses the critical as well as the moral precisely because, to quote Shelley, it most directly "administers to the effect by acting upon the causes."[55]

As it happens, Dewey was no clearer about what this means than Shelley had been; but like Shelley, Dewey assumed that the imagination can replace morality as the chief instrument of the good because its function is to liberate all the meanings of which experience—any experience, all experience—is capable. And the liberation of all the meanings of which experience is capable—which for Shelley as well as for Dewey constitutes the true business of culture—requires the development of forms, at once reflexive and expressive, that provide the fullest possible realization of all that is potential to, as well as actualized within, experience itself.

Here is where the political radicalism of Dewey's view of art, and hence of culture, finally reveals itself. Not only does his view of art as potential experience, and of experience as art in potential, furnish the possibility of reconciling the ordinary with the exceptional and the prosaic with the poetic. By defining art and its attendant critical disciplines as forms of culture whose purpose is to enable the actual to be viewed in light of its own potential, Dewey's aesthetics, no less than his politics, joins the diagnostic with the revisionary and the deconstructive with the heuristic. It does so by showing how culture itself is, or should be, comprised of forms not only critical of previous cultural closures but also potentially creative of further extensions and realizations of experience itself. What therefore marks such a culture as at once democratic *and* critical has less to do with its professions than with its practices, and the character of its practices, Dewey maintained, depends in the last analysis on the intellectual test it always puts to itself, as to all forms of social existence: to what extent do its conclusions, when they are referred back to the experiences of ordinary life, and its processes of associated living, render those experiences "more significant" and "more luminous," and thus "make our dealings with them more fruitful."[56]

5

Pragmatism and the Renovation of Liberalism: Richard Rorty's *Novum Organum*

★

When will men pass from the illusion of the intellectual, limited to sapless reason, and bow to the intelligent, juicy with the succulent science of life.

Alice James

★

In a variety of books from *Philosophy and the Mirror of Nature* to *Contingency, Irony, and Solidarity* and a spate of influential articles, Richard Rorty has mounted a far-reaching critique of what might be called our contemporary intellectual *pseudodoxia*. That term, Francis Bacon's, was employed to refer to various notions in the human mind that stand in the way of the advancement of human knowledge. These notions, or *Idols*, were, he said, of four kinds, and they needed to be overcome in the furtherance of knowledge: "Idols of the Tribe," being "inherent in human nature," seduce us into believing that sensory perception can give us direct knowledge of reality rather than knowledge relative to the standpoint and coloration of the senses and refracted through the mind's own desire for coherence and regularity; "Idols of the Den" reflect the "particular and singular disposition" of individual perceivers and the fact that their interpretations are dependent upon what is reflected in the cave of their own experience; "Idols of the Marketplace" refer to the symbolic forms of human commerce and exchange and their susceptibility to debasement whenever their inherent "plurisignificance," in Philip Wheelright's coinage, is discounted or words are taken for things, language confused with actual entities; and "Idols of the Theatre," which Bacon associated with the purely inventive dogmas of various philosophical systems that sow the seeds of error in human minds by operating not as lenses through which to see the universe as it actually is but as stage plays designed to produce particular effects on an audience.[1]

For our purposes, it matters scarcely at all that Bacon prescribed as the antidote to these toxins what many intellectuals would now describe as but another poison. By insisting that human beings could regain mastery over the natural world only through the application of the scientific method for gathering data, classifying material, conducting experiments, interpreting results, and generalizing inductively, Bacon was merely displacing one of the "Idols of the Theatre" with what Rorty would describe as another, and one whose blandishments, like those of religion and philosophy before it, we no longer need. What is more remarkable is that, despite the foundationalist pretensions of Bacon's "Great Instauration," his diagnosis of modern idolatry carried within itself the clue to what many modern intellectuals, Rorty among them, would now accept as effective vaccines for these disorders. To counter the influence of the "Idols of the Tribe," Bacon recommended an epistemological skepticism toward all that is seemingly mirrored by our faculties of perception. To resist the temptations of the "Idols of the Den," he counseled "suspicion" of whatever the mind "seizes and dwells upon with peculiar satisfaction." As a prosthetic for the "Idols of the Marketplace," he urged a new respect for the differences between language and its referents and a new appreciation of the equivocality of words. And, finally, as a preventive against the "Idols of the Theatre," he advised the cultivation of a studied disbelief, holding that the nostrums of philosophy, and particularly that kind of philosophy which confuses itself with the onto-gymnastics of theology, springs from the same "absurd mixture of matters divine and human" as "heretical religion." [2]

Bacon's prescience in these matters is by no means a sign of Rorty's belatedness. It is rather a way of underscoring the scope and, more importantly, the essential significance, of Rorty's philosophical project. Rorty is deeply opposed to putting science or reason in the place where religious faith or belief once were, and he views all attempts to defend theory in what Stanley Fish calls the "strong" sense—by developing a general model of hermeneutics that would be free of "contingencies," "contextual circumstances," and "interested judgments"—as beside the point. [3] And yet he is as committed as Bacon ever was to challenging the way we currently think about thought—or, rather, the way we think about the relations between intellect and experience. He wants to delineate what deserves to be called a new model of the constituents of this process and a different, not to say more useful, way of relating ourselves to it and extending its benefits—personally, morally, and socially. So conceived, Rorty's project is part of the ongoing revision of American philosophical and cultural pragmatism. As we can now appreciate, the project amounts to the most important critical and political attempt since John Dewey to resituate the tradition of American pragmatism within the broader framework of modern Western liberalism. It deserves to be described as at least a "modest instauration" to replace Bacon's "great" one because Rorty's project assumes that this resituating will require a fundamental alteration in the goal of liberal society itself and the creation of a new set of intellectual techniques for pursuing the mastery it affords.

The word "resituate" is no accident here. In much recent literary criticism—no small amount of it influenced by the position Rorty takes so powerfully in *Consequences of Pragmatism*—pragmatism, or neopragmatism as it is now called, has come to be associated with cultural currents that are thought to be postliberal, if not antiliberal, in some very specific ways. It aligns itself—as does Rorty in such influential essays as "Philosophy as a Kind of Writing" and "Nineteenth-century Idealism and Twentieth-century Textualism"—with the postmodernist and poststructuralist repudiation of culture as an expression of individual consciousness woven into patterns of consensus and dissent, of conformity and conflict, and it prefers to view culture as an intertextual system of signs that can be infinitely redescribed. It has thus positioned the critical recovery of pragmatist discourse essentially beyond the kinds of disputes that used to vex liberal criticism theoretically. The old disputes concerning the relation between the universal and the particular, the absolute and the relative, the political and the personal, the necessary and the contingent, the self-creative and the socially reconstructive, the ethical and the artistic are deemed by the neopragmatist to be either false or irrelevant.

Whichever the case, there immediately follows a rejection of the first term in each pair in favor of an embrace of the second, and a subsequent assertion that pragmatic thinking is antifoundationalist, anti-essentialist, anti-intentionalist, and antirepresentational. It is a pragmatism committed ultimately and exclusively to the effectual—or to what Barbara Herrnstein Smith describes more elegantly in *Contingencies of Value* as "the local figuring/working out, as well as we, heterogeneously, can, of what seems to work better rather than worse."[4] It may therefore be described, in Smith's version, as the most ideologically unillusioned and politically unmotivated of critical theories, or, as in the version proposed by Walter Benn Michaels and Stephen Knapp in their celebrated essay "Against Theory," as no theory at all. Rather, it is a name for that kind of practice which is critical of all other practices that resort to theory for the sake of trying to govern practice from a position mistakenly assumed to exist outside of it.[5]

Rorty's relation to this postmodernist pragmatist revisioning has become increasingly complex. While supporting and, as we shall see, in certain ways furthering the ironization of discourse to which this has led, he has at the same time distanced himself from the wholesale critique of democratic individualism, or what C. B. McPherson calls "possessive individualism," that goes along with so much of it, whether in Derrida or Foucault, in Nietzsche or Heidegger.[6] Siding with those who accentuate the historicity and relativism of all cultural practices, he nonetheless insists that some practices, like art and ethnography and, one would suppose, certain kinds of investigative journalism, are much more humanly beneficial than others, such as theology or, let us say, advertising. Even as he dismisses all talk of history as an evolutionary process, he still believes that intellectual and moral progress can be measured by the history of increasingly useful metaphors. Insisting that conscience, as Freud taught us, is a product of no more than the accidents of upbringing, he yet writes a prose that is recurrently hortatory and determinedly edifying.

These paradoxes would be more disconcerting if they weren't managed with such disarming candor and panache. Rorty reminds me somewhat of Kenneth Burke's injunction to "use all there is to use," but here there is nothing eclectic about the "all." By putting his "all" to selective as well as effective use, Rorty is more like the philosopher who, as Wallace Stevens once noted in a helpful distinction, is "intent on making sure of every foot of the way" than like the poet whose attention is always diverted because "the sense of the certainty of the presences about him is as nothing to the presences themselves."[7] Rorty's version of pragmatism is clearly less interested than are some of its other newer variants in repudiating its ties with the history of Western liberalism. He wants to recuperate, albeit cautiously, what may have been glossed in this process of postmodernist revisioning. This has recently entailed a change, or at least a sharpening, of focus in his own thinking about the pragmatic legacy itself; at any rate, it has led to an important extension and development of some of his earlier ideas, particularly as they bear upon his interests in the culture of democracy.

In its Rortian, postmodernist form, pragmatism is premised on the contingencies, as Rorty describes them successively in the first three chapters of a recent book, of language, selfhood, and community. Each of these terms is large with complexities, but Rorty is masterful in threading his way through them. Pairing each term with a major thinker who serves less as a guide (Rorty has assumed this Virgilian role for himself) than as a kind of benchmark—Davidson with language, Freud with self, and a combination of Isaiah Berlin, Joseph Schumpeter, Michael Oakeshott, John Rawls, and, in the immediate

background, John Dewey, with community—Rorty proceeds to delineate the main elements of his proposal for the reconstitution of intellectual method.

★

The contingency of language commits Rorty to the idea that truth is
no longer "out there" in a reality beyond language but "in here," so to
speak, in the relations among our sentences. Truth is something we
make with metaphors; it is not already "there" waiting to be found
with words. Just as nothing possesses an intrinsic nature—neither
words, selves, nor the world (Rorty thinks of this as the residue of the
notion that reality is the creation of a divine person)—so understanding brings us no closer to the way things truly are. It only moves us
into a more useful figurative or tropological relation with them. In this
conception, language is a medium neither exactly of representation
nor of expression. It is rather an instrument of redescription:

Davidson lets us think of the history of language, and thus of culture, as Dar-
win taught us to think of the history of a coral reef. Old metaphors are constantly dying off into literalness, and then serving as a platform and foil for
new metaphors.[8]

To accept this analogy is for Rorty to believe that a recognition of
the contingency of language is tied inextricably to the dedivinization
of the self and the world. This is the point made by intellectual historians like Hans Blumenberg who narrativize such connections by arguing that they are the product of a sequence of transformations.
Where "once upon a time we felt a need to worship something which
lay beyond the visible world," as Rorty summarizes the story Blumenberg tells in *The Legitimacy of the Modern Age,* by the seventeenth century we began to worship something that lay within the world, and
thus decided to substitute the love of truth for the love of God. By the
end of the eighteenth century, however, the love of truth was compelled to give way to the love of self, as human beings transferred their
worship from the quasi-divinity of the world described by science to
the quasi-divinity of their own spiritual nature. But by the end of the
nineteenth century and the beginning of the twentieth, the idealistic or
romantic worship of the self was to be displaced by the realization,
variously phrased by Nietzsche, Freud, and Wittgenstein, that we
don't, in fact, need to worship anything as divine once we recognize
that "*everything*—our language, our conscience, our community—" is
"a product of time and chance."[9]

This is a narrative that lends considerable credence to the assumption that the self is linguistically constructed and that reality is largely unaffected by the language we attach to it. It also supports the view that cultural change has a lot more to do with alterations in language than with revolutions in belief:

As Kuhn argues in *The Copernican Revolution,* we did not decide on the basis of some telescopic observations, or on the basis of anything else, that the earth was not the center of the universe, that macroscopic behavior could be explained on the basis of microstructural motion, and that prediction and control should be the principal aim of scientific theorizing. Rather, after a hundred years of inconclusive muddle, the Europeans found themselves speaking in a way which took these interlocked theses for granted.[10]

Language in this view is more like a set of tools for performing a task than a medium for getting something straight. But, as Rorty points out, the creators of new languages, the inventors of new vocabularies, unlike the masters of various crafts, may not know what it is that they want to do before they have created a language with which to do it. Thus the problem of adequation still remains, but it is now solved—or, better, dissolved—differently. The question is no longer how to secure agreement between one's language and something that stands beyond it, such as fact, truth, or reality—"the world offers no criteria for comparing alternative metaphors"[11]—but how to get over one way of talking and acquire the habit of another.

This is pragmatism with a vengeance, and Rorty is nothing if not consistent in practicing it. Since the key to changing minds is not better arguments but alternative vocabularies, his chief discursive tactic is to make the positions he opposes look bad by showing how limited and brittle they are, and to cast his own position in the most favorable light possible by revealing how many different issues it can illumine. Either way, the oft-noted frustrations of Rorty's prose—frustrations, it should be remarked, that have nothing to do with the lucidity of his sentences, the deftness of his moves, or the elegance of his examples— begin to make sense. His occasional simplifications of opposing arguments, his constant tacking in the face of counterevidence, his rapid narrative surveys of immense historical stretches, his agile but also disconcerting transitions from one analogy to another, his incisive, almost aphoristic, synopses of supporting positions, his constant and always slightly altered redescriptions of central points—all find their justification in an Emersonian conviction that deference to the language of one's ancestors, or at least to the inherited descriptions of their contingencies, amounts to a kind of mortuary practice, what Rorty describes, in another arresting figure, as "worship" of "the corpses of their metaphors." [12]

★

This Emersonian iconoclasm—thinking of Rorty no less than of Emerson, it could as easily be described as an antinomian intransigence—is nowhere more vividly exemplified than in the practice of the so-called strong poet. Rorty applies this term more broadly than does Harold Bloom to the originator of any new words, the founder of any new languages; but like Bloom (and Emerson before him), he conceives this figure, a little hyperbolically, as "the vanguard of the species." [13] All strong poets are ironists, according to Rorty, because of their understanding "that anything can be made to look good or bad by being redescribed, and their renunciation of the attempt to formulate criteria of choice between final vocabularies." They are to be distinguished from the rest of us ironists by their ability to re-create what Nietzsche called the "all 'it was' into a 'thus I willed it.'" [14]

The strong poet is thus the kind of self who refuses to be a "copy," who is horrified at the thought of being, in Bloom's wording, "a replica." [15] The question is whether a self terrorized by the thought of living off the capital of other peoples' creativity is more prepared than any other self to accept the fact of its own contingency. Indeed, by couching the terms of his or her self-invention in language usually reserved for the deity, Rorty's strong poet seems in danger of the opposite: of hypostasizing its own sense of being rather than provisionalizing it. To put this more directly, if the portentous capacity to will oneself, and presumably all else, into life can lead in one direction to something as benign as an Emersonian, or, better, a Franklinesque experiment in self-creation, can it not lead in another direction toward a Zarathustrian exercise in self-deification?

Despite the fact that we are all by now alerted to the significance of this kind of terminological instability, Rorty can be occasionally obtuse about the referential equivocality it implies. To Rorty such verbal ambiguity is more often than not the sign of an epistemological playfulness that derives from the conviction that the self and the world have been emptied of intrinsic significance, have become "dedivinized," so to speak, leaving the field to those whose aim is not to develop "The One Right Description," as he calls it, but "an expanding repertoire of alternative descriptions." [16] Here the exemplary text is the first part of Derrida's *The Post Card* entitled "Envois" whose whimsical "fantasizing" strikes Rorty as "the end product of ironist theorizing." [17] But to the careful reader of some of Rorty's own equivocations about Heidegger and Nabokov, such verbal escapades—Rorty calls them the privatization of the sublime—may signal instead a certain moral insensibility about the way in which play can become simply frivolous and possibly banal, redescription evasive, reweaving narcissistic.

To Rorty such reservations as these almost fail to matter. The importance culture heroes possess for us—Derrida being one of his—is more often associated with the names of their books, and the styles of self-perfection those books represent for us, than with how well they live up to their own self-images. But this begs several questions. One is whether there is always consensus about what those self-images actually consist of. In the celebrated cases of Heidegger and, say, Paul de Man, there seems to be a good deal of confusion on the part of their defenders and detractors alike as to what it was they meant to represent in the first place. Another has to do with whether our caring—or not caring—about the integrity of our culture heroes remains the same no matter what they represent. Again, it would seem that the de Man and Heidegger affairs belie the view that the issue of integrity is irrelevant: all parties to all sides of the current debate about these figures seem to care about nothing other than the relation between the images of self projected by their work and the actual lives they led.

Not that Rorty finds all strong poets admirable, any more than he believes all redescribers are invincible. If the world and the self have been deprived of their divinity, this means neither that the world and the self have lost their power over us nor that the experts in human redescription will always invent self-images we will want to emulate. Rorty is acutely sensitive to the fact that the world can overcome us, that other selves can betray and destroy us, that our own vulnerability to despair, grief, and rage can engulf us. But in adding that the only remedy to such hazards lies, as so many strong poets have attested over the centuries, in our ability to acknowledge contingency, pain, and otherness for what they are, he may be slighting the other half of their testimony. This is the half that stresses the problematic relationship between the invention of the self and the abjection of the self. In other words, their realism, whether comic or tragic, has not stopped short of acknowledging that the self, in its very desire to achieve autonomy and redefinition, is often the author of its own embarrassments, the creator of its own pain, the parent of its own misery. Nor was this insight lost on the figure most central to Rorty's discussion of the self. Freud's theory of human nature acquired its immense modern authority not simply because it verified the fairly recent discovery that human beings are products of the contingencies of their upbringing; what set it apart from all other equally historicistic and positivist contemporary theories was that it also confirmed the more traditional and tragic view that in their desire to escape or overcome these contingencies, human beings simultaneously become the muses of their own unmaking.

This lacuna in Rorty's understanding of Freud, and by extension in his appreciation of the legacy of strong poets, does not deter him from ascribing large but measured importance to that class of what might be called secondary redescribers, such as literary and cultural critics. Comparers rather than explainers or inventors, contextualizers more than evaluators or creators, the Arnolds and Trillings and Sontags and Spivaks of this world are experts in placing books in relation to other books. Hence their range of acquaintance is more important than their deep readings. By constantly enlarging the sphere of the cultural conversation, they help us resist the seductions of any one, final vocabulary.

It is worth observing that Rorty extends the notion of "literature" to include any works that critics discuss, any works "that might conceivably have moral relevance—might conceivably alter one's sense of what is possible and important." Literary criticism thus becomes regrafted on the branch of what was once called moral philosophy. But in critical terms moral philosophy then becomes, to a discouraging extent, largely academicized. The critic is no longer obliged to determine the "literary" merits or the moral worth of any work but can content him- or herself with encouraging ethical reflection "by suggesting revisions in the canon of moral exemplars and advisors, and suggesting ways in which the tensions within this canon may be eased—or, where necessary, sharpened." [18]

*

If strong poets like Hegel, Nietzsche, Heidegger, Derrida, and Foucault afford us models of self-perfection, of individual salvation, Rorty finds their usefulness in social reconstruction very much more limited. While they are of enormous assistance in freeing the self for redescription and thus in helping liberal society exchange the dream of rationalizing for that of poetizing itself, they are "pretty much useless when it comes to politics." [19] Their central social task is restricted to furthering the dedivinization of liberal culture by showing how the languages of moral responsibility and social purpose are always contingent. But they have little to contribute to the actual restructuring of society. For that we must turn to an entirely different line of thinkers, to authors such as Marx, Mill, Dewey, and Habermas, who have made the public sphere and not the private the subject of their reflections.

Interestingly enough, Rorty writes as though the public sphere is in little or no need of conceptual redescription. Though he takes many of his cues from modern social thinkers like Michael Oakeshott and John Rawls, philosophers who have retained "Enlightenment liberalism while dropping Enlightenment rationalism," he writes that "J. S. Mill's suggestion that governments devote themselves to optimizing the balance between leaving people's private lives alone and preventing suffering seems to me pretty much the last word." [20] The ideal citizen of this new world of revisionary American liberalism will therefore be an ironist who combines an acceptance of the contingency of all political perspectives with a belief that whatever is meant by the good and the true in liberal societies will always be a function of free discussion.

Rorty has read too much of the Frankfurt school, and Marxist theory generally, to believe that freedom is ever innocent of ideological coloring. All he asks for, or thinks we need, is the standard bourgeois kind of criticism that is possible "when the press, the judiciary, the elections, and the universities are free, social mobility is frequent and rapid, literacy is universal, higher education is common, and peace and wealth have made possible the leisure necessary to listen to lots of different people and think about what they say." [21] While such freedoms may have nothing more to recommend them than the kind of support history shows they have furnished for private agendas of self-recreation, Rorty thinks that they can, and do, generate distinctive public debates about two issues central to the creation and maintenance of democratic society. The first is how to balance the private need for individual self-fulfillment with the public need to leave people alone to use or abuse such personal opportunities as they will. The second is how the desires democracies typically create for wealth, freedom, and peace can be adjusted to the fact that those desires cannot be equally accommodated economically, socially, and politically.

Rorty's liberal is thus not without convictions. Drawing on Judith Sklar's definition of the liberal as a person who thinks that "cruelty is the worst thing we do," he adds to this a corollary belief of his own that solidarity is the best thing we do. [22] As a liberal Rorty accounts these convictions socially and ethically salutary; as an ironist he knows that this cannot be proved. The liberal is therefore placed in the paradoxical situation of having to grant, as Isaiah Berlin once quoted Joseph Schumpeter as saying, "'the relative validity of [his or her own] convictions and yet stand for them unflinchingly.'" [23] Schumpeter conceived of this paradox as the difference between barbarism and civilization. Berlin is more circumspect. While he is prepared to admit the "deep metaphysical need" for greater ontological certainty, he is equally convinced that to allow this need to determine one's life is symptomatic "of an equally deep, and more dangerous, moral and political immaturity." [24]

Rorty understands this admonition to mean—or, at any rate, to give him license to say—that the aim of liberal society should be to "cure us" of the dependence on metaphysics (by which he also means metaphysical theory) altogether. Berlin merely says that we shouldn't let it get the better of us. The difference in interpretation is revealing. What Rorty characterizes as a disease from which we should all be healed, Berlin regards as conceivably a basic human desideratum which should not be misapplied. Therefore what the liberalism of Berlin is willing to tolerate so long as it can be constrained, the liberalism of Rorty is intent on expunging before it infects us. Hence Rorty's liberalism is anything but socially passive, and it is also anything but consistently ironic. If on the public side it is committed to extending solidarity to those who are presently, and injuriously, excluded from it, on the private side it is resolved that we can only make "the best selves of ourselves as we can" if we turn antimetaphysics into the intellectual architectonic of a New Cultural Dispensation and construe dedivinization as its new method, essentially its new rhetoric, of salvation. [25]

There are serious difficulties with both these commitments. Rorty has a firm grasp of the one, but only a tentative grip on the other. On the political side, he realizes that the desire to demarginalize the excluded can only carry us so far in the direction of social renewal because the languages of personal hope and public responsibility are philosophically incommensurable. By this he means that if solidarity is the best thing we do—and Rorty is emphatic on this point—there is no way of satisfactorily explaining its relationship with self-creation. On the contrary, Rorty is convinced—and in many respects is convincing—that more than twenty centuries' worth of attempts to reconcile the language of personal fulfillment and the language of social obligation have ended in the sand. The only alternative is to keep these languages as separate as possible and to live with the compromise this entails. The compromise situates him, he believes, almost directly between the Foucaults of this world, who are too ironic to be liberal, and the Habermases, who are too liberal to be ironic. Such a person is willing to live with the tension of believing with the Nietzschean-Foucauldian line that most of our social ills derive from turning private, provisional vocabularies into public, final ones, while also acknowledging with the tradition from Mill and Dewey to Habermas that the social goal of reducing pain and humiliation may be more commanding than any necessity for individual redefinition.

The reason he can't bring these two lines of reflection into closer conversation is because he is convinced that the radical metaphysical suspicions of the one undercut the inevitable metaphysical pretensions of the other. But this is to forget that Dewey, who is another of Rorty's culture heroes, described metaphysics as simply another form of re-description, and then went on to show, if not in *Experience and Nature,* the text that served as the basis for Rorty's famous repudiation of metaphysics, then in *Art as Experience,* how in a truly poetized or aestheticized universe, metaphysics furnishes the motive force for re-describing itself.[26] Dewey's procedure was to argue that to aestheticize or poetize experience is to define it as a process whose realizations, completions, or "consummations," as Dewey termed them, possess as part of their nature the tendency to generate more such experiences like them. This was Dewey's way of acknowledging that an aesthetic model of experience guarantees that there can be no last words, no final closures, no ultimate endings, because the processes which occur there are always being translated into something more, something dif-ferent. Redescription, then, simply becomes what life is like when lived under the sign of the poem.

But Dewey did not stop there. For he knew that the sign of the poem, the agon of aesthetics, is always social rather than solitary. It is social both because its rhetorical aim is to communicate and because it springs from a shared fund of experience. Dewey's aestheticism thus confirmed his liberalism by showing that fraternity can never be dis-sociated, as Rorty thinks it must, from liberty and equality. Unless we grant that our private life with ourselves is dependent upon our shared life with others, we have no way of accounting for why we should either be concerned about others or want to change ourselves. Rorty is much too serious a thinker to leave these things to chance, and yet this is precisely what he does by allowing his postmodernist commitment to contingency and irony to eviscerate his notion of community. This finally leaves us, as we shall see, with a liberalism disconcertingly rem-iniscent of the caricature of its recent leftist critics: a liberalism whose sense of freedom verges on being another name for selfishness and whose conception of solidarity is to a very large degree based wholly on mutual suffering.

Rorty is not afraid of criticism from the left since he thinks that the politics of liberalism, like its ethics, can only be justified in terms of what Wilfrid Sellars calls "we-intentions." In the language of "we-intentions," the bourgeois liberal is simply someone whose special sense of "we," from the late eighteenth century to the present, has been predicated, at least partially, on what Nathaniel Hawthorne, speaking of his own art, once described as a series of "attempts, and very imperfectly successful ones, to open an intercourse with the world." [27] However, Rorty does not think of this either as an ancient human disposition or a universal one.

It is associated primarily with Europe and America in the last three hundred years. It is not associated with any power larger than that embodied in a concrete historical situation, for example, the power of the rich European and American democracies to disseminate their customs to other parts of the world, a power which was enlarged by certain past contingencies and has been diminished by certain more recent contingencies. [28]

In this instance, loyalty to our own society is, as Rorty said in his essay "Postmodern Bourgeois Liberalism," "loyalty enough . . . ; it need be responsible only to its own traditions." [29]

*

Such sentiments, really prejudices, nonetheless leave Rorty in an awkward position. In a book that seeks, among other things, to spell out for the postmodern era the new terms of the social compact, he seems to be defending what looks like ethnocentrism. Clifford Geertz, in what has already become a classic essay entitled "The Uses of Diversity," charges that Rorty is in fact trying "to make the world safe for condescension." [30] This charge produced a response from Rorty ("On Ethnocentricism: A Reply to Clifford Geertz") that goes a long way toward clarifying what remains problematic about Rorty's insistence on maintaining the distinction between the individual and the social, the personal and the political, or what he calls, in the essay just named, "private narcissism and public pragmatism." [31] An exchange that is centered on what Rorty means by "anti-anti-ethnocentrism," it turns essentially, as I read it, around two questions. The first is whether self-knowledge, and thus the quest, through redescription, for individual realization, is at all possible without learning how to think rather differently about the social other. The second is whether procedural justice, as Rorty would practice it, is for the liberal a satisfactory antidote to the social misery caused both by our innate proclivities to be cruel and by our equally habitual inattention to suffering when it occurs in places or among people unfamiliar to us.

To take them one at a time, there are at least two reasons for Geertz's skepticism about the way Rorty divorces self-knowledge from social awareness. One derives from the character of contemporary experience itself, where the social boundaries between self and other, between familiar and foreign, between private and public, have now become infinitely more blurred, unstable, and ambiguous than they once were. With foreignness now beginning at the skin's edge, as Geertz puts it, rather than the water's, experience has taken on the aspect of an "enormous collage," making "the world . . . at each of its local points . . . look more like a Kuwaiti bazaar than like a English Gentlemen's Club." [32] Rorty agrees, but insists that the development of the bazaar has not brought an end to the clubs for gentlemen. If anything, it has only made the virtues of such clubs that much more apparent: "after a hard day's haggling," in which "you smile a lot, [and] make the best deals you can," they offer a place of retreat where you can "be comforted by the companionship of your moral equals." [33]

Rorty thus remains undaunted by the prospect that contemporary existence has turned into an exotic marketplace where most of the participants would rather die than share the beliefs of most of those with whom they must dicker on a daily basis. While this social situation will never encourage the creation of the kind of community longed for by liberalism's critics, the Gemeinschaft of a Robert Bellah or an Alasdair MacIntyre, it will certainly not discourage the creation of "a civil society of the democratic sort. All you need," Rorty adds, "is the ability to control your feelings when people who strike you as irredeemably different show up at the *Hotel de Ville,* or the greengrocers, or the bazaar." [34] Geertz, on the other hand, is of the opinion that such control will prove a very inadequate instrument of social cohesion indeed, when the liberal discovers that the club has also been politicized and now confronts him or her with the same social situation represented by the bazaar: a world composed of "irremovable strangenesses [he or she] can't keep clear of." [35]

A second reason for Geertz's skepticism results from the fact that, even if we think we live in a society where social and cultural boundaries still remain carefully drawn and comfortably coincident, the real boundaries of the self, as Arthur Danto points out in an article on which Geertz draws, are defined instead by "the gaps between me and those who think differently than I—which is to say everyone, and not simply those segregated by differences in generations, sex, nationality, sect, and even race." [36] Without a perception of such gaps and the asymmetries they represent, we have no way of "discovering," as Geertz puts out, "at what sort of angle . . . we stand to the world." [37] And lacking such knowledge, we are powerless either to determine where we really are, or what it feels like to occupy such a place, or whether on reflection we might like to change our location. Thus Geertz concludes:

To obscure those gaps and those asymmetries by relegating them to a realm of repressible or ignorable difference, mere unlikeness, which is what ethnocentrism does and is designed to do, . . . is to cut us off from such knowledge and such possibility: the possibility of quite literally, and quite thoroughly, changing our minds.[38]

This would be a less damaging criticism if Rorty's position weren't everywhere predicated on the possibility of our knowing who "we" (and "they") are, and of being able to change our minds (through re-description) if we want to. But it doesn't seem to bother Rorty in the least because he is convinced that such distinctions and desires depend not on destroying enthnocentricism but rather on maintaining it. To "wet liberals" presumably like Geertz, the supposition that "the exclusivity of the private club might be a *crucial* feature of an ideal world order" will undoubtedly look like "a betrayal of the Enlightenment."[39] To dry liberals like Rorty, by contrast, it is the Enlightenment that originally betrayed us by encouraging us to try to create a world based upon a common human nature and shared moral aspirations. If we abandon hopes for a universal culture based upon a univocal sense of the human, we will then see, as thick describers like Geertz himself have taught us, that such exclusivity is merely "a necessary and proper condition of selfhood," and one that when assumed by a liberal "we" such as our own, a "we" that has been raised to be suspicious of ethnocentrism to begin with, may well prove to be just what is needed to keep "the bazaar open," to keep "the institutions of procedural justice functioning."[40]

This brings us to the second point of contention between Geertz and Rorty, which has to do with whether procedural justice as presently conceived is an adequate instrument for the relief of human suffering and humiliation. Rorty clearly thinks it is, but admits that some clubs, like ours, will view procedural justice as a moral commitment, while others (e.g., theirs) will construe it simply as a matter of social and political expediency. Geertz is considerably more dubious and offers as an example of its cultural and moral limitations "The Case of the Drunken Indian and the Kidney Machine." This case turns on the conflict between a native American, who is unwilling to abandon his alcoholism after being placed on dialysis, and the medical protocols governing the use of such therapy, a conflict that reflects deep moral assumptions on the part of society generally about who deserves to have access to the therapy.

So far as Geertz is concerned, the point of the story is that the lack of understanding on both sides of this divide about what it means to be on the opposite side prevented either party from understanding even its own position. While, to be sure, a rough kind of justice was served, inasmuch as the Indian was permitted to stay on the machine until he died, all sorts of procedures had to be waived, because of the general social inability to understand variant subjectivities and therefore to comprehend why the rules must often be changed to accommodate new cases.

So far as Rorty is concerned, however, Geertz's reading manages to get things pretty much reversed. Whatever measure of justice was achieved in this case—and it was as much, he thinks, as could be decently hoped for—resulted directly from the integrity and not the deficiency of the procedures involved. Further understanding of moral diversities and asymmetries would have only gotten in the way. Rorty is therefore "cheered" rather than "depressed" by this little fable. To him it shows just how well the system works when the tasks of understanding—of knowing how the Indian's victimization at the hands of whites, together with his own ethnic traditions, may have contributed to both his alcoholism and his rebellion—are left to the "connoisseurs of diversity" or "agents of love," as Rorty somewhat patronizingly describes ethnographers, novelists, journalists, and their kind, and when the tasks of social implementation—of making sure that everyone gets treated the same once they have been demarginalized—is left to the "guardians of universality" or "agents of justice," as he describes the lawyers, politicians, and corporate managers who run the system. Rorty is eager to keep lots of the "agents of love" around because he knows that they are essential to enlarging the liberal sense of "we." And yet he is convinced that the world would not function at all without an abundance of the "agents of justice," if only because the bias of their own liberal procedures, particularly if they are ironists, has the practical advantage of "allowing individuals and cultures to get along together without intruding on each other's privacy, without meddling with each other's conception of the good."[41]

★

Rorty's position about the Indian and dialysis, like his view of solidarity generally, is of a piece with his desire to move the Enlightenment tradition away from its original concern with rationalism, rights, and moral obligations and toward a more liberal concern with finitude, contingency, and redescription. This is a move designed to turn solidarity into "a matter of imaginative identification with the details of others' lives, rather than a recognition of something antecedently shared."[42] The problem with this aspiration is that Rorty is of two minds about which details, however meticulously described, might make other selves seem "one of us," and he resists the idea that "thick describers" like novelists possess any magical formulas for making such details move us.

In the last chapter of *Contingency, Irony, and Solidarity,* for example, as well as in the essay "On Ethnocentricism," the details that seem to matter most to him are those that stress the most obvious resemblance between us and them, those that suggest a shared membership in the same set of clubs—ethnic, economic, social, political, religious. In most of the rest of the book, however, the more salient details appear to be those that speak to our common vulnerability to adversity. Either way, Rorty sees little or no bearing on our sense of solidarity of that entire spectrum of details that Stanley Cavell, thinking of Emerson and Thoreau but sounding more like William James, calls "the ordinary." Constituted of commonplace tasks and quotidian pleasures, the "ordinary" may represent a range of experiences we mostly take for granted; but it is also a range of experiences whose deprivation we can least afford to suffer because it is so closely tied to the sensed humanity we share with others. Such, at any rate, is the testimony of Salman Rushdie whose cruel confinement because of Ayatollah Khoumeni's death sentence has robbed him of such routine privileges as shopping for groceries, taking a walk, going to a movie, browsing at a magazine rack, or driving a car. "What I miss is just that, these tiny little things. When you have them you think they're completely unimportant or even chores, . . . but when you can't do them you realize that in fact that's what life is, that's real life."[43]

To say that people may possess more of a capacity to identify with the details of dailiness than with the details of adversity (or, for that matter, of mutual affiliation) is neither to suggest that human beings share a common nature nor to imply that thick describers such as novelists should abandon the effort to sensitize us to woe and hurt wherever they occur. It is merely to point out that for various psychological and cultural reasons it may be more difficult to empathize, much less sympathize, with the painful and the pitiless than with the prosaic.

*

Rorty's blindness about this seems to follow from the distinction he everywhere posits but never quite manages to sustain, except rhetorically, between private hope and public responsibility, between the demands of self-creation and those of human bonding. It is a distinction he frequently tries to enforce by associating it with other oppositions that are equally indifferent to the claims of the ordinary, like those between justice and love, or irony and common sense, or force and persuasion. As it happens, all these distinctions live an odd life in Rorty's prose. Whatever their function as counters in his arguments, they tend to assume the status of quasi-absolutes in his prose. Not content to absolutize these oppositions, he also absolutizes their opposition—or, what amounts to the same thing, he rarely entertains the possibility that their opposition may itself be a product of contingency and may thus be in no sense philosophically or terminologically given. To concede that their relations are themselves contingent, Rorty would have to be more attentive to their historicity, to the different kinds of calculus that, as critical coordinates, they make possible in different discursive contexts and successive cultural eras.

Would the historical record bear him out, for instance, in his contention that the vocabulary of self-creation is always and inevitably private, the vocabulary of justice always and necessarily public? Isn't this precisely the kind of distinction that has become so frequently opaque or occluded in, if not before, the postmodern fiction of a Gabriel Garcia Marquez, a Jamaica Kincaid, a Milan Kundera, a Thomas Pynchon, or even a more traditional modernist like Nadine Gordimer? Or to take another example: In a world so wholly organized and coordinated in terms of simulacra, of images that are simply copies of other images—a world where nation-states justify foreign policies, as Carlos Fuentes has recently pointed out, by appealing to the trope of individual self-description popularized by the Frank Sinatra lyric about "doing it my way"[44]—is it any longer possible to differentiate clearly, say, between force and persuasion, or between power and inducement, or between indoctrination and influence? Why, for that matter, is common sense, which Charles Saunders Peirce associated with "those ideas and beliefs that man's situation absolutely forces upon him,"[45] so constantly identified with "the husks of dead metaphors" when so many historians of everyday life have just as often shown it to represent the musculature of live ones?

These queries raise troubling issues about the narrow or angled interpretation Rorty gives to some of his key terms. His notion of the contingent, for instance, is curiously unweighted, allowing all particular historical contingencies, from the haphazard and accidental to the fated and inevitable, to sink to the same level in his prose. His concept of irony is so closely affiliated with doubt, skepticism, and disbelief that it loses all contact with such related concepts as the discrepant, the gratuitous, and the incongruous. It is for that reason never allowed to curve toward the comic, where we might well see how it serves as a corrective for the effects not only of essentialism but also of pride and stupidity. Even Rorty's notion of language suffers deformation when he assumes that Wittgenstein's claim about all feeling and thought being grounded in some form of life simply means that the limits of our world have now been reduced to the limits of our language. As Geertz has noted in "The Uses of Diversity," this "is not exactly what the man said":

What he said . . . was that the limits of my language are the limits of my world, which implies not that the reach of our minds, of what we can say, think, appreciate, and judge, is trapped within the borders of our society, our country, our class, or our time, but that the reach of our minds, the range of signs we can manage somehow to interpret, is what defines the intellectual, emotional and moral space within which we live.[46]

This is why an increase in the number and kind of cultural symbols people are able to interpret can lead to an enlargement of the mind with which they try to grasp them, a broadening of the sympathies with which they try to engage them. Change the language people use, the symbols they employ, and you can, as we have learned since the Berlin Wall came down, alter the world they inhabit.

But Rorty wants to keep these alterations within well-defined cultural and linguistic borders. Hence his skepticism about the possibility of any moments when, as James and Dewey both maintained, we can stand beyond language, or at least beyond any of its conventional mediations, without necessarily standing beyond experience—even the experience of which language is sometimes, but only sometimes, a part. James was initially prepared to locate this possibility in something that stands beyond the reach of language altogether, the experience of which is "entirely unparalleled by anything in verbal thought." He was referring to experiential moments, as he said in a passage originally prepared as the opening paragraph of his Gifford lectures on "the varieties of religious experience" but which he subsequently omitted, that seem to be alive in a way that language, patently, is not. Unlike language, which leans together "laterally for support, in chains and propositions, and there is never a proposition that does not require other propositions after it, to amplify it, restrict it, or in some way save it from the fatality by defect or excess which it contains," these moments possess what Emerson could have called "somewhat of absolute that needs no lateral support."

James's description of these moments is so felicitous, and the passage so little known, that it deserves to be quoted in entirety:

Their meaning seems to well up from out of their very centre, in a way impossible verbally to describe. If you take a disk painted with a concentric spiral pattern and make it revolve, it will seem to be growing continuously and indefinitely, and yet to take in nothing from without; and to remain, if you pay attention to its actual size, always of the *same* size. Something as paradoxical as this lies in every present moment of life. Here or nowhere, as Emerson says, is the whole fact. The moment stands and contains and sums up all things; and all change is within it, much as the developing landscape with all its growth falls forever within the rear windowpane of the last car of a train that is speeding on its headlong way. This self-sustaining in the midst of self-removal, which characterizes all reality and fact, is something absolutely foreign to the nature of language, and even to the nature of logic, commonly so-called. Something forever exceeds, escapes from statement, withdraws from definition, must be glimpsed and felt, not told. No one knows this like your genuine professor of philosophy. For what glimmers and twinkles like a bird's wing in the sunshine it is his business to snatch and fix. And every time he fires his volley of new vocables out of his philosophic shot-gun, whatever surface-flush of success he may feel, he secretly kens at the same time the finer hollowness and irrelevance.[47]

At the risk of digression, it is worth noting how much of the heritage of pragmatism that Rorty has found problematic is packed into this statement. One could begin with James's acknowledgment of the salutary distinctiveness of the ordinary, or at any rate of some aspects of the ordinary, which he traces back to Emerson but which could easily be seen as extending to Thoreau and even to Whitman. Then there is the recognition that as aspects of experience, presence and absence are not simple opposites of one another but are integrally related as elements within the same continuum. Still further, there is James's cognizance of the frailty and duplicity of our verbal instruments. And finally, the passage reflects James's realization that the success of philosophy, and of the critical enterprise generally, rests on an awareness of its futility, or what he calls "the finer hollowness and irrelevancy."

But as James developed his ideas about radical empiricism, he was to qualify this almost transcendental view of the relationship between language and experience. In his later thought, experience transcends language by virtue of a conjunctive process of which language itself reminds us. Kierkegaard once said that we live forward and think backward, but James knew that everyday words like "and," "with," "near," and "toward" suggested otherwise. All our thinking, like our living, is anticipatory: toward "a 'more' to come, and before the more *has* come, the transition, nevertheless, is directed towards it." The life of experience is therefore one of constant movement beyond the linguistic formulations to which it gives rise, and it makes no difference to the reality of our experience that we have no names for its connective and transformative tissue. Its processes of relation and transition are still as real and as consequential as the places where they carry us.

We can not, it is true, name our different living "ands" or "withs" except by naming the different terms towards which they are moving us, but we *live* their specifications and differences before those terms explcitly arrive. Thus, though the various "ands" are all bilateral relations, each requiring a term *ad quem* to define it when viewed in retrospect and articulately conceived, yet in its living moment any one of them may be treated as if it "stuck out" from its term *a quo* and pointed in a special direction, much as a compass-needle . . . points at the pole, even though it stirs not from its box.[48]

As to whether this propellant force within language that enables language to take us beyond it is to be called "religious," or "humanistic," or something else, James was comparatively indifferent. Merely a verbal dispute over terms, James believed that the essential question, as he stressed in an article on "Is Radical Empiricism Solipsistic?," is whether one can concede the reality of the relational and often affective mechanisms that make it possible.

Call it self-transcendency or call it pointing, whichever you like—it makes no difference so long as real transitions towards real goals are admitted as things given *in* experience, and among experience's most indefeasible parts. Radical empiricism, unable to close its eyes to the transitions caught *in actu,* accounts for the self-transcendency or the pointing (whichever you may call it) as a process that occurs within experience, as an empirically mediated thing of which a perfectly definite description can be given.[49]

Dewey, on the other hand, sees the possibility of transcending language without transcending experience as deriving from something associated not with language as such but rather with thought, and in particular with thinking's attempt to follow out the possible implications of any given act. Confronted with the prospect of where actions may lead, of how far ultimately they reach in the direction of some larger, if only hypothetical, totality or composite whole, the mind confronts what cannot be expressed in language, and hence conceptualized in ideas, but what can be experienced imaginatively, and thus comprehended as intuition or insight. This is the perception of every act's infinite extensionability of implication, which is "vast, immeasurable, unthinkable." Employing a vocabulary that sounds more like the Royce of *The Sources of Religious Insight* than the Dewey of *Human Nature and Conduct,* he refers to this "unthinkable" reach or scope of action as "ideal," meaning thereby only that while our sense of the unfathomable, undecidable range of connections that lend each act its infinite import is not a concept that can be intellectually formulated, it remains potential to and ingredient within the fabric of every living thought. It is there if only as a significance to be felt, an intimation to be sensed, a potentiality to be appreciated.

Dewey sees it as the task of art and of religion, and sometimes of art and religion together, to evoke such felt understandings—"to enhance and steady them till they are wrought into the texture of our lives"—but this task is inevitably thwarted whenever, as Rorty does, "philosophers define religious consciousness as beginning where moral and intellectual consciousness leave off." The religious consciousness is then conceived as something that comes after the experience of mental labor, that emerges only when critical reflection reaches its limit and commences what, thinking of William James, Dewey called a "moral holiday, an excursion beyond the utmost flight of legitimate thought and endeavor." [50] Dewey's rejoinder is that this is to misconstrue the activity of thought itself: ". . . there is a point in *every* intelligent activity where effort ceases; where thought and doing fall back upon a course of events which effort and reflection cannot touch. There is a point *in* deliberate action where definite thought faces into the ineffable and undefinable—into emotion." [51]

Rorty would interpret such moments, whether they be cognitive or affective or, as most experiences are, a combination of both, as merely symptomatic of the religious delusion that we can achieve contact with a power that is not ourselves. All I would think such moments presuppose or need represent are perceptual occasions, no doubt often induced by language, that currently resist incorporation within our traditionally inherited vocabularies and verbal technologies. In any event, whether described as experiences of the ineffable, the unthinkable, the undecidable, or simply the vague, they are often produced, as Richard Poirier has pointed out in *The Renewal of Literature,* by the tropological behavior of language itself. Indeed, this is one way of describing the office of the strong poet: someone whose redescriptions are predicated on the human ability through language to avail us of possibilities for understanding that language itself cannot name.

By remaining distrustful of, or indifferent to, such capacities and the moments they make available to the imagination, Rorty is compelled to reduce severely the heuristic value of art, and particularly the novel, to a largely diagnostic function—either to reveal the seeds of cruelty within ourselves or to disclose hidden sites of pain and suffering in others. What gets lost in this truncation of the poetic dimension of Rorty's project is something more than art's ability to describe all that James Agee meant by "the cruel radiance of what is." [52] What disappears is the belief that art, poetry, fiction can sometimes lift us out of ourselves, or compel us into a new relation to ourselves, as when we see or feel experience, or a portion of it, from the partial perspective of someone else. Solidarity can be achieved in no other way. And no proposal for the renovation of intellectual inquiry and the reformation of society as ambitious or acute as Rorty's can furnish us with sufficient mastery of our postmodern predicament that does not show us how to enhance it.

PART TWO

PRAGMATIC REVISIONINGS

6

The Pragmatist Turn: Religion and the Enlightenment in Nineteenth- and Twentieth-Century American Letters

*

We thank thee, Father, for these strange minds that enamor us against thee.

Emily Dickinson

I feel along the edges of life for a way that leads to open land.

David Ignatow

*

The story I wish to tell about religion and the Enlightenment in the American literature of the last two centuries is a fairly familiar one, though it has never been told, so far as I know, from the point of view I wish to use. That point of view belongs predominantly, but not exclusively, to the American Enlightenment, or at least to certain selective and extended emphases within it. Like all narratives, mine is inevitably a distortion but a distortion created not to deform the truth so much as to try to divine a portion of it that has been obscured. I take this to be the motive as well behind an important set of counternarratives to the dominant story about American literature, constructed in this case by feminist and African-American critics, who need to be taken very seriously if the full fictive capabilities and interpretive dimensions of the American materials are to be adequately appreciated.

My own narrative reflects the ambivalence sedimented in both of my epigraphs as well as the tension between them. Like the Dickinson passage, those who seek to challenge the religious legacy in America testify at the same time to the power that once gave it life by virtue of the terms in which they cast their spiritual rebellion, as though in that act of resistance, to borrow some lines from Robert Frost, "regret were in it/And were sacred." Like the passage from Ignatow, those released from love of the conventional source or sources of religious devotion who set off on antinomian quests for a new life can only

119

imagine that life in terms of the limitations they must overcome, the boundaries they must cross, to find what is yet unbounded, limitless, free. There is, moreover, the tension between the retrospective, nostalgic echo of the first passage by Dickinson (Who can fail to hear the note of remorse in Ahab's curses?) and the wariness of the prospective outlook of the second passage from David Ignatow (Who isn't afraid of the open independence of his or her sea?). As John Berryman in "Dream Song #325" ruefully remarks for the pessimists in both camps, the American soul is divided, "headed both fore & aft and guess which soul will swamp & lose:/that hoping forward, brisk & vivid one/of which nothing will ever be heard again."

But something, of course, always is heard of that other soul again because even its own darkness is double, paradoxical, mixed. So Berryman's poetic protagonist in the "Dream Songs," the antic but besieged "Henry" can do no less than split the difference by urging an "Advance into the past!" And thus the poem ends, where so many American journeys, like the narrative I shall try to tell, seem to begin: "Henry made lists of his surviving friends/& of the vanished on their uncanny errands/and took a deep breath."

*

Such a narrative must begin with the difficulty of beginning itself, or at least with the difficulty of beginning here. There are, in fact, two such difficulties. The first concerns the reference of the two constitutive terms of this inquiry, religion and the Enlightenment. Even if we confine religion to the basic tenets of American Protestantism in the first two centuries of colonial settlement, and restrict our understanding of the Enlightenment to the core of epistemological, anthropological, and cosmological ideas shared by the Founding Fathers, there is considerable variation in the way such principles and axioms were interpreted by representative figures of each so-called camp.[1] For example, the theological affirmations of the Synod of Dort—unconditional election, limited atonement, total depravity, irresistible grace, the perseverance of the saints—were by no means accepted by all Protestant Christians in the seventeenth and eighteenth centuries, any more than Voltaire's cynicism, Hume's skepticism, or Dugald Stewart's common sense can be flattened out into a characterization of the beliefs of all members of the Enlightenment. Just as colonial Christians differed greatly over their views on everything from the nature of God, the ineradicability of sin, the universality of redemption, and the order of worship to the proper organization of the church, so the American Enlightenment, as Henry F. May has shown, was composed of at least four discriminable traditions that ranged in ethos and method from the moderation, rationality, and balance of figures like Locke, Newton, and Franklin, through the skepticism and critique of Voltaire, Hume, and Holbach, to the utopian optimism and revolutionary millennialism that begins in Rousseau and continues through Jefferson, Paine, and Godwin, to, finally, the didacticism of Scottish Common Sense philosophy associated with Thomas Reid and Lord Kames.[2]

In addition to this, it must be noted that the Enlightenment constituted itself not as a historical movement in reaction to religion, and thus by nature opposed to religion, but rather, as Crane Brinton was among the first to note, as itself an alternative to or substitute for religion.[3] Hence religion and reason, belief and doubt, faith and freedom are never opposed, or at least opposed as absolutes, in the writings of the Founding Fathers, but are each opposed instead, particularly as one moves closer to the American Revolution, to what Jonathan Mayhew described as "Tyranny, PRIEST-CRAFT, and Nonsense."[4]

Since so much of the concern about liberty and democracy in the eighteenth century, no less than the suspicions of authoritarianism, originated in debates about explicitly theological issues and was nourished by evangelical interests, this is, or should be, scarcely surprising.[5] The Founders came by their ability to mix secular and religious rhetoric in their writing naturally, as it were, and they exploited that ability for reasons other than political expediency. As in the changes the signers of the Declaration of Independence made in Jefferson's initial draft, they felt that they could not convey their theological sense of the cosmic significance of the events in which they were participating unless they added to the phrase about "the laws of nature and of nature's God" an appeal "to the supreme judge of the world for the rectitude of our intentions." One can try to discount this kind of appeal as merely the hegemonic effort of a dominant group to appropriate the theological language of its residual precursor, but as Robert A. Ferguson, whose reflections on these matters I have been following, has noted, the Founders' need for such discourse was anything but disingenuous or simply calculating:

Irrespective of belief, the frame of mind within which the Founders operated has a vital religious component, and that component is richly connotative. "In God we trust" is more than just the motto of American republicanism; it points back in time to a central promise in the language of national creation.[6]

Nevertheless, there are important distinctions to be made between the spiritual legacy associated with the Protestant tradition of thought and feeling in America and that associated with the American Enlightenment, distinctions which, for purposes of discussion, can be formulated as follows. By religion I shall mean, first, the predisposition to view all human problems not traceable to natural accidents as reducible to the perfidiousness of human nature; second, the predilection to view the perfidiousness of human nature as unamenable to satisfactory redress by any agencies such as reason, will, or feeling intrinsic to human nature itself; and third, the tendency to view access to any agencies of empowerment transcendent to human nature as possible only through faith rather than works, including the efforts of the human mind to secure through analysis, criticism, or imaginative projection relief from such problems. By the Enlightenment I shall mean, on the contrary, the inclination to view all human problems amenable to any kind of redress, whether they derive from human nature or not, as dependent for resolution on the human capacity to think about them critically and to validate critically the insights achieved by the intellect through wider appeal to general human experience.[7]

These provisional definitions sometimes—though not necessarily always—carry with them certain other associations. Religion is often linked with belief in a sovereign God, dependence on a personal savior, the existence of original sin, the treachery of reason, the need for justification and absolution, the intercession of the sanctified, or the immortality of the soul. The Enlightenment is frequently related to convictions about historical progress, the beneficence of nature, the reliability of ordinary human understanding, the salience of criticism, the existence of inalienable rights, the virtues of free inquiry, and the pursuit of happiness. But the key to the difference between Protestant Christianity and the Enlightenment, as I am defining them here, is the question of whether relief of the human estate is dependent upon powers that originate in, and derive their authority from, realms of experience beyond the boundaries of its own agencies and capacities or within them.[8]

The second difficulty that attends the problem of beginning an inquiry into the relations between religion and the Enlightenment in nineteenth- and twentieth-century American literature has to do with the state of late twentieth-century scholarship. The problem can be put very simply. While elements of religion and the Enlightenment have both exerted a measurable and significant cultural pressure on the shape of literary life in the United States during the last two centuries, their mutual influence has not been equally assessed. Indeed, American literary historians have turned the account of Protestant, and particularly Puritan, pressures on the subsequent development of nineteenth- and twentieth-century writing into what, by some estimates, has been their principal postwar undertaking while, at the same time, leaving the study of the Enlightenment's influence on the shaping of the later tradition only superficially explored and almost completely unwritten. This phenomenon is the more surprising just because evidence of the pressures exerted by both spiritual legacies, as well as of the tensions between them, is everywhere visible in the American literature of the last two centuries.

Traces of those different pressures, and of the tensions between them, are plainly discernible, for instance, in Poe's vacillation between experiments with the associationist psychology of David Hartley in nature poems like "Tamerlane," or his more radical commitment to reason in such "tales of ratiocination" as "The Murders in the Rue Morgue," "A Descent into the Maelstrom," and "The Gold Bug" and the residual religious Gothicism of other tales like "The Fall of the House of Usher" or "The Cask of Amontillado" and poems such as "The Raven," "Ulalume," and "Annabel Lee." But marks of this tension between Enlightenment interests in reason, freedom, and individual fulfillment and Protestant Christian commitments to faith, obedience, and self-renunciation are even more visible in a writer like Nathaniel Hawthorne. So often and correctly acknowledged as our best historian of American Puritanism, Hawthorne was also a child of the eighteenth century who, for all of his anguished misgivings about the rights and responsibilities of the detached observer, was incapable of subordinating his quasi-scientific interest in the psychological complexities of human nature to any residual religious scruples about their moral impropriety or experiential belatedness. Employing ethical and religious allegory in his best work only to suspend and often to deconstruct it, Hawthorne risked the "specular gaze," as we have come to call it, because in the last analysis he was as convinced as any of his Enlightenment forebears that the only way we can see at all is by first looking intently, remorselessly, at the empirical facts of human behavior themselves—even if, in a reflex action deferential to his own conscience, he quickly added that the act of looking out and looking at required the ironic correction of an equally intense and unforgiving look within.

In a different and less tortured form, this tension is also present in the writings of "the autocrat of the breakfast table." An early imitator of Lawrence Sterne and a devoted scientist as well as a distinguished physician, Oliver Wendell Holmes could be adamant in his opposition to the harshness of Calvinist doctrines like predestination in *Elsie Venner* and yet in "The Deacon's Masterpiece; or, The Wonderful 'One-Hoss Shay'" indulge in playful satire on the logic of Jonathan Edwards. But Holmes's more characteristic stance is expressed in poems like "The Chambered Nautilus" and "The Secret of Stars" where science and faith are shown to be perfectly compatible, where religious and Enlightenment concerns can, like the lamb and lion of Isaiah, lie down together.

This more irenic position sometimes found a correspondent resonance in the work of several of Holmes's other nearly forgotten contemporaries, such as Henry Wadsworth Longfellow and John Greenleaf Whittier, but it was not until after the War between the States that strong Enlightenment concerns, still colored by religious ideality but also chastened with a strong dose of Scottish Common Sense, found their way back into the center of literary culture and seemed to displace religion, or at least the religion of American Protestantism, altogether. The Enlightenment's return was mapped by a somewhat disparate group of writers that included the poet Edmund Clarence Stedman, novelist-editors like Thomas Bailey Aldrich and Charles Dudley Warner, and better-known figures such as William Dean Howells and even Henry James, men of letters who for all their diversity of talents and accomplishments helped create, in the second half of the nineteenth century, what has recently been described accurately as perhaps the closest thing the United States has ever achieved to "a coherent national literary culture."[9] Easily dismissed for its sometimes tepid spirituality, its latent didacticism, and its reliance, at least in writers like Howells, on common sense, the Genteel tradition not only gave new life to Enlightenment perspectives and postures but also extended itself deep into the present century. Its descendants include, among their number, the New Humanists of the 1920s, many of the Southern Agrarians and New Critics of the 1930s and 1940s, and even, it should be noted, several of the more prominent cultural critics of the 1940s and 1950s, like Edmund Wilson and Lionel Trilling, who, while deeply suspicious of the Genteel tradition's overly optimistic assessment of human nature, were no less indebted to some of the Enlightenment values of balance, variousness, complexity, possibility, modulation, and mind it consistently emphasized.

However, there were other major writers in the later nineteenth century who worked to one side of the Genteel tradition and expended much of their energy puncturing its pretentions. In these writers—I am thinking in particular of Mark Twain and Henry Adams—the dialectic, or at any rate the dispute, between what was left of the Calvinist roots of American religion and what remained of the Enlightenment origins of American skepticism left an indelible imprint on late nineteenth-century American literary culture. Think only of *The Ad-*

ventures of Huckleberry Finn, which reduced the posturings of a debased Calvinism to the theatrical fraudulencies of the Duke and the Dauphin, or Mark Twain's most enigmatic novel, *Puddn'Head Wilson,* which mounted a withering satire against the emergent religion of Jim Crowism through a defense of the empirical temper. All the more interesting, if not surprising, that in his last years the Calvinism that Mark Twain had earlier spurned in its specious versions of racist sentimentality and spiritual soporifics tended to turn against him by darkening his view of humanity and generating the quiet but corrosive bitterness of "The War Prayer" and *The Mysterious Stranger.*

In Adams, it could be said, the Enlightenment confronted its old Calvinist antagonist more directly than it had for an entire century. But it was a confrontation that takes place not in the realm of ideas so much as in the medium of temperament, when a child of New England resistance ("The atmosphere of education in which he lived was colonial, revolutionary, almost Cromwellian, as though he were steeped, from his greatest grandmother's birth, in the odor of political crime") seeks to measure the value of an eighteenth-century education for living, and serving, in a later nineteenth-century world.[10] *The Education of Henry Adams* is simultaneously one of the genuine masterworks of American literature and one of the few fully self-conscious assessments of the two moral, intellectual, and spiritual legacies that have shaped its past. In this *The Education* not only sums up a century but also seeks to rescue a divided past, or at least to assess what has been irretrievably lost to it.

Mention of Adams's central achievement in *The Education* returns us again to the puzzlement, really the paradox, with which we began: Why has the Enlightenment disappeared so quickly and, seemingly, so irretrievably from our modern calculus of the religious meanings of nineteenth- and twentieth-century literary culture? Why has the Enlightenment been so singularly effaced in modern literary historiography, even when critics and scholars have continued to employ distinctions that evoke the difference between the American religious heritage and the American Enlightenment heritage, distinctions between piety and rationalism, or enthusiasm and skepticism, or sense and sensibility, to structure their understanding of the past?

★

Looming above all other reasons has to be the primacy we have given to the geographical region known as New England and to the experience of its seventeenth-century Protestant spokesmen in American literary history. Ever since the appearance in 1939 of the first volume of

Perry Miller's *The New England Mind,* American literary historians have maintained, and often in the face of considerable counterevidence, that the European colonization of America took its most fateful root around Massachusetts Bay, and that the most socially significant as well as intellectually articulate members of the colonial enterprise not only spoke, but also thought and felt, almost exclusively in the language of Christian, and at that a very selective kind of Christian, theology. Moreover, by the time Miller had published the second volume of *The New England Mind* in 1953, and complemented it in 1956 with the enormously influential collection of essays that made his view of this "errand into the wilderness" fully accessible to literary scholars, it had become possible to see how this significant immigration of peoples and ideas across the Atlantic had also made its way temporally across the centuries as well as spatially across the water.

Miller's case for the existence of Puritan continuities of experience capable of surviving the successive articulation of ideas for three centuries owed its credibility to the brilliant intellectual and cultural links that he forged in various of his chapters between, say, "the marrow of Puritan Divinity," or the federal theology of the seventeenth century, and the eighteenth-century metaphysics of Jonathan Edwards, or between Jonathan Edwards's latter-day Puritanism and the nineteenth-century transcendentalism of Ralph Waldo Emerson, or between Emerson's conversion of America into the trope of "Nature's nation" and modern millennialist expectations exasperated by the threat of a nuclear apocalypse in the Cold War era. But now it seems to matter little or not at all that critics have shown many of these associations to be more rhetorical than historical, or that numerous later students of the period have found Miller's view of Puritanism, or for that matter his interpretation of the whole legacy of early American spirituality, to be highly intellectualistic and extremely selective.[11] Seventeenth-century New England, and the theological precepts for which it became known, have continued to hold priority of place, to exert hegemonic authority, at every turn. Listen to the way one of American Puritanism's first great modern students, and one of Miller's predecessors at Harvard, Kenneth Murdock, dismissed the Enlightenment, even as he truncated it, in his discussion of the "Puritan legacy" at the end of his important study of 1951 on *Literature and Theology in Colonial New England:*

If . . . the phenomenon of religious experience is still real for some men; if there is a place for a faith transcending what unaided reason, logic, or science can supply; if there is still value in the prayer and worship which proceed from deep inward emotion, then scientific manuals, polite moral essays, and popular novels will not suffice. There will be need for more intellectually incisive and more emotionally effective expression of contemporary religious life; there will be need for some myth in which to symbolize and concretize its values.[12]

With its grand themes of Creation, Damnation, Election, and Sanctification, seventeenth-century American Protestantism clearly lent itself to the provision of such a myth "to symbolize and concretize its values" in a way that the Enlightenment's eighteenth-century preoccupation with rights, reasons, and rectitude never could. Just as important, the central tenets of early American religion were far more susceptible to demythologization in terms consonant with the modernist-existentialist spirit of the immediate postwar age than those of the American Enlightenment. To reduce Franklin's beliefs about a divine providence whose rule guarantees the immortality of the soul, and whose service is to be found in doing good to others, to any set of precepts or prescriptions more elemental than the terms in which they were expressed in Franklin's own prose was to risk caricaturing them as wholly prudential and self-serving, or as what Van Wyck Brooks and D. H. Lawrence called, respectively, "catchpenny realities" and "moral machinery."[13] By contrast, Miller's identification of the whole of seventeenth-century religion with what he called the "Augustinian strain of piety," and his translation of this strain into what he described as a subjective mood or frame of mind that in his *New England Mind* converted Puritan metaphysics into a prefiguration of romantic metaphysics and in his intellectual biography of Jonathan Edwards made Puritanism sound instead like a metaphysical precursor of modernism—such reductions only succeeded in rendering Puritan spirituality more rather than less intellectually attractive in the cultural climate of the postwar era. One could, of course, merely conclude that Puritanism has been better served by its modern interpreters than has the Enlightenment, but this would be to gloss several other factors that have delimited our historical ability to perceive the Enlightenment's after-effects in the last two centuries of literary expression.

★

One of them derives from the assessment literary and cultural historians have made of these traditions' different spiritual legacies. For example, it is generally assumed that American Protestantism, at any rate in its Calvinist form, has left as its chief legacy in America something like an inherited penchant for self-criticism that at its best is capable of correcting even its own excesses. This assessment of the spiritual legacy of American Protestantism is often explained by reference

to Melville's famous review of Hawthorne's *Mosses from an Old Manse,*
where Melville attributes the force of Hawthorne's appeal to "a blackness, ten times black" that shrouds, or at least casts into deep shadow,
the "Indian-summer sunlight" of Hawthorne's historical romances.
Melville is not prepared to say whether Hawthorne has availed himself
of this "mystic blackness" merely to secure his marvelous chiaroscuro
effects or is really afflicted with "a touch of Puritanic gloom," but he is
convinced that the power of this blackness in Hawthorne ultimately
derives from its reference to an intuition that no deeply feeling,
thoughtful person who attempts to "weigh this world" and "strike an
uneven balance" can do without for long. This is an intuition of
"something, somehow" like "that Calvinistic sense of Innate Depravity and Original Sin, from whose visitations, in some shape or other,
no deeply thinking mind is always and wholly free." [14]

Melville's emphasis on the indefinite pronouns—"something,
somewhat"—is what makes, and always has made, all the difference in
the way this statement has offered itself to later generations. While it
permits him to appropriate a sense of evil as a principle of moral and
spiritual correction, it enables him at the same time to dissociate this
sense from the necessity of any conscious assent to the theological doctrine in which it was first expressed. The cultural utility of the principle continues to engender respect for the tradition which first generated it without requiring that anyone believe in the specific tenets of
that tradition itself. Thus Melville and his cultural heirs can remain—
and have remained—Puritans at heart while at the same time spurning
Puritan dogmas with their mind.

By comparison, the cultural heirs of the Enlightenment have not
been similarly favored. To embrace the Enlightenment in almost any
form in the postwar period has been tantamount to affirming virtually
all of the liberal republican ideals, from freedom, autonomy, individualism, and rationalism to the self-reliance, democracy, and free-
market capitalism in which they have been thought to issue. But to
affirm as diverse, ultimately as vague, and potentially as conflicting a
set of ideals as these has been to advocate something very much like
what editorial writers, no less than historical scholars on both the extreme right and the extreme left, take to be America's official ideological version of itself. Thus where the Calvinist legacy has frequently
been interpreted as the intellectual and spiritual source of whatever real
cultural criticism has been produced in America, the Enlightenment
legacy has as readily been dismissed as the moral and philosophical
source of American cultural consensus and complacency.

Yet another factor contributing to the increasing opaqueness of the

Enlightenment in twentieth-century literary scholarship is the fairly widespread conviction that its chief aesthetic assumptions exerted an essentially negative influence on subsequent literary practice in the United States. Their influence is held to have been essentially negative because it is still supposed generally that these aesthetic assumptions derived from the Scottish Common Sense philosophers who were in the habit of restricting the creative arts, and particularly the writing of fiction, to the provision of moral exempla.[15] As the story goes, the effect of such strictures was to compel gifted young antebellum writers like Hawthorne and Simms to abandon the writing of novels altogether in favor of creating, in reaction to the restraints of eighteenth-century common sense, an alternative fictive form. This fictive form was, and is, known as the romance and in time came to be defined as a kind of counteraesthetic to the Enlightenment. But such a development would have made little difference to any but a few historians of early nineteenth-century fiction if after World War II the romance had not been reinterpreted as virtually the only authentic fictive form in America. The key text was no doubt Richard Chase's *The American Novel and Its Tradition,* published in 1957, but it was supported by countless other studies that not only defined the romance aesthetically as a form antagonistic to the Enlightenment but also helped transform postwar nineteenth- and twentieth-century literary history into an outright repudiation of Enlightenment values.[16]

Finally, there is the historical prescience of the Enlightenment's last great representative in the nineteenth century and the accuracy of his diagnosis about the ways experience was to change in the twentieth. I am referring once more to Henry Adams, and to the book he pointedly did not wish to refer to as his autobiography, where the reader is forced to contemplate something far more shattering than the discovery that an eighteenth-century education, however painstakingly acquired and brilliantly adapted, no longer prepares a person to live a life of useful and productive service in the nineteenth century. What breaks Adams's historical neck as he looks up at the forty-foot dynamos in the Gallery of Machines at the Great Exposition of 1900 in Paris is the discovery of "an irruption of forces totally new" that plunges him into what one of his later chapters calls "an abyss of ignorance." What was once a carefully ordered universe has become a haphazard and chaotic multiverse, and when Adams tries to imagine what kind of new education would suit this New World, he is confounded:

He found himself in a land where no one had ever penetrated before; where order was an accidental relation obnoxious to nature; artificial compulsion imposed on motion; against which every free energy of the universe revolted; and which, being merely occasional, resolved itself back into anarchy at last. He could not deny that the law of the new multiverse explained much that had been most obscure, especially the persistently fiendish treatment of man by man; the perpetual effort of society to establish law, and the perpetual revolt of society against the law it had established; the perpetual building up of authority by force, and the perpetual appeal to force to overthrow it; the perpetual symbolism of a higher law, and the perpetual relapse to a lower one; the perpetual victory of the principles of freedom, and their perpetual conversion into principles of power; but the staggering problem was the outlook ahead into the despotism of artificial order which nature abhorred. The physicists had a phrase for it, unintelligible to the vulgar: "All that we win is a battle—lost in advance—with the irreversible phenomena in the background of nature." [17]

The problem for Adams was not simply that the constellation of physical energies had changed, or that a new grammar of motives had been introduced; the real rupture had occurred in the idiom of experience itself and in the kinds of moral and spiritual calculus required to measure its consequences. In scientific parlance, this amounted to a paradigm change, in critical terms to a revolution in metaphor. But to Adams the question of what to call it was less disturbing than the issue of what to make of it. The only analogue he could imagine to the cataclysmic changes foreshadowed in 1900 was the year 310, when the Emperor Constantine began to establish Christianity as the official religion of the Roman Empire. For Adams, then, all the intellectual and ethical coordinates were rendered impotent after 1900, and Alfred Kazin has argued that much of American writing since has been an attempt to register the experiential meanings of this change that Adams was the first to describe and to devise strategies for coming to terms with it. [18]

Theodore Dreiser provides one of the most powerful representations of this newly reconfigured world in his sympathetic portrayal of Clyde Griffiths as a "wisp in the wind of social forces" in *An American Tragedy,* F. Scott Fitzgerald another in his depiction of the pulverization of James Gatz at the hands of Tom Buchanan's brutal power and Daisy Fay's cruel indifference in *The Great Gatsby.* But force, power, and energy are also the essential metaphors of Ernest Hemingway's experiments with the short story in *In Our Time,* and they figure as elements only intermittently suppressable—and then often with disastrous and not fully comprehended consequences—in Willa Cather's novels of the Nebraska prairies. Power becomes the explosive feature that must be prevented from turning suicidal, or at least self-hating, in confessional poets like Robert Lowell, Sylvia Plath, and Anne Sexton; it constitutes the factor whose social and political transvaluation is the only antidote to its racist and sexist misuse in the writings of African-Americans like Ralph Ellison and James Baldwin and women generally; and it is synonymous with the component that is running down in Thomas Pynchon's fantasies of entelechy.

A world so completely organized around and dominated by power, by sheer potency, is a world no longer susceptible to understanding in terms of such Enlightenment values as balance, reasonableness, adaptation, freedom, skepticism, happiness, autonomy, and optimism. It is a world comprehensible only in terms of religious myths of catastrophe, of metaphysical narratives of rupture, division, and disinheritance. As a consequence, the Enlightenment has become the absent, or at least the forgotten, integer in the American equation of the relationship between faith and knowledge. There is no chapter, for instance, either on the Enlightenment or on the legacy of Enlightenment thinking and feeling in the recent *Columbia Literary History of the United States*. There is not even a single entry on the Enlightenment in any of the five editions of *The Oxford Companion to American Literature*. In comparison with the astonishing number of major monographs that explore the religious dimensions of nineteenth- and twentieth-century American literature,[19] one is pressed to come up with a single text, other than fugitive remarks sprinkled through Howard Mumford Jones's *O Strange New World* and his *Belief and Disbelief in American Literature*, that does the same thing for the Enlightenment and American writing.

The one recent exception, surely, is the criticism of Lewis Simpson, and particularly *The Brazen Face of History*, where it is argued that American literature has been obsessed (as William Ellery Channing predicted it would be in his 1831 "Remarks on a National Literature") with "the perfectibility of mind in America," though in a decidedly negative way; "Its force (as [John] Adams may be said to have forecast) is to be estimated in terms of the ironic challenging of it in our letters rather than its literary affirmation."[20] Thus among the many characters who have their origination in the mind but then experience the mind's inability to gain dominion over nature and history—the list begins, according to Simpson, with Cooper's Leatherstocking and passes on to Poe's Roderick Usher, Hawthorne's Robin Molineux, Melville's Ishmael, Mark Twain's Huckleberry Finn, Hemingway's Jake Barnes, Fitzgerald's Jay Gatsby, Faulkner's Quentin Compson III, and Robert Penn Warren's Jack Burden—all attest to the literary questioning of the Enlightenment paradigm. But otherwise Puritanism, or at least Calvinism, has carried the day, managing to be connected by historians and critics to an enormous company of American writers that includes Franklin, Emerson, Thoreau, Theodore Parker, Francis Parkman, Frederick Douglass, Hawthorne, Melville, Dickinson, Jones Very, the later Mark Twain, Henry James, Henry Adams, Edwin Arlington Robinson, Wendell Phillips, Vachel Lindsay, Paul Elmer More, Irving Babbitt, Robert Frost, Sinclair Lewis, Ernest Hemingway, T. S. Eliot, Marianne Moore, Wallace Stevens, William Faulkner, Katherine Anne Porter, Robert Penn Warren, James Baldwin, Robert Lowell, James Agee, Flannery O'Connor, and various others.

★

Thus it should come as no surprise that the conventional way of telling the story about post-Enlightenment American literature in the post-war period is to leave the Enlightenment pretty well out of it and to treat religion as an attribute of the imagination and an aspect of form. Religion thus becomes associated with a quality of mind obsessed with moral oppositions and suspicious of thematic closure, indeed, skepti-cal of all metanarratives—a mind that characteristically tends to ex-plore extreme ranges of experience and to rest in dichotomous, even conflicting or contradictory, frames of thought. Far from seeking through Christian strategies of redemptive catharsis to reconcile divi-sion and dissonance, the American literary imagination, male and fe-male, so this narrative goes, has concentrated its most important ener-gies on exploring the aesthetic and even religious possibility of forms of alienation and disorder, and often in morally equivocal ways.[21] Hence even in a standard work like *The Scarlet Letter,* where transgres-sion and repentance, autonomy and submission, and freedom and ser-vitude constitute the principal poles between which much of the action oscillates, the novel resists all impulses toward intellectual or spiritual resolution by terminating, finally, in an image of tragic separation. Hester and Dimmesdale both remain true, but their fidelity merely succeeds in condemning them to opposite or, at the very least, to hardly apposite ways of being.

The customary way of reading the religious meaning of nineteenth- and twentieth-century literature has consequently gone something like this. If the representative American literary imagination displays char-acteristics that are undeniably Manichaean, these internal divisions have not resulted from its absorption with the predicament of human iniquity and its transcendence, or with the problem of sexual domina-tion and its displacement. They have derived instead from its preoc-cupation with the problem of human freedom and the impediments to its realization. And when this preoccupation has taken narrative form, it has typically produced narratives that diverge sharply from the traditional pattern of the Protestant story about repentance and possible regeneration through faith, even when they use many of its presiding symbols, for the sake of telling a tale about the limitations of selfhood and their heuristic value. This is a narrative, then, that makes only the faintest gesture backward toward the Enlightenment's ideology of mediated freedom before attempting to reconcile a later romantic quest for unmediated being with the residue of an earlier Puritan, or at any rate Protestant, sense of human impotence and the need for self-abasement.

Tony Tanner has captured the religious essence of this story about as well as anyone else by noting that it is predicated on "an abiding dream . . . that an unpatterned, unconditioned life is possible in which your moments of stillness, choices and repudiations are all your own."[22] This is what, for example, Isabel Archer seems to express when, in *The Portrait of a Lady,* she confesses that "nothing that belongs to me is any measure of me, everything, on the contrary, is a limit and a perfectly arbitrary one." It is the same conviction that in Faulkner's *Absalom, Absalom* solidifies Thomas Sutpen's desire to wrest a house and a dynasty from 100 square miles of Mississippi wilderness, as though, like the central figures in *The Great Gatsby* or "Song of Myself," he was born of some Platonic conception in his own mind. It is the dream of an individual who, like Captain Ahab in *Moby-Dick,* would be "free as the air" but discovers that "he is down in all the world's books."

The corollary to this romantic dream amounts to a correspondent and not un-Calvinist dread, to quote Tanner again, "that someone else is patterning your life, that there are all sorts of invisible plots afoot to rob you of your autonomy of thought and action, that conditioning is ubiquitous."[23] Thus Hawthorne again, in Chillingworth's self-excusing confession to Hester: "My old faith, long forgotten, comes back to me, and explains all that we do and all that we suffer. By thy first step awry, thou didst plant the germ of evil; but, since that moment, it has all been a dark necessity." Or the narrator in Faulkner's *Light in August,* who tends to view Joe Christmas and Percy Grimm as pawns on a chessboard drawn ever closer to their fated confrontation by an invisible Player.

The traditional American strategy for dealing with this situation and narratively encompassing it is to submit the dreamer to the dread to determine what, if anything, he or she can learn from the experience. But because this experiment in what might be called liberal self-revisioning usually takes place in idyllic natural surroundings set at some distance from the world of women and children, and in the company of social others whose moral and spiritual attributes simply mirror the values their protagonists long to acquire even when they can nowhere be seriously applied, it has been criticized as dangerously antinomian and imperialistic by some critics and characterized as a "melodrama of beset manhood" by others.[24]

★

We now know that this way of constructing and reading the story of nineteenth- and twentieth-century American literature and its relation to religion, and particularly to Protestant Christianity, isn't quite accurate, or, at any rate, doesn't comprise the whole story. Owing largely to the work of feminist critics, we know, for example, that Protestant orthodoxy has played a much more active role in the formation of at least some post-Enlightenment literature than was formerly acknowledged, and that within this literature it has been as committed to serious cultural criticism and renewal as the revisionary liberalism associated with many of the writers of the more predominantly male canon. Interestingly enough, the reinstatement of Protestant religious orthodoxy in this feminist counternarrative to the canonical story has been secured only at the expense of more or less completely discrediting the Enlightenment altogether.

The feminist counternarrative construes the Enlightenment, and particularly its stereotypical attitudes toward reason, nature, gender, liberty, and the realm of the personal and the intimate, as expressions of a patriarchial structure that had to be challenged, and in considerable measure displaced, if women were to assume something like a position of equality within the economy of human affairs. The instrument of their empowerment in this counternarrative turns out to be the religion of early nineteenth-century Protestantism once its redemptive energies were released in the evangelical enthusiasm of the Second Great Awakening. Those energies helped legitimate a new sentimentalization of American piety that resituated the institutions of the family at the center of American society and redefined motherhood and the rituals of homemaking and child-rearing as central mysteries in a new feminist, almost Eleusinian, cult of domesticity.

Told most vividly in the writings of critics like Jane Tompkins and Cathy N. Davidson, this story finds abundant exemplification in the antebellum soteriology of sentimental novels ranging from Susanna Rowson's *Charlotte Temple,* Hannah Foster's *The Coquette,* and Catherine Sedgwick's *Hope Leslie* to Susan Warner's *The Wide, Wide World,* and it achieves a kind of consummation in Harriet Beecher Stowe's *Uncle Tom's Cabin*.[25] Here Christian self-sacrifice—Little Eva's no less than Uncle Tom's—performs, at least for women, an invaluable kind of cultural work whose subtly dialectical patterns of critique and recovery, of repudiation and resurrection, can be traced as well in such later works as Elizabeth Stoddard's *The Morgesons*, Kate Chopin's *The Awakening*, and Sarah Orne Jewett's *The Country of the Pointed Firs*. As feminists point out, this is a literature that explicitly in some cases, implicitly in others, questions the prevailing image of culture as dominated by upper-class white males who use the instruments of rationality, moderation, common sense, and civic virtue to consolidate their power over women. This literature seeks to replace it with a more sentimental image of culture as a kind of family held together by the sacrificial action of females whose heroic submission to the procreative and nurturing responsibilities of the household can, and should, be interpreted as a symbol of strength rather than of weakness—a symbol with the power to transform the family into a source of moral and spiritual rebirth for society as a whole.

According to some feminists, however, this feminist counternarrative never quite manages to escape the pull of the masculine, and thus the Enlightenment, values that it would repudiate. Even if the piety of a little Eva eludes Ann Douglas's charge that Christianity in *Uncle Tom's Cabin*, like religion in the sentimental novel generally, runs the risk of functioning for its readers as "camp," as a form of narcissistic nostalgic, the counternarrative itself never succeeds, as Elizabeth Fox-Genovese has recently pointed out, in freeing women from the culture of men. By politicizing the culture of sentimentality, the feminist counternarrative, like the fiction that illustrates it, merely reinscribes the values of white, male, elite individuality, and the ideology of dominance it supports, in the religious sensibility of women.

This becomes clear, Fox-Genovese maintains, when one compares the writings of women in the northeast with those from the south where, as it turns out, many women writers, both black and white, were made as uncomfortable by prevailing models of womanhood—particularly if those models sought to resegregate women in a gendered ghetto of religious sensibility isolated from the world of men—as they were by the images that men were trying to impose on them. No less assiduous than their northern counterparts in exploring their own identity and independence, these southern writers nonetheless were just as emphatically opposed to "the northeastern model of individualism"—Augusta Jane Evans's spectacularly popular *Beulah* is the example Fox-Genovese invokes—"and celebrated woman's acceptance of her proper role within marriage and, above all, her willing subordination to God who guaranteed any worthy social order." [26] Thus if empowerment is what many southern women sought, they did not find it either by dissociating themselves from the world of men or by repudiating the dominant culture men had created to maintain, through religious and secular values, their control over women. Rather, they achieved it by using that cultural world for their own purposes:

Women and African-Americans, including African-American women, have developed their own ways of criticizing the attitudes and institutions that hedged them in. Confronted with rigidly class-, race-, and gender-specific models of acceptability, they have manipulated the language to speak in a double tongue, simultaneously associating themselves with and distancing themselves from the dominant models of respectability. Their continuous negotiation with the possibilities that the culture has afforded them has had nothing to do with a mindless acceptance of themselves as lesser. It has had everything to do with their determination to translate the traditions and values of their own communities into a language that would make them visible to others—and with their own determination to participate in American culture. [27]

Why were women of all colors, both north and south, to say nothing of many men, unable to find, either in the feminist narratives of the northeast and the south or in the male narrative of the traditional canon, a language into which "to translate the traditions and values of their own communities" so that they might become "visible to others"? I would contend that at least one of the reasons is that both of those narratives may have misconstrued the literary relations between colonial American religion and the American Enlightenment and, more particularly, may have misconceived, or at least underestimated, what was achieved as a consequence. This is a large claim that would require for its support the writing of an entirely different book; all I can do here is sketch some of its main elements and hope that its further refinements and necessary extensions can be inferred by the discerning reader.

★

In this revisionist narrative, which is in truth less interested in countering its feminist and male canonical competitors than in complementing them, the Enlightenment is accorded an importance rather different from contemporary estimates. The contemporary estimate is the one furnished by Henry F. May, which assumes that the Enlightenment's largest impact on the formation of post-Enlightenment literary and intellectual culture in the United States derived from those traditions that emphasized moderation and common sense, what May calls the Rational and Didactic Enlightenments, and exercised the slightest influence through those traditions that were utopian and critical, namely, the Revolutionary and, most especially, the Skeptical Enlightenments. Indeed, May is convinced that the tradition of the village atheist that descends from Voltaire and Diderot, and runs in America from Abner Kneeland to Clarence Darrow, has never led more than a minority, and distinctly paradoxical, existence in this country, since religious iconoclasm here has rarely amounted to a questioning of all moral values, and the deeper skepticism associated with David Hume that is prepared to doubt the operations of all minds "and the validity of all general principles" has, at least until very recently, found no fertile soil in America at all.[28]

In the narrative I propose, the relative contribution of these several strains needs to be reversed almost exactly. The Enlightenments that seem to have played the most influential role in shaping American literature in the modern age were the Revolutionary and, particularly, the Skeptical Enlightenments, and they did so often by combining forces to challenge, and eventually to undermine, the very foundations of Protestant thinking in much nineteenth-century literature. Thus skepticism of the Humean variety, which puts all mental operations in doubt, has erupted intermittently but recurrently throughout nineteenth- and twentieth-century American writing and can be found in works ranging from "The Narrative of Arthur Gordon Pym" and *Pierre* to Quentin Compson's anguished meditations in *Absalom, Absalom* or the torments of many of John Berryman's Henry poems. And the trope of the village atheist was given a new cynical twist in the nineteenth-century with the emergence of the figure of the confidence man, a figure first anticipated by some of the stratagems Benjamin Franklin reports adopting as a young man in his *Autobiography*, then memorialized in Melville's novel by that title, later given feminine coloration in some of Emily Dickinson's poems on God's duplicity, carried forward in that admonitory strain of Robert Frost's poetry that includes "Design," "Fire and Ice," and "Provide, Provide," subsequently rendered comical and mordant (or both) in Wallace Stevens's "The Emperor of Ice-Cream" and "A High-toned Old Christian Woman," and eventually pushed to brilliant extreme in Ralph Ellison's portrait of Rinehart the Runner in *Invisible Man*. Furthermore, these currents of religious skepticism, as David S. Reynolds has shown in reference to the writers of the American Renaissance, have always been fed by a vast underground literature that is by turns witty, derisive, caustic, iconoclastic, subversive, and parodic.[29]

Another way of saying this would be to suggest that some of the most important work of the Skeptical or Critical Enlightenment in France and England, if not the Revolutionary Enlightenment as well, was accomplished not in the eighteenth century but rather in the nineteenth, and not on that side of the Atlantic but on this. It was work that proceeded, at least from a literary perspective, toward the dismantling of virtually all of the religious assumptions on which American literary culture was then based. At the beginning of the century it was assumed that the chief representational function of literary art was to legitimate a world centered on God and illustrative of His purposes, particularly as they were revealed in the orderly processes of Nature and as they were worked out in the unfolding salvific pattern of History. This theory of representation is perfectly exemplified in the "prospect" or "rising glory" poems of the misnamed "Connecticut Wits" where, in texts like *The Rising Glory of America, The Conquest of Canaan, Greenfield Hill,* and *The Columbiad,* poets such as Philip Freneau, Timothy Dwight, and Joel Barlow envisaged a redemptive future for the United States whose symbolic outlines were to become even more familiar much later in such concepts as the Monroe Doctrine and Manifest Destiny.[30] By the end of the century, it would be fair to say that in critical terms the only thing left of this theory was a belief in the importance of representation itself and in the perceptual instrumentalities which made it possible. Those instrumentalities amounted to what was variously meant by the term "consciousness," and consciousness, now understood not as an entity so much as a function, was in turn held to be accountable for representing little more than the processes and perspectives that made it up.

*

This story is one version of what I have been calling the pragmatist narrative, and virtually the whole of it is proleptically present in what is generally conceded to be America's greatest epic, Herman Melville's *Moby-Dick.* Often interpreted as a representation of the nineteenth century's absorption with the issue of deicide, *Moby-Dick* has too rarely been read as also a prefiguration of the kind of pragmatic consciousness that was, in the later nineteenth and subsequently the twentieth century, to take its place. More than this, the roots of much of the text devoted to Ahab's concerns in the theological world of seventeenth-century Puritan metaphysics are nicely balanced by its structural reliance, during many of the stretches when Ishmael's voice becomes ascendant, on the literary form that was so often reappropriated in the intellectualized, ironic, satiric world of the eighteenth century, the form known as the anatomy.[31]

From a pragmatist point of view, the problems that afflict Ahab are those of a latter-day Puritan who inherits a system of belief that can no longer answer or evade the questions he puts to it but who cannot escape the tyranny of the system itself. Ahab is the last and fullest and most perverse flowering of the high Calvinist tradition in America, a tradition which now, in its death throes, and in the name of Christian values that Ahab himself constantly transgresses, turns against itself by calling God Himself to account. When God fails to listen, or, from the text's perspective, appears to be indifferent, the tradition then destroys itself in a maddened act of self-immolation.

This is not, of course, how Ahab experiences his own predicament. Ahab's experiences his own predicament as a desire to determine what lies behind the pasteboard mask of appearance that has been shoved so brutally in his face. But this desire is endlessly frustrated because of the impenetrability of the mask whose nearness only compounds the outrage. "That inscrutible thing is chiefly what I hate," says Ahab, meaning, as Charles Feidelson long ago remarked, "the ambiguity of the meanings that lure him on and the resistance that objects present to the inquiring mind."[32] The only way that Ahab can end this torture is by terminating the voyage in quest of truth, and the only way he can do this is by settling for only one definition, or set of definitions, of the pasteboard mask and then hurling himself, all mutilated and mutilating, against it.

Ishmael's predicament seems to be the very opposite of Ahab's, or eventually becomes so. Initially daunted by the indefiniteness of the novel's quest for the mystery that lies behind the pasteboard mask—an indefiniteness Ishmael recurrently experiences in the earlier parts of the book as the ultimate horror of a world that constantly blurs all distinctions in an insubstantial medium that seems, as he notes in "The Whiteness of the Whale," purposefully deceptive—Ishmael himself becomes in time the vehicle through which we discover a world whose insubstantiality is but the reverse side of its diversity and procreativity. Such a world can be comprehended only by a frame of mind that is the very opposite of Ahab's. If Ahab's mind, outraged by a world that defies its quest for certainty, traffics in signs, equivalences, and linked analogies that are supposed to represent the thing that they name, Ishmael's mind, undismayed as it finally becomes by the multitudinous expressivity of the world's plurality, trades in images, metaphors, and symbols that acknowledge the surplus of meanings that language carries within itself when it is used tropologically rather than allegorically.

The book's major movement is the transition from Ahab's mind to Ishmael's, from the "old consciousness," in D. H. Lawrence's terminology, that Ishmael initially shares with Ahab, and that must be sloughed off, to the "new consciousness" that is forming underneath. The outmoded consciousness that we identify with Ahab, and that Ishmael shares with him at the beginning, is a theocentric, monologistic, and moralistic consciousness that is predicated on the possibility of dividing up the principalities and powers that comprise experience into opposing elements of divine and demonic, good and evil, love and hate, life and death, male and female. The new consciousness that begins to emerge underneath in the polyphonous, polymorphous discourse of Ishmael's narrative is one that views these traditional oppositions as "interweavingly" intermixed in experience and responds by adopting an attitude that is tentative, experimental, provisional, improvisatory, eclectic, synoptic, changeable, and even contradictory.[33]

This consciousness is in many parts of the book no more than a matter of style, of an idiom as various and fluid as the circumstances of experience itself, but it is not too much to say that its creation and elaboration eventually become, as Daniel Hoffman was among the first to realize, the book's real spiritual destination.[34] That consciousness is identical with the style of Ishmael's bouyant, metaphoric voice as he records his "doubts of all things earthly" and his "intuitions of some things heavenly," while at the same time "knowing this combination makes neither believer nor infidel," but a person "who regards them both with equal eye." This is the idiom of a consciousness that is far less interested in preaching a message or developing a philosophy than in exploring another way to be. This way of being could easily be called comic if it weren't at the same time so close to the tragic. Founded on similar perceptions of life's cross-purposes, it simply recommends that we respond to them differently. While tragedy says that there is no help for the misfortune it brings us save in that recognition itself, a recognition which ennobles those who are capable of it even as it seals their doom, comedy in the Melvillean mode replies that we dare not dwell on these facts in outworn terms of thought. In other words, we need some possibility for corrective discounting. Ahab's story shows what happens when, through the atrophy of consciousness, we lack one; Ishmael's story shows us how, through the adaptations of consciousness, we can stylistically create one. "In its vast assimilations, its seemingly opportunistic eclecticism, its prag-

matic and improvisatory nonchalance, its capacious grandiloquence
and demotic humour it is indeed a style for America—the style of
America."[35]

★

So defined, consciousness in its late-nineteenth-century variants was
what the Enlightenment either had left out of its conception of the
mind altogether or had too often truncated in it; it was also what a
certain group of American philosophers and other intellectuals could
not resist transforming into a new subject of intellectual and aesthetic
investigation. With help from useful adversaries such as Josiah Royce
and important precursors such as Charles Sanders Peirce, William
James, along with other pragmatists, was able to show how the Enlightenment's confidence in the work of the mind might yet yield ad-
ditional discoveries into what had once been thought to be the sole
property of American religion. It all depended on developing a
method of intellectual inquiry that would permit consciousness to explore what yet remained ineffable and undecidable but still irrepress-
ible on its own borders. James spoke of this as "the re-instatement of
the vague to its proper place in our mental life."[36] What he meant by
"the vague" was that whole mysterious shadow world of feeling, intuition, implication, conjunction, disjunction, and change that under-
girds cognition and motivates action but that continues to remain invisible or discredited in so many late nineteenth- and early-twentieth-
century versions of experience.

"Every thing," as Emerson had noted in his *Journals* for June 1847,
"teaches transition, transference, metamorphosis: therein is human
power, in transference, not in creation & therein is human destiny, not
in longevity but in removal. We dive & reappear in new places."[37] This
was the kernel of the perspective James was to convert into his theory
of radical empiricism, a theory which, in addition to insisting that the
only things worth debating are definable in terms that are drawn from
experience itself, holds that the parts of experience hang together,
without need of transempirical support, in "a concatenated or continuous structure" of their own because the relations between parts are
just as much an element of experience as the parts themselves.[38] Less a
philosophical theory than a way of thinking, a form of mentality,
James's pragmatic method for exploring experience that eventuated, in
the notion of radical empiricism, in a doctrine of experience itself
amounted, in other terms, to what has usefully been called a special
kind of "consciousness *of* consciousness—an awareness that philosophical speculation, hitherto forbidding and remote, was suddenly

justification for the imaginative act of mind operating on the produce of the common day." [39]

James's turn toward the "consciousness *of* consciousness" was thus a turn toward a new theory of representation, but a theory that now supposed that the reality in need of representation was not "substantive," to use James's words again, but "transitive." What awaited full exploration and expression was the whole realm of conjunctive relations, a reality of experience that the Enlightenment, with its more restricted understanding of mentality, had tended to discount and that religion, with its more urgent requirements for certainty, often tended to engulf. This was a theory of representation, then, that drew on an interest in the practical, the immediate, and the concrete that goes back directly to the antimetaphysical bias of some of the most radical Enlightenment philosophers. [40] But it was also indebted to the experiential tenor of much seventeenth- and eighteenth-century American religion, and particularly to its concern with the problem of transcendence.

Thus we can summarize by suggesting that American philosophical pragmatism, at least as it began to work itself out in literary terms, was by implication a theory of representation that attempted to reconcile what was still epistemologically viable about the Enlightenment's quest for a sense of reality as personal, palpable, and publicly accessible with what was still culturally compelling and believable about American religion's imagination of an otherness that cannot be put by. Hence, as a theory of representation, American pragmatism was also a theory of belief. It was a theory about the nature of the real which postulated that if the real lies neither wholly beyond the self, in some hypostasizable world set over against it, nor wholly within the self, in some unitary core of spiritual being or deposit of biological essence independent of the occasions of its actualizations, then the real can still be found in the experience of those processes, events, and actions by which the self and the world interact. These are processes which, when understood in relation to the human agency that motivates them, are defined by the term "imagination" and, when understood in relation to the forms in which this agency realizes itself, are called "style."

At the risk of oversimplification, this is the theory of reality that was variously put to the test in that kind of twentieth-century American literature we traditionally refer to as modern or modernist. The test itself ultimately was to turn on the question of how imagination and style are to be represented when their function is redefined as a symbolization of the concourse between a self that is no longer singular but plural, or at least diffuse, and a world that is no longer fixed but changing, or at least unstable. This was a test that obviously took a variety of forms, ranging from Hemingway's attempts to convey "what really happened in action; what the actual things were which produced the emotion you experienced," to Faulkner's efforts to recover the "presentness of the past" in fictions whose elaborate methods of technique—unreliable narration, stream-of-consciousness writing, mythic parallels, chronological disorientation, historical flashbacks, montage effects, philosophical brooding, and structures of detection— were intended to historicize his readers' sense of the present. In some cases, the test involved parsing something as indefinable as what Stevens meant by his reference in "The Snow Man" to the "Nothing that is not there and the nothingness that is." In others, it amounted to determining what happens when, as Eliot wrote in "Burnt Norton," "Words strain,/Crack and sometimes break, under the burden,/Under the tension, slip, slide, perish,/Decay with imprecision, will not stay in place,/Will not stay still."

One of the most radical responses to this test was to be made by William's brother, Henry, a fact that would have been more obvious and richly appreciated if Henry's relation to the pragmatic tradition had not been constantly missed or suppressed by all but a few critics and scholars.[41] This is the more surprising because Henry made no secret of his intellectual indebtedness to William. When he finished reading his brother's *Pragmatism,* he immediately confessed himself in a letter to be "lost in the wonder of the extent to which all my life I have (like M. Jourdain) unconsciously pragmatised."[42] And upon finishing William's *The Meaning of Truth,* Henry was even more effusive and confessional:

You surely make philosophy more interesting and living than anyone has *ever* made it before, and by a real creative and undemolishable making; whereby all you write plays into *my* poor "creative" consciousness and artistic vision and pretension with the most extraordinary suggestiveness and force of application and inspiration. Thank the powers—that is thank *yours!*—for a relevant and assimilable and *referable* philosophy, which is related to the rest of one's intellectual life otherwise and more conveniently than a fowl is related to a fish. In short, dearest William, the effect of these collected papers of your present volume . . . seems to me exquisitely and adorably cumulative and, so to speak, consecrating; so that I, for my part feel Pragmatic invulnerability constituted.[43]

These are admissions that should have made more of a difference to our reading of Henry James than they have. Much of the mystery, though little of the magic, surrounding a complicated text like *The*

Turn of the Screw would be disspelled if critics were more sensitive to these remarks. As in so much of his later fiction, Henry is investigating the experience of things that exist, as William would have said, on the very edge of consciousness and, from a pragmatist perspective, challenging the kind of residually religious interpretive intelligence that is tempted not merely to essentialize the putative sources of those experiences but also to demonize them. On this reading, it matters far less to the outcome of the story whether the ghosts are real or the children are truly corrupted by thinking they are. What matters is that from motives at once psychosexual and religious the governess is compelled to imagine that they can be nothing else and is thereby corrupted herself, being transformed by the end of the story, but without her realizing it, into a beast from hell. Similarly, in *The Beast in the Jungle* Henry explores the moral failure of a character who refuses, in effect, to become a radical empiricist; John Marcher's sin can be summarized as a continuous rejection of the numerous opportunities presented him to follow the pointings of his own experience with May Bartram, to connect, if we can think of this in the broad sense, the subjects of his sentences with the predicates they imply.

While none of this is expressed discursively, James renders it dramatically by (to give pragmatism another name) the "ambulatory" method he shared with William. This is the method that enables us, as William stated, to move toward a knowable object by means of the impulse, and not the content, which the idea of it communicates to us. A trenchant description of the method that Henry perfected in his later writing, pragmatic ambulation is premised epistemologically on the belief that reality is made, not found, and that the greatest threat to the inquiring mind is the temptation to interrupt the process of its continuous construction and reconstruction by arresting and isolating some moment from the ongoing process and taking it for an image of the whole. Seeking what Wallace Stevens called the "ghostlier demarcations" and "keener sounds" of consciousness in motion, the later fiction of Henry James, like, in so different a manner, Marianne Moore's poetic experiments in exacting attention or Katherine Anne Porter's fictional reproductions of the technology of memory, was an attempt stylistically to represent life *in actu*.

Thus as a theory of representation, the pragmatist conception of consciousness, or, rather, of the consciousness *of* consciousness, could still survive the tests put to it by modern circumstances, even in such desperate gestures of self-definition as Adrienne Rich's "Diving into the Wreck" or such self-doubting acts of social investigation as James Agee's *Let Us Now Praise Famous Men*. It could survive so long as the spirit of an increasing late-modernist skepticism could be prevented from rebelling against consciousness itself, from calling into question its belief that imagination or style represent not, as Robert Frost put it in "The Most of It," their "own love back in copy speech,/But counter-love, original response." Yet when the spirit of a more radicalized criticism began to invade the precincts of consciousness itself, its contents no less than its creations were quickly reduced, as in the stories of Donald Barthelme, to a series of clichés, what Barthelme calls the "dreck" of contemporary society, or to mere critical and aesthetic "junk," what John Barth portrays in *The Sot-Weed Factor* as the "refuse" of literary history.

Such postmodernist works as these tend to presume that consciousness is no more than a construct comprised of "used" components that, like the cigarette butts, old Kleenex tissues, and discarded food wrappers left behind in secondhand cars when they are traded in, symbolize only, as Thomas Pynchon suggests in *The Crying of Lot 49,* the pathos of their own enervated disposability. In a world composed of little more than trash, or what Pynchon wittily refers to as "W.A.S.T.E.," the objects that consciousness was once held to represent—feelings, relations, passages, intuitions, interruptions, aporias—dissolve into thin air, to be replaced by gestures, signs, marks as innocently empty of significance and as infinitely replicable and replaceable as the mind of Chance the gardener, whom the television producers rename Chauncy Gardener, in Jerzy Kozinski's *Being There,* or as indeterminate and sometimes unreadable as the "art of distilling/ Weird fragrances out of nothing" which constitutes the subject of John Ashbery's *Self-Portrait in a Convex Mirror* and other poems.

*

If this suggests the emergence of a new postmodernist literary culture that is now bent on confounding what I have called the pragmatist project—the project of regrafting those parts of the liberal, if not rationalist, heritage that survived the seductions of essentialism onto those elements of the religious heritage that resisted the soporifics of certainty—it may still be a culture that, for all of its alienation from the religious enthusiasm surrounding it, has not seen the last of the Enlightenment. In late-modernist and postmodernist American literature—or, better, in our present academicized understanding of it—the Critical or Skeptical Enlightenment is, in one of its forms, clearly in the process of seeking to avenge itself against its own earlier principal achievement. That achievement was the creation of the philosophical subject known as "Man" which in former eras underwrote such serious projects as democratic politics, Freudian psychology, and the humanistic tradition (and is still recognizable in James's notion of the pluralistic self), but which in ours tends to be viewed as just another corrupt technique by which human beings reinvent themselves as privileged objects of study.

This act of critical self-consumption has, to be sure, cleared the intellectual and cultural field of much of the metaphysical and moral debris that had accumulated there over the last several centuries, but at the same time it has left the field morally and spiritually eviscerated. To some intellectuals, this may merely signify America's return to the state of moral and spiritual poverty that has, on the reading of various pragmatists as well, always been its natural condition, or that, according to some interpretations, has always been the condition most propitious for its creative development. Stanley Cavell, who is clearly a close cousin to the pragmatists if not one himself, has turned this double conviction into what is probably the most powerful defense ever mounted of an American philosophical tradition that originates with Emerson and was expanded by Thoreau, a tradition in search of what, after Emerson, Cavell calls, in the title of a recent book, "this new yet unapproachable America."

Cavell's argument centers around the question of why America is "unapproachable." It is "unapproachable" in a negative sense because its official culture, such as it is, is conformist, which is the same thing as saying that for Emerson it is unoriginal. Being unoriginal, American culture does not, at least in its "official" formations, know what it might or could originate, does not even have a language to speak of such things. In this sense, America is "unapproachable" because it is undiscussable, and it is undiscussable because it offers no terms of approach to what it has not yet begun to be, to the experience, as Cavell says another way, that it has not had of what it has yet to experience. This may be as simple a matter as saying that America has—or at least until Emerson's time had—no language of its own, but Cavell questions whether, according to this logic, this can really be said or shown. Cavell's way out of this dilemma is to turn back to the project of Emerson himself for what amounts to a description of his own philosophical practice in America's continuing economy of cultural scarcity:

The classical British Empiricists had interpreted what we call experience as made up of impressions and the ideas derived from impressions. What Emerson wishes to show, in these terms, is that, for all our empiricism, nothing (now) makes an impression on us, that we accordingly have no experience (of our own), that we are inexperienced. Hence Emerson's writing is meant as the provision of experience for these shores, of our trials, perils, essays.[44]

Making a virtue of necessity is Cavell's way, like Emerson's perhaps, of rendering unapproachability approachable. But even if one is persuaded, as I sometimes am, by this sanguine assumption that America's cultural opportunities are to be found in the discovery of its comparative cultural deprivation, there is no gainsaying that now, to use Stevens's metaphor, "the theatre has changed," and with it the kind of play that can be staged there. The scene may still pit religion against the Enlightenment, setting something like a religiously residual sense of solidarity with all those people that official cultures tend to marginalize over against the ministrations of a "later Reason" that has at heart only its own self-redescriptions. But intellectuals like Richard Rorty, who think this way, are now convinced that these traditions have little or nothing to say to one another and, in fact, may never have had. As resources for helping us cultivate the kind of ironic perspective that will provide the greatest scope for personal self-creation or the greatest inducement to notice the pain and suffering of others, both the American Enlightenment and the traditions of American religion have, by Rorty's lights, pretty well spent themselves.

By this Rorty does not mean to imply that we have derived no moral benefit from Christianity and the Enlightenment. All he intends to maintain—though for him, as for many others like him, it is everything—is that those benefits—an increased sensitivity to the suffering of others in the one case, an enhanced appreciation of the need and importance of personal freedom on the other—are no longer tied to the world views that were initially developed to express them and are of little further help to us so long as they continue to obscure or repress the contingency of their own origins. Our need to relate ourselves to something larger than the self may be no less urgent than our need for better models of self-description, but these two needs now possess only attenuated connections with traditions once vital in the past and can in no sense be integrated with each other, despite centuries of philosophical and theological effort. This is as much as to suggest that the old contest between religion and the Enlightenment is essentially over, not because either side won, but only because most intellectuals and artists no longer see themselves as actors in that drama. The old problematics of their relationship have not so much been solved as dissolved. And so the story ends, the poet said, not with a bang but a whimper.

*

But the story for pragmatism, and particularly for pragmatism as one way of resolving the relations between religion and the Enlightenment in American letters, has no ending; that, in fact, is one of its main themes. The object of the pragmatist narrative is not to reach closure so much as to suspend its achievement indefinitely for the sake of keeping the narrative from terminating before all the voices implicated in it, all the parties with a vested interest in its outcome, get to be heard. This is a world, so pragmatism maintains, whose evidence isn't all in yet and never will be so long as anyone with a claim on its meaning has yet to be understood. This in effect is to say that the Enlightenment still lives, at least so long as we continue to believe that a republic of opinions, no matter how various and even contestatious, is to be preferred to an oligarchy of truths, no matter how coherent or benign. By the same token, this is not to say that religion is dead, unless we are prepared to concede that all experience is subsumable within some biological, graphological, or ideological template. Religion and the Enlightenment continue to survive just insofar as we continue to have experiences capable of being shared, of being communicated, which exceed our rational grasp precisely at the point where our need to express their singularity and salience, their distinctiveness and decisiveness, surpasses our ability to say what they mean.

Another way of putting this would be to say that the pragmatic tradition in American writing has conceived for itself a different kind of consummation altogether, one that Stanley Cavell has tried to imagine for the relations between religion and the Enlightenment through his efforts to recover "the uncanniness of the ordinary" and that Richard Poirier has invoked through his suggestive notion of "writing off the self." [45] Fantasies of self-annihilation are, as Poirier well knows, hardly novel in Western literary history, just as he also knows that until the recent past they have most often been associated with dreams of redemption. But Poirier is interested in the project of self-evacuation and renewal neither as, in Christian understanding, a propaedeutic to salvation nor as, in Nietzsche and Foucault, a response to the bankruptcy of those organizations or forms of life that have turned human beings into the chief objects of their own study. In opposition to both the Christian and the modern view of self-erasure, Poirier intends to define an American tradition that discovers the vitality of human presence in forms so alien to its traditional interests and sites of valorization as almost to link the human with energies that deny it.

This is a tradition, so Poirier maintains, that begins in America with Emerson and includes Thoreau and Whitman but also extends through the elder Henry James and his son, William, to such moderns as Stein, Frost, and Stevens, and to such contemporaries as Ashbery and, possibly, O'Hara. This is a series of thinkers and artists whose associations with the intellectual habits and assumptions of American pragmatism come out in a variety of ways, from their faith in the materials of ordinary experience, their distrust of absolutes, their delight in process, mutability, and activity, and their conviction that truth is fabricated rather than found, to their belief that America's richest cultural resource may consist in what other interpreters of the American scene, most notably Henry James, have described as its most serious cultural deficiency: namely, the comparative thinness and barrenness of American social circumstance. Yet what most unites this often-misunderstood tradition that refuses to associate the problems of writing with our inherited cultural life is its predilection for moments, as Cavell notes, when the ordinary becomes exceptional, the familiar strange, the habitual "other," without at the same time being made available to ideology.

Poirier is convinced that these are moments produced as often as not by the metaphorical capacities of language itself, when those capacities that enable language to swerve away from its own inherited meanings, to resist tropologically the technology of its own traditional usages, are seen as a source of empowerment that needs no sanctions, religious or otherwise, for the sense of personal enhancement that accompanies them. In the moment when punning, joking, and troping break the grip of institutionalized terminologies, self-emancipation is effected merely by the way the writing calls attention to the performative presence of the self even in gestures of its own dissolution or self-effacement. Thus in Whitman's "As I Ebb'd with the Ocean of Life," or Stevens's "The River of Rivers in Connecticut," or Bishop's "At the Fishhouses," we become aware of how "it is possible to confer value on moments of transformation or dissolution without looking ahead toward a narrative of fulfillment. The moment is endowed with something as vague as wonder or beauty, empty of the desire to translate these into knowledge." [46]

The idea that human presence can be revealed in those very processes and projects that apparently deny it has long been entertained by works of literature and just as assiduously avoided in works of criticism. Poirier attributes this avoidance to our seduction by a simple "either/or": either the Judeo-Christian self whose creaturely identity as a substantial entity is guaranteed by the metaphorical appellation "child of God," or the view Emerson enunciates in "Circles" where, by seeing every fact as the beginning of another series for which there is no necessary circumference, the self seeking realization in language is always dissolving, "since language has no fixed or ultimately rationalizing terms." [47] The seduction, in other words, has been by the view that religion and the Enlightenment are unalterably opposed in America. The alternative possibility that American literature so often invites us to explore, even though so few readers ever do, involves "discovering a form of the human which emerges from the very *denial* of its will to become articulate, or of looking at a landscape from which the familiar human presence has been banished and of enjoying this vista without thinking of deprivation."[48]

Poirier's reiteration that such moments do not need to be preceded by crisis or catastrophe—or, for that matter, viewed as deprivational, as they are for someone like Harold Bloom—but can be elicited by means of the metamorphic capacity of language itself raises a question as to why so few women figure in his view of this tradition.[49] With all due allowance for the sexually specific ways in which this occurs, moments when the self risks disappearance, or at least radical metamorphosis into something historically unrecognizable, as language first resists and then overcomes its own resistance to the tropological opportunity to turn in what Poirier calls "directions or detours it seemed destined to avoid"[50]—can be found even at the very commencement of the American literary tradition in some of the marriage poems of Anne Bradstreet. In addition to being our first major poet in America, Bradstreet was also the first of our writers to experience America initially as no more than a great emptiness, "at which my heart rose," before subsequently transforming a portion of that emptiness into the richest resource of her poetry. But there are further and more spectacular exhibitions of the same cycle—almost dialectic—of resistance and accommodation, now used as a literary strategy in the poetry of Emily Dickinson. In Dickinson, the penchant for self-eradication reveals itself less in her sudden predisposition to forsake the insights of the quotidian for visionary instants than in her willingness to "work" the threatened disappointments of both kinds of knowledge into a mode of cautionary, almost minatory, "knowing," really knowingness, that is registered in such lines of lowered, nearly menacing, expectation as "Better an ignis fatuus/Than no illume at all."

Here knowing becomes precisely the kind of "work" that Poirier associates with Frost and Stevens: "The human presence can make itself felt only by and in its actions, even while the results of those actions, the texts and other bodies it produces, will be obliterated by the power it is trying to interpret."[51] On such occasions the pragmatic narrative, as I am calling it, transmutes the dialectic between religion and the Enlightenment not into another "myth of eternal return," such as the one Eliot envisioned at the end of "Little Gidding" (where the end of our exploration is to arrive "where we started/And know the place for the first time"), but into a new access to the unexpected, a new exposure to the alterity of our own, if not of someone or something else's, oddness. If this doesn't quite manage to convert the philosopher into what Cavell touchingly describes as "the hobo of thought," it does transform the thinker into what Thoreau described as a kind of "saunterer."[52] This is a person whose mental and imaginative vocation is to seek, far enough out beyond the conventional boundaries of thought, beyond the traditional oppositions of the intellect, for a "somewhere" where we may "witness our own limits transgressed, and some life pasturing freely where we never wander."

Is this how, as Cavell thinks, philosophy is successful or how philosophy is transcended? It scarcely seems to matter. The secret to being, as he and Poirier and Melville, not to say Whitman, would agree, is to be found on the open road of experience itself, a road that will lead to edification, enhancement, self-realization only insofar as we learn to respond to moments when the actual is rendered extraordinary, the prosaic mysterious, the commonplace sublime, because it "is imagined," as Poirier states, "as if it were not less but, because extemporized within and also against existent forms, immeasurably more than the result of some 'arrangements of knowledge.'"[53]

7

The Kingdoms of Theory and the New Historicism in America: A Pragmatist Response

*

The past is never dead. It's not even past.

William Faulkner

History deals with the past, but this past is the history of the present.

John Dewey

*

Theory has become ubiquitous in literary and cultural studies, and it is sometimes difficult not to feel under siege. The study of verbal texts, like the study of cultural forms of almost any kind, has in many ways become a beleaguered enterprise in which the establishment of methodological and theoretical credentials now often takes precedence over all other intellectual procedures. "The aim of interpretation," as E. D. Hirsch once termed it, is more often than not to validate the system of thought that presumably serves as its premises.[1] No longer are texts, for example, or things that can be "read" as "texts," always studied as intentional forms whose meaning can be inferred from a reconstruction of the putative conditions to which they are a response and the cognitive and affective associations to which they give rise; more and more they are being converted into "sites" for the testing of theories. What was once assumed to yield a "conflict of interpretations," in Paul Ricoeur's phrase, has given way to something that looks more like a contest of concepts, where the object is not to see what can be learned from the debate but to determine how completely the terms of discussion can be subsumed within a single discourse. The text is in danger of being displaced not by context but by metacritical template.

Such aggressions, where they have occurred, have proved daunting to interpretative traditionalists of almost every stripe. The omniverousness of theory has taken on for many humanists the enormity of a moral offense, even of religious blasphemy. So much of what earlier generations of literary and cultural interpreters once held sacred about the integrity of the object under investigation—the object, to quote Matthew Arnold, "as in itself it really is"—is now felt by many to have been profaned by this new enculturation of theory or, worse, actually desecrated, and the victims are not just texts themselves but whole traditions, indeed, the entire canon of Western literature.

But interpretive traditionalists can sometimes suffer from periodic lapses of memory. While there is no gainsaying that the current fascination (some would say obsession) with theory often carries with it a suspicion of traditional forms of knowledge and scholarship, theory was used no more than a generation ago to defend the tradition of Western humanism against its detractors. In this instance, the theory belonged not to the poststructuralists or the neo-Marxists but to the American New Critics who, with their formalist allies in other countries, were bent on resisting both the pedantries of various kinds of philological and historical specialists and the reductionisms of everyone from New Humanists to old-fashioned Marxists.

But critical theories have come to the aid of literary humanism and its traditions almost from the commencement of its organized, institutional study in America, and in each of the successive conflicts that have characterized its history, as Gerald Graff has pointed out, their influence has proved determining.[2] Theoretical concerns were present in the early nineteenth century, for example, when modern language scholars battled classicists over whether vernacular literatures should be given primacy over ancient literatures in the college curriculum. They resurfaced again after the Civil War when belletrists found themselves under attack by the new scientific-research investigators who had come under the influence of German models of scholarship. They emerged yet again as determinative in various twentieth-century disputes, first, between historical scholars and a new generation of literary critics who came of age immediately before and after World War I; then between the New Humanists and the New Critics during the interwar period; and, finally, in the recurrent clashes after World War II between the academic descendants of the New Criticism and those social and cultural critics who held out for a more contextualized study of literature. Thus when the institutional consensus established by the New Criticism ultimately collapsed in the early 1960s under a variety of pressures at once political, social, sexual, ethnic, and methodological, little had changed but the names of the opposing parties. Theories still provided the terms of the dispute, but now the party opposed by scholar-critics both within the academy and outside was held to be the party of theory as such.

This is not to suggest that everything remains the same. If the most recent critical debate between traditionalists and theorists is still driven by ideas, the ground being contested has changed. Heretofore something like Arnold's view of humanism and the literary traditions that sustain it had never been questioned; the only real issue was how best to study and preserve it. Now the issue is more nearly with which parts of the tradition are worth studying at all, with what a tradition is to begin with, and with whether all forms of study are inevitably privileged and therefore suspect, if not specious. More specifically, the critical questions that presently vex theoretical discussion circle around the problematic nature of literature itself, whether there is as such a "discipline" for studying it, how interpretation and evaluation are interlinked, and what the relation is between the intrinsic domain of literature and extrinsic realms that often bear upon its production, interpretation, and absorption, from institutions like publishing, marketing, and teaching to other disciplines like pyschology, philosophy, sociology, and religion.

Graff suggests that the one issue that may encompass all of these previous theoretical disputes concerns the possibility of historicizing literature itself by assimilating it to social and political contexts. But if much of the present-day theoretical ferment on both the right and the left is being drawn toward "a new historicism," it is not only a historicism rather different from the kind announced by Wesley Morris in his 1972 book by that title, but one whose potential for conflict among its various proponents—African-Americanists, feminists, neo-Marxists, ethnohistorians, gender critics, quantitative social historians, and others—may be more far-reaching than anything yet seen in the development of literary studies in America.[3] According to its critics, the new historicism's potential for conflict derives in large part from the fact that its understanding of the social and political is so largely internal and academic. According to its sympathizers, such criticism tends to overlook the fact that the new historicism proposes to redefine such things as "the social" and "the political" by historically resituating them within the material sites of their textual production, representation, and appropriation.

As both its friends and its enemies are prepared to concede, to do this is to do something not only to conventional notions of society and politics but also to inherited conceptions of history, and the new historicism makes no bones about it. Drawing heavily on the work of Michel Foucault, and particularly on his theory of discursive formations, which posits "a body of anonymous, historical rules, always determined in the time and space that have defined a given period, and for a given social, economic, geographical, or linguistic area," the new historicism presents a potentially severe set of challenges not only to traditional conceptions of the historical but also to conventional formulations of the boundaries between disciplines.[4] When history is reconceived as an interlinked system of institutions and discursive practices dispersed throughout its structures but often related only disjunctively with all that has gone before or with all that may come after, what is put at risk is not only the disciplinary subspecialties— intellectual, literary, political, diplomatic, religious, social, economic, biographic, folkloric—by which historical material has traditionally been made accessible to scholarship but also the cultural myths of coherence, continuity, and progress that the study of history has traditionally served.

Graff's point is that in the history of literary study in the United States we have rarely allowed such critical conflicts to come out into the open, and even where, as with the new historicism, we have not tried to mask or suppress them, their failure time and again to find institutional embodiment in the organized study of literature itself has impaired their heuristic value. Indeed, for well over a century, Graff maintains, the invisibility of these theoretical disputes about the structure and purpose of the literary curriculum to all but those participating in them has not only determined the patterns of literary professionalization but has also kept alive the notion that literature can, at it were, teach itself, that the traditions of humanism on which much of the canon is based are self-authenticating. Only expose young people to the canonical texts, said John Erskine of Columbia in 1907—enunciating a hope that the radical supporters of General Education in the 1930s would institutionalize in the undergraduate curriculum not only at Columbia but also at such places as Harvard and Chicago—and by a process of educated inference "the great books" will, as Erskine put it, "speak for [themselves]." What Erskine meant was that the literary classic "needs no screen of historical and critical apparatus to make it available to students or general readers."[5]

Complementing this "humanist myth," as Graff calls it, was a second factor that masked these conflicts and prevented them from becoming absorbed within the educational curriculum itself as part of what should be taught and studied. This was the "field-coverage model" of departmental organization which developed toward the end of the nineteenth century. Organizing the departmental study of literature by historical and generic fields staffed by experts not only insured that instructors would by and large leave one another alone to preside over their own specializations, but also enabled departments to assimilate new subjects and theories with comparatively little disruption. What could have proved ideologically challenging or methodologically competitive was, in effect, co-opted through a kind of institutional pluralism that adjusted to the new and different simply by increasing the aggregate of fields and approaches.

Nevertheless, the cost of such assimilation, according to Graff, has been very high. Instead of exploiting the heuristic value of such conflicts and the assumptions on which they are based, the institutions of literary study have more regularly been employed to suppress or dismiss them, and the loss to students, he thinks, has been incalculable. Where literary study might have served to introduce students to the issues at stake in contemporary critical and theoretical disputes, they have been organized instead chiefly to acquaint students with their results. This has predisposed most students to construe controversies over principles like most of their teachers do, as digressive or invasive, and has thus helped reinforce the more general public view that art is essentially an affair of affect rather than of ideas, that education has more to do with mastering the chief values of a tradition than with comprehending the conflicts that produced them.[6] Graff is of the opinion that this latter practice has been institutionalized almost nowhere in the history of American higher education but at Harvard University where, at the turn of the century, William James, Josiah Royce, George Santayana, George Herbert Palmer, and others managed to transform the Department of Philosophy into one of the most creative discursive communities in the world by treating their intellectual differences as part of the substance of the curriculum fashioned and nourished by their dialogue rather than as one of its more unfortunate by-products.[7]

The experience of the rise of American philosophy at Harvard thus gives credence to the view that the real enemy of the humanistic tradition is not theory per se, however inimical certain theories may be to humanistic values, but those kinds of traditional literary orientation that shun all discussion of aims, principles, and norms. Theory in this sense is neutral with respect to the humanistic tradition and simply refers to any discourse that treats such issues as integral to literary study, or, conversely, any discourse that views literature as in some sense problematic and attempts to formulate the nature of that problematic in general terms.[8] Either way, while theory may include metacritical speculation, it does not end there. Its essential object is to throw into relief for systematic reflection those general questions that arise in the study of all verbal texts and, by extension, all semiotic systems. To this extent, as Graff wittily notes, the English department is itself a theory, or the product of a theory, and part of the purpose of his institutional history is to expose the whole "operational totality" of this theory not simply by criticizing principles and practices but also by revealing the contradictions and confusions that have attended their professional absorption.[9]

Theory for Graff therefore serves both an elucidatory function and a constructive one: it helps to illumine what has been obscured and at the same time assists in the recovery of that cultural text which exists not so much behind the literary text as within it by showing us how to construe every work of literature as a response to an ongoing cultural conversation. This cultural text, which is currently occluded by the divisions that presently organize both the literature department and the university, "separating periods, genres, and fields, criticism, creative writing, and composition," can be recovered only if we shift the constitutive question of the discipline. The question should be not "Whose overview gets to be the big umbrella?"—a question which in this form, as Graff aptly notes, is "unanswerable"—but "How do we institutionalize the conflict of interpretations and overviews itself?"[10]

Graff's proposal to foreground conflict and dissent may sound like the by-now-familiar association of consensus with a politics of repression, but he is careful to distance himself from any "social control" theories of literary studies because the "radical" view of their institutionalization often turns out in practice to be the same thing as the "honorific"—the radicals have simply reinscribed the traditionalists' model of institutional history in an accusatory vocabulary—and, in any case, is based on wishful thinking. Whether espoused by feminists seeking to challenge the hegemony of the "male" canon or deconstructionists attempting to dismantle rhetorical idealizations in the direction of the conflicts that constitute them, the "radical" view, on his reading, tends to attribute to literary studies a measure of success in legitimating the dominant political ideology that in actuality it clearly hasn't achieved. This is not to say that Graff takes any comfort in the political arrangements tacitly endorsed by the practice of contemporary American literary studies, but merely to underscore that for him their chief political failing has been not to reflect the wrong ideology but to submit to institutional arrangements that prevent the various discourses on which they draw from confronting one another.

*

To see how this has occurred and continues to occur, one need merely consult another "institutional history" like Kermit Vanderbilt's richly detailed *American Literature and the Academy*. Vanderbilt's survey covers virtually the same period as Graff's, from the early years of the Nationalist era to the breakup of the New Critical consensus and the emergence of the American Studies movement in the late fifties, but it tells a very different story. Graff's tale, which, to be sure, takes in the whole of literary studies rather than American literature alone, is the story of a profession developing at times almost in spite of itself; Vanderbilt's, though I am not sure that he intends it to be, is the chronicle of a profession emerging, albeit out of struggle and anguish and much dogged persistence, essentially to reify itself. The profession of American literary studies comes of age by creating a canon designed in the main to be self-mirroring, or at least to provide a mimetic representation of its own institutional consensus. In Vanderbilt's treatment the canon and the profession are creations of each other. The disciplinary categories and classifications of the canon constitute the field they render authoritative or "classic"; the establishment of the canon, first with the publication of the *Cambridge History of American Literature* from 1917–21, and then, later, with the appearance in 1948 of *The Literary History of the United States,* climaxes, at least in Vanderbilt's interpretation, the two formative moments in the profession's rite de passage toward institutional adulthood. Describing the *Cambridge History* as a summary of the first century of American literary scholarship, Vanderbilt intends his readers to accept the publication of the *Literary History* as "in a number of respects . . . the foremost event in American literary studies," embodying "twenty-five years and more of professional self-consciousness—and over 150 years of an American literary self-awareness." [11]

Yet both projects, it should be noted—both the CHAL and the LHUS—were the creation of a highly selective group of historical scholars who, for the most part, were members of the Modern Language Association's American Literature Group, and among the leaders of that group closely associated with the editing of the *Literary History* there was considerable unanimity. As Vanderbilt admits, only a small number of the eighty-one articles prepared for the volume represented anything like distinguished scholarship, and those that did were often written by people like Henry Nash Smith, critics who had comparatively little sympathy with the relatively conservative historical and literary principles that had guided the development of the project and who wrote on subjects that, being more social than aesthetic, were somewhat offbeat. Furthermore, despite its breadth of detail and evenhandedness, Vanderbilt's narrative leaves almost entirely out of account many of the texts and figures that during the same years, or the years immediately following, contributed to the creation of what Graff refers to as "the theory of American literature"—F. O. Matthiessen,

Perry Miller, Yvor Winters, Alfred Kazin, Lionel Trilling, Newton Arvin, Richard Chase, Charles Feidelson, Jr., R.W.B. Lewis, and, later, Leslie Fiedler, Leo Marx, and others.

Graff includes an important chapter on these critics and their work in *Professing Literature* because they did so much both to extend and, theoretically and culturally, to deepen the academic study of American literature initiated by Vanderbilt's scholars and critics and professionally legitimated in the pages of the *Literary History of the United States.* But Graff is also interested in asking why their achievements in creating a field of "American Studies" failed to produce what their enterprise promised: a reorganization of literary studies in America that could overcome the old compartmentalizations and fragmentations by redefining the study of literature as a form of cultural studies. According to Graff, the answer lies primarily in the institutional organization of literary studies as a whole, where there existed a strong predilection to view the study of American writing as simply one more field among others. He would concede that other problems contributed as well—the tendentiousness of certain theories, the narrow range and number of texts on which most theoretical generalizations were based, the temptation to reduce the diversity of American writing to a simple unity often conceived in dualistic terms, the lack of historicity in the analysis—but none were as decisive as the field-coverage principle that enabled departments of English to add any new field to the aggregate without responding to its most challenging discoveries about the nature of literature itself.

★

In a book whose historical ambitions come closer to reducing literary study to social and political contexts than to assimilating it to them, Russell Reising is prepared to dispute this. He thinks that cultural critics like Yvor Winters, Perry Miller, F. O. Matthiessen, Charles Feidelson, Jr., R.W.B. Lewis, Leo Marx, Leslie Fiedler, and others, along with later critics like Richard Poirier, Sacvan Bercovitch, and John T. Irwin, all failed to reshape the study of literature in the American academy because they only succeeded in furnishing us with what Reising rather glibly describes, in a recent book, as "The Unusable Past." This amounts to arguing that they were poor historians because they failed to recover a past that is sufficiently social and political. Either they neglected or discounted works and writers that make explicit social reference (preferring, say, *The Spoils of Poynton* to *The Hazard of New Fortunes*), or, as with the mimetic properties of Puritan jeremiads or the cetological chapters of *Moby-Dick,* they treated the muted social reference in works ranging from seventeenth-century sermons to twentieth-century fiction as a non- or antireferential element. Even where (as was often the case) these theorists attempted to define American literature in opposition to American life—or rather, as do Yvor Winters and Sacvan Bercovitch, they define it in complicity with various moral and rhetorical simplifications of national experience—they failed to integrate literary interpretation and significance with political and social significance. Thus Reising can conclude that these critics all remain hostage to the bourgeois culture they think they have transcended because they possess no other terms but the ones supplied by that culture itself with which to define those "worlds elsewhere" in which American writers have purportedly managed to secure their fictive independence.

This view of cultural hegemony is, as I have already discussed in chapter 2, not without its difficulties. In its most extreme contemporary forms, such as the deconstructionist claim that the semiotic system to be opposed can never be escaped so long as its repressions remain the subject of the discourse, it possesses an element of intellectual, if not a social, legitimacy, if only because of the lengths to which it is carried and the rigor with which it is applied. But in much revisionist cultural criticism of a less scrupulous kind, where the purpose of invoking it is essentially (as here) to imply that all cultural opposition is therefore by definition moot, it does not. It is one thing to argue that the culture of late corporate capitalism has effectively absorbed, or at least essentially trivialized, many of the intellectual terms with which it might be resisted, thus threatening to turn radical thought itself into intellectual chic through the co-option of the space once reserved for it. On the other hand, it is but another example of intellectual chic itself to deduce from this that with all opposition to the culture of bourgeois capitalism supposedly rendered futile, or at any rate ineffectual, its chief critics are nothing more than dupes of the system.

Reising's susceptibility to modishness carries over to his penchant for pigeonholing, which permits him to argue that postwar theories of American literature neatly organize themselves into three groups, each with a famous progenitor and all with a series of distinguished representatives—Puritan-origin theories, taking their bearings from the work of Perry Miller, which have been developed by everyone from Yvor Winters, Richard Chase, and Leslie Fiedler to Sacvan Bercovitch; culture theories, inspired by the criticism of Lionel Trilling, which have found expression in R.W.B Lewis, Richard Chase, Leslie Fiedler, and Leo Marx; and self-reflexive theories, originating in the work of

F. O. Matthiessen and, before him, D. H. Lawrence, which have been expressed in successive generations of scholarship by Charles Feidelson, Jr., Richard Poirier, and John T. Irwin. The difficulties with this kind of classificatory scheme are perhaps obvious and nowhere were better diagnosed than by Foucault. Even in a critic as purportedly savvy about such matters as Reising himself, the categories tend to control the interpretation or, as the case may be, misinterpretation rather than the other way around. Richard Chase and Leslie Fiedler as Puritan-origin theorists? F. O. Matthiessen and D. H. Lawrence as self-reflexive theorists? The problem here is not simply with the classifications this permits but with the categories themselves.

The most interesting example of the kind of historical confusion to which this leads is Reising's identification of Matthiessen with the genesis of self-reflexive theories, which is almost as misleading as the parallel temptation that, to his credit, Reising for the most part resists: to imply that Matthiessen is the sole author of the mid-nineteenth-century American canon.[12] Even if the term "self-reflexive" were the most felicitous description for the set of theories Reising has in mind, true title to the authorship of this trend surely belongs to Charles Feidelson's *Symbolism and American Literature,* and it does so on its own account. Feidelson noted himself that the real bent of Matthiessen's book was sociological and political and in his introduction to *Symbolism and American Literature* gently admonished Matthiessen for allowing his "concern with . . . cultural history . . . to lead him away from specifically aesthetic problems."[13] Feidelson intended his own study to provide the appropriate corrective to this tendency, but what we now know, and what Reising's categorizations tend to blur, is that Feidelson's argument in behalf of what he called the writers' "attitude toward their medium, . . . their . . . devotion to the possibilities of symbolism," not only carried the critical day, so to speak, but also effectively determined the way Matthiessen's own book would be subsequently construed.[14]

This is one element in the history of these texts that Reising never quite manages to write, though his own political orientation should have made him more sensitive to its importance. A second aspect of the history of these texts that Reising too often obscures or discounts has to do with the critical and cultural situations to which they themselves were variously—and often quite distinctly, not to say obliquely—a response. Though Reising makes a very useful detour at one point in the direction of the criticism of Mikhail Bakhtin in order to suggest a model for how the study of American literature might be "dialogized" to "reaccentuate" its true "heterogeneity," he never

wholly succeeds in absorbing what Graff, echoing Bakhtin, has referred to as "the lesson of recent criticism": "that no text is an island,
that every work of literature [and criticism] is a rejoinder in a conversation or dialogue that it presupposes but may or may not mention." [15]
Had he done so, he would have seen that the only way to historicize
these theoretical texts in American criticism is to provide a more detailed treatment of the Progressive view of the past to which so many
of his theorists were reacting—a view which, again on Graff's reading,
was scarcely an improvement over the Genteel image of the past it replaced—and he would also have had to question the ideological assumptions of his own categorical scheme.

For example, even if it could be demonstrated that American critics
have used such theories to gloss or suppress the sociopolitical dimensions of American literature—either by assuming, as "Puritan-origin
theorists" purportedly do, that American literature inevitably enjoys
an adversarial relation to a culture that is inimical in its organization to
the interests of the individual self; or by arguing with "culture theorists" that the American literary imagination is alone capable of reconciling the tensions and contradictions that compose the culture on its
own deepest levels; or by maintaining, after the fashion of "self-
reflexive theorists," that American writers have created symbolic or
rhetorical forms capable of encompassing the aspirations to freedom
that constitute our exceptionality as a people—there is nothing inherent in these critical formulations themselves, much less in the literary
texts recurrently used (or, better, overused) to support them, that dis-
qualifies literature from mediating aspects of the social and political.

Indeed, Reising himself seems to concede as much when he observes perceptively that many of the writers who furnish the basis of
Poirier's speculations about the intransigent antinomianism of the
American literary imagination actually seem in certain ways to contra-
dict it. Far from creating "worlds elsewhere" for their characters to
inhabit, writers like Hawthorne, James, Eliot, and Fitzgerald could
just as easily be interpreted as attempting to "socialize" them by exposing the dangers of their solipsistic gestures. Reising therefore concludes that there may very well be two traditions in American writing,
or two impulses within the same tradition, that live in dialectical tension with one another. A critic like Richard Poirier has chosen to accentuate one such tradition in *A World Elsewhere,* but Reising apparently means to say that there is nothing to prevent a different reading
of the same writers which accentuates the other. If this reasoning displays something of the self-contradictory ideology of Reising's own

leftism, it also reveals some of the balance that on occasion derives from his sympathies with the "new historicism" in literary studies.

★

A somewhat inexact designation that stands for the desire to reinscribe the social and the political in our notion of the literary and its study, the new historicism reflects a variety of perspectives—Marxist, deconstructive, feminist, psychoanalytic, and materialist, among them—but is inevitably revisionist in motive. Its characteristic aim is to unmask ideological factors that have influenced the shaping of the canon, to deconstruct the idealized oppositions between innocence and experience, machine and garden, civilization and wilderness, or novel and romance by which the canon has been established and defended, and to resituate texts in the sociopolitical and economic sites of their creation and reception. While its gains have been considerable, its problems, as is now becoming apparent, are real. At its best, the new historicism offers an opportunity to bring the ideological into fruitful relations with the aesthetic; at its worst, it furnishes an excuse for confusing or conflating them.

The new historicism can be differentiated from the old by virtue of the way it construes the text as the site of a particular kind of production rather than a specific kind of reflection. The "old historicism" was—and is—defined most simply, and not inaccurately, in the well-known words from the preface to Edmund Wilson's *Axel's Castle,* as the attempt to provide "a history of man's ideas and imaginings in the setting of the conditions which shaped them." [16] Most old historicists, Erich Auerbach no less than Perry Miller, M. H. Abrams and Walter Jackson Bate no less than Joseph Warren Beach and Roy Harvey Pearce, have also understood this kind of history to be, in its way, broadly moral: they have assessed the value of what Wilson called "man's ideas and imaginings" in direct proportion to the amount of resistance they offer to their shaping conditions. Where these historicists have differed among themselves is over the question of what sorts of resistances the intellect and the imagination encounter in any given period, and what sorts of strategies, gestures, and achievements constitute an overcoming of them.

An excellent example of the old historicism in something like contemporary dress is provided by Alfred Kazin's *An American Procession.* Published more than four decades after *On Native Grounds,* his first book recently reissued in a Fortieth Anniversary Edition, *An American Procession* is idiosyncratic only in that, like so much of Kazin's criticism, it is intransigently personal as well as historically perspicacious. Eschewing much of the machinery, though not necessarily the insights, of modern scholarship—there are few footnotes in the book and no citations, and previous critical discussion is rarely mentioned—*An American Procession* reflects the view that criticism should aspire to the status of *histoire morale*. This is the kind of criticism that in the old historicist mode "sums up the spirit of the age in which we live and then asks us to transcend it, . . . that in the way of Marx on Greek philosopohy, of Kierkegaard on Mozart, of Nietzsche on the birth of tragedy, of Shaw on Ibsen, of Lawrence on American literature, asks us—in light not only of man's history but of his whole striving—to create a future in keeping with man's imagination." [17]

This ambition plays itself out in the way *An American Procession* defines its subject. The book turns on the question of what happened when certain nineteenth-century American writers discovered that the old god or gods had died and that if a replacement or substitute was needed they would have to create one for themselves. This realization—for Kazin it was their "shock of recognition"—transformed them into modernists in spirit nearly a century before their time and converted their writing into a species of what R. P. Blackmur, thinking of all the great European moderns, once described as a form of "irregular metaphysics." *An American Procession* tries to determine what sustained them morally and intellectually through this continuing crisis of belief, a crisis that has shaped so much of the craft, the technique and style, of what many take to be our most representative literature in America, and for that matter, of our representative visual art as well. According to Kazin, they were sustained by a certain emphatic and highly calibrated sense of self, or form of consciousness, which became for so many of these writers their surrogate for the sacred.

This is, of course, a story that has been told many times before in the history of modern American literature. What lends special drama and novelty to Kazin's narrative is the way he shows how this modern sense of self deepened, darkened, and then suffered deprecation under the impress of the new social, political, and economic conditions that amassed toward the end of the nineteenth century and became endemic in American life early in the twentieth. Kazin uses the writing and example of Henry Adams to explain what these portentous conditions amounted to. From one perspective, they amounted to something like a new sense of history itself, or, rather, a new sense of what history could mean. Their combined effect, as Adams experienced it, was to convince him that the history which had shaped him—the history for which, as a young man, he had been trained to take responsibility, and

over which, as an older man, he had exercized such masterful understanding—was no longer relevant. These senses of history had been
replaced by circumstances so momentous, so unprecedented, and so
irresistible as to make the past seem wholly anachronistic, almost fos-
silized.

From another perspective, the new conditions to which Adams and
so many of the other members of Kazin's grand procession were exposed—from Emerson, Whitman, and Melville through Mark Twain,
the two James brothers, Stephen Crane, and Theodore Dreiser to such
well-known moderns as Eliot, Pound, Hemingway, Faulkner, and Dos
Passos—meant that history as it has been known, history as an image
or idea of collective experience in which patterns of social action and
belief are seen to compose a moral design—history in this different
sense was, in effect, over. For Adams no less than for the Hemingway
of "The Killers" and "A Clean, Well-Lighted Place," or the Eliot of
"Gerontion," or the Faulkner of *The Sound and the Fury,* history was
and is a tale told by an idiot which was rendered meaningless by the
way the idiom of the self had been subverted and displaced by the
idiom of force, by energy in its aspect as a kind of power that is both
uncontrolled and uncontrollable.

As Kazin interprets it, this was more than a figurative displacement
even if it was to generate profound metaphorical consequences. In
sum, it was a displacement of one of America's presiding "ideas of
order," of the nineteenth century's Supreme Fiction, and we are still
living with the implications for both art and life alike. Yet here is
where, on Kazin's reading, the writers of "the crucial century," as he
calls them, have helped us, and where his narrative makes a move so
characteristic of the old historicism rather than the new. The meaning
of his grand company of writers is to be found, finally, in their capacity not only to register such changes, and thereby to anticipate the kind
of physical and metaphysical environment that has now engulfed us,
but also to resist, and even to surmount them, by developing in their
work various strategies, inevitably stylistic, for surviving them at least
imaginatively.

Kazin's way of bringing this out is very much his own and is not to
be confused with the way other old historicists might do it. He seems
to be writing something that is not quite critical biography and certainly not in any accepted sense a history of literary texts and traditions. His book is more like a history of artistic achievement that centers around selected writers whose accomplishment is measured, at
least partially, in terms of the circumstantial, temperamental, and cultural obstacles they were obliged to overcome. To do this well requires

a good deal of verbal painting, of evocative description. Kazin has always taken pleasure in spectacle, and here he is better than ever at eliciting the sense of some specific situation, at defining the character of some singular moment, at depicting some particular scene. But the nature of Kazin's historicism dictates that the rich if selective tapestry of life is described not only for its own sake but also to better illumine the careers played off against it. It is the full arc of artistic exertion and expression that most arrests and compels him, and so he seeks the axis of vision on which it turns.

Thus of Emerson, he writes: "He could subsist outside the church because, living in his mind and being responsive to its every prompting, he was satisfied that the 'active soul' was an actual mirror of the world";[18] of Melville, that his "basic image" was "the inconclusive nature of reality, man forever driven back on himself as he seeks a fixed point";[19] of Hawthorne, that what made him "special" was "the belief that though no moral order may exist, the responsibility for it has fallen on the sinner himself";[20] of Dickinson, that "her aim is not Thoreau's conversion of Nature into her own mind . . . [but] the minuteness, the exact shading, of an actual human cycle forever reenacting itself within a domestic setting";[21] of Dreiser, that "the background of all his works . . . was his sense that injustice makes society possible";[22] of Hemingway, that his "greatest gift, the foundation of all his marvelous pictorial effects, was his sense . . . of some fundamental wrongness at the heart of things, to which an American can still rise, and which he will endure (and describe) as a hero." [23]

These passages not only convey Kazin's "genius for the essential," as he once remarked of Emerson, but also reveal his capacity for "perception," to borrow Henry James's great phrase, "at the pitch of passion." It is not that intensity in criticism is everything; the critic in Kazin would say that the intensity without the perception is pure sentimentality; but the historicist in Kazin would add that the perception without the intensity, without a commitment to the kind of future which is commensurate with the human capacity to imagine a different, if not a better, world is simply sterile. This is where Kazin's historicism comes together with his romanticism. In tone and character so like those of F. Scott Fitzgerald, who in similar fashion included the meaning of America within them, Kazin and Fitzgerald each finds the completion of their historicism and their romanticism, not surprisingly, in the capacity to love. Thus Kazin can indicate both the power of his historicism and also something of its pathos by reserving a special place in his book for Thoreau's panegyric: "All that a man has to say or do that can possibly concern mankind, is in some shape or other to tell the story of his love—to sing; and, if he is fortunate and keeps alive, he will be forever in love. This alone is to be alive to the extremities." [24]

★

How different from all this is the mood of much of the new historicism. Where the old historicism seeks, finally, out of admiration, or at least out of hope, to salvage and recuperate the past, the new historicism seeks out of something closer to suspicion and disillusionment to demystify the past. These are not mere differences of emphasis; they take in and reflect an entire realignment of sensibility, a major alteration in the structure of intellectual desire. The new historicism is based on the premise that to understand any representative human actions and aspirations historically is to come to terms with the way they are sedimented with, in Wittgenstein's sense, all the past "forms of life" that went into any given formulation of the principles informing them. To historicize them, then, is to see them configured both as products of meaning and also as processes for its creation. The new historicism aspires to subvert continually our tendency to foregound and possibly reify specific facts or objects of study (say, a literary text) by displacing "the immediately given fact," as Alan Trachtenberg has written, "with the profoundly mediated [cultural] process" by which it comes to us. [25] The object is to resituate the text in the sociopolitical and economic sites of its production and thus to unmask the ideological factors that have concealed its true purpose.

The new historicism therefore always entails an interpretive rewriting of the literary text itself. But this rewriting assumes that the text is itself a rewriting of an ideological or historical subtext, "it being always understood that that 'subtext' is not immediately present as such, not some common-sense external reality, nor even the conventional narratives of history manuals, but rather must itself always be (re)constructed after the fact." [26] But how does one do this? How does one reconstruct after the fact the process by which the literary text rewrites or restructures the historical or ideological subtext, thus in part disguising its own productive operations? According to Fredric Jameson, the answer involves a fundamental reconception of historiographic method. To reconceive the text as an exemplification of the production of meaning and not merely of its reflection, one cannot conceive of the text as emerging from a prior moment in some developmental process. Nor can one define the text in relation to some external ground or context that is assumed to lie beyond it. To reconceive the text as a representation of meaning production, one must interro-

gate its materials for their formal and conceptual conditions of possibility. "Such analysis," Jameson writes, "thus involves the hypothetical
reconstruction of the materials—content, narrative paradigms, stylistic
and linguistic practices—which had to have been given in advance in
order for that partial text to be produced in its unique historical specificity." [27]

From this perspective, the ideological is not something added onto
or inserted into the aesthetic. It should be conceived rather as something inscribed within the aesthetic in a way that makes aesthetic creation, and therefore literary production as a whole, an ideological act in
and of itself. Unless I am mistaken, however, to reconceive their relationship in this way also transforms the historical recovery of ideology
itself into a fundamentally aesthetic act, since the historical reconstruction of the ideological is essentially an act of the imagination. And this
reconstruction of the material conditions of possibility for the emergence of any text with this unique historical specificity produces what
Jameson concludes is simply another "hypothetical" structure.

Hence the point for the new historicist is not to establish a theoretical or critical perspective beyond the ideological but to resituate critical and theoretical reflection wholly within it. Yet this only raises all
over again the question as to whether the critic can ever escape the
ideological contamination of his or her own processes of reflection. If
he or she can, then the practices of ideological criticism confute its
own premises. If he or she cannot, then the moral aim of cultural criticism (to the degree that moral discrimination remains a meaningful
critical activity to begin with) is reduced to little more than the unmasking of the mendacious.

*

A good example of a book that can't quite manage to make up its mind
about this, and therefore seems to vacillate between delivering us from
a past it would deidealize and revalidating a past we have misappropriated, is Donald Pease's daring but also disturbing *Visionary Compacts*. Like much of the recent criticism of American literature that is
fascinated, after the fashion of the new historicists, with the social and
political sedimentation of subjective representations, Pease's book is
devoted to the writers of the American Renaissance. Unlike many new
historicists, however, Pease is content to leave the canon essentially as
is. Devoting a long, and not wholly successful, chapter to the retrieval
of Edgar Allen Poe, "the lost soul of the American tradition," and
omitting any treatment of Thoreau, he is otherwise prepared to accept
the tradition established by others, the tradition of Emerson, Haw-

thorne, Whitman, and Melville, as central. Nevertheless, his book is professedly revisionist, even reproachful, arguing that these writers have been consistently misinterpreted by a generation of scholars who failed to appreciate their relation to America's unfinished past.

Pease's quarrel, then, is not, like that of so many American new historicists, with the writers of the mid-nineteenth century themselves but with their mid-twentieth-century critics. Indifferent as the latter have been to such nineteenth-century issues as slavery, expansionism, union, free trade, and national conscription, modern critics have completely suppressed the concern these mid-nineteenth-century writers expressed over the possibility of civil war and the pains they took to prevent it by creating in their art what Pease calls "visionary compacts." These covenants, of which D. H. Lawrence's *Studies in Classic American Literature* is a later but for Pease a normative example, were designed to help fulfill America's still-unrealized historical promise through a restoration of those civic bonds creative of a common life in which all Americans could share. In short, visionary compacts were reimaginations of an American social contract now imperilled by sectionalism and material self-interest.

Pease is a good enough critic—and sometimes very good indeed—to know that his five writers devised fairly distinct versions of this visionary contract and, accordingly, he does not blink their differences. His thesis itself seems to work most effectively with Whitman and Hawthorne—the chapter on Whitman may well present the definitive case for the moral and political integrity of Whitman's attempt to create a "New World metaphysics," and his discussion of D. H. Lawrence and "the sense of place" is perhaps the best thing ever written on the subject—and somewhat less well with Emerson, Poe, and, for other reasons, Melville. But even with Emerson, Pease can be extraordinarily acute, as when he demonstrates how Emerson transformed self-reliance into a virtue that transcends the individual and the social precisely where, and how, it "directs the individual as well as the culture to a vision of the innermost principles underlying both. When Emerson opposed the Fugitive Slave Bill, his person became transparent so that the principle of liberty could speak all the more forcibly through it." [28]

Pease's interpretation of Emerson is particularly remarkable because he manages to defend the latter's engagement with some of the chief social and political crises of his era on virtually the same grounds that other critics like Poirier and Harold Bloom, in defining Emerson as a cultural antinomian, even as a kind of visionary proto-modernist, have explained his indifference to them. Nonetheless, Pease's book, his title notwithstanding, is oddly, not to say aggressively, antimodernist, which amounts in this case to the same thing as being antiantinomian. Such ideological bias might be justified simply as an expression of Pease's own historicist assumptions if *Visionary Compacts* were not at the same time, and in several different respects, so curiously anti-historical. Its aversion to history reveals itself most clearly in its critique of the way these writers have been interpreted by so-called modernist critics.

Pease's critique of the tradition of modernist interpretation of the American Renaissance is based on an ingenious parallel he thinks he can establish between the generation of newly created citizens following the American Revolution and the generation of critics who came of age intellectually nearly two centuries later in Cold War America. According to Pease, both generations were advocates of something that could be called "negative freedom." Constituting more of a "freedom from" than a "freedom for," this negative view permitted each of these generations, separated as they were by more than 150 years, to use the mythos developing—or already developed—around the American Revolution to establish for themselves a sense of their own identity. But this sense of themselves, built as it was upon a confusion of the idea of freedom with a feeling of liberation from all institutional constraints, created for members of both generations, so Pease contends, a similar crisis of cultural identity. By grounding personal as well as national identity on what Pease considers to have been a virtually complete repudiation of the institutions of the past, the representative members of both generations were left without any foundation on which to develop a sense of shared obligations, of moral solidarity, with other generations before or after them.

In response to this crisis of what Pease terms "cultural legitimacy," the post-Revolutionary generation developed a mythos of the Revolution which their modernist descendants merely reprised. According to this Revolutionary mythos, cultural legitimacy can only be achieved by displacing public interest, and the needs of the commonweal, with self-interest, and then by founding citizenship on the principle of opposition as such—"to family, environment, cultural antecedents, and even their former selves." [29] However, to the writers of the American Renaissance, as Pease reads them, this response to the crisis of cultural legitimacy spelled disaster for both the civil order and the idea of national union. Thus to avert political catastrophe, they bent their various talents to creating in their art alternative social compacts, albeit "visionary" or figurative ones, in which all Americans might discover their places in a sociopolitical world and assume the responsibilities of citizenship.

This is the ideological history of mid-nineteenth-century American literature that was suppressed by such postwar or "Cold War" critics as Richard Chase, Harold Bloom, and Richard Poirier. But Pease reserves his severest criticism for F. O. Matthiessen, whose landmark book entitled *American Renaissance* gave a name to this nineteenth-century period, even if it can scarcely be added, as it has become recherché to say, that he "authored" it. In fact, Matthiessen didn't even invent the phrase—that honor going instead to Samuel Knapp, whose 1829 *Lectures on American Literature* first introduced the idea of a nineteenth-century cultural "naissance"—and the term was subsequently to take on a kind of canonical authority only later, when critics and scholars converted it into a field of study capable of being taught and examined by its own cadre of specialists and textually represented by its own anthologies. Needless to say, for all of Matthiessen's excitement over, and commitment to, the release of imaginative energy that, on his reading at least, occurred during the middle years of the nineteenth century, he would have been, had he lived long enough, deeply distressed by the association of his own writings with a critical position that is supposedly blind or indifferent to the claims of social and political mindsets. After all, Matthiessen was merely writing about a five-year span in American literary history, albeit to him an extraordinarily fertile and significant one for aesthetic, political, and moral reasons, and he took great pains to complicate and qualify its cultural authority by viewing that period against a background of almost four centuries of literary and intellectual accomplishment. He was particularly eager to resituate these American developments in an Atlantic cultural context, and far from masking his motives for undertaking the book when he did—*American Renaissance* was begun in the middle thirties and published in 1941—he made no bones about trying to furnish an embattled, and weakened, and what now seems a then already outdated, democratic humanism with a usable past.

All of this should help to explain why, after World War II, and for several decades thereafter, Matthiessen's book could take on the authority of a scholarly classic even as his interpretations of most of his five writers were being systematically neglected.[30] In the period of postwar recovery, liberalism emerged triumphant in a form Matthiessen and other leftist critics found repulsive, and it allied itself in the academy with a critical formalism far more consistent with one side of Feidelson's book than with any side of Matthiessen's. That formalism, and the sense of cultural legitimacy that went with it, proved extremely determinative of how Matthiessen's book was, and wasn't, taken, and it influenced to an extent we have yet to fathom what was, and wasn't, made of the new canon he was attempting to wrest from the grasp of the Progressive historians and some of their Marxist descendants. But of so much of this history Pease seems indifferent—it is scarcely possible that he is unaware of it—because, like various other new Americanists, he is more interested in historicizing the rhetoric of Matthiessen's text than in rhetorically engaging its historicity. In fact, Pease goes so far as to turn Matthiessen's reading of *Moby-Dick* into a "site of cultural persuasion" for Cold War rhetoric. To do this requires nothing short of a kind of allegorical sleight-of-hand: Matthiessen is charged with reducing the text to a moral tale, almost an exemplum, of how a free man named Ishmael was able to survive the destructive actions of a tyrant named Ahab, whereupon *Moby-Dick* becomes, so Pease argues, little more than a prefiguration of "America's power to get the free world through [and beyond] a war." [31]

The interest of this kind of criticism is not unrelated to its dangers. By assimilating all "modernist" or postwar theories of American literature to a model of history that foregrounds dominance, control, disciplinary power, and manipulation, it looks like it is "out-lefting" the competition. [32] Yet by reducing all the messiness and complexity and ambiguity that normally accompany the social and the political to the level of simple allegory, it makes a gesture that is often strangely conservative, even retrograde. But this is neither an isolated problem in Pease nor, I am persuaded, a calculated one; it simply comes from breathing perhaps too deeply what Lionel Trilling would have called "the haunted air" of our time, in which the whole of politics is compressed into the abstractions of ideology and the historical is collapsed into the textual. The result of such conjunctions is, in any case, all too predictable. In much of the revisionist criticism that centers around the American Renaissance, Matthiessen becomes the victim of a kind of historicism turned inside out. Instead of faulting him for the way he may have effaced or confused, as in places he no doubt did, the historical conflicts and tensions that related the work of his five writers to both their own time and his, this new revisionism has tended to criticize him for the confusions and falsifications that have developed around *American Renaissance* from Matthiessen's time to our own. In effect, this is to hold Matthiessen responsible for the way his book has been appropriated or, as the case may be, misappropriated, but this only risks producing a revisionist reading of the past that is not so much, as in Reising's sense, "unusable" as, in Nietzsche's sense, "abused."

While abuse of the past is what such criticism neither necessarily intends nor in any case inevitably entails, Nietzsche's view of history is much to the point here. The historicism of new Americanists, as Crews calls them, like Tompkins, Arac, and Pease, or Walter Benn Michaels, Philip Fisher, and Myra Jehlen, is essentially and rightly suspicious of all expressions of what Nietzsche called "monumental history" and seeks to displace it with what he termed "critical history." That is to say, the new historicism is distrustful of all attempts to idealize the past by finding models of heroism that can provide inspiration to face the challenges of the present and the future and aims instead to deidealize and deconstruct the past in order to deliver the present and the future from its bondage.

Part of the difficulty with this model of historical work is that the project of ideological emancipation which it serves depends, to a considerable degree, on the new historicism's frequent reliance on the tactics of what Nietzsche described as "antiquarian history." But this creates several problems. The first is that by placing so much emphasis on the retrieval of the forgotten detail, the seemingly gratuitous relationship, the unremarked parallel, much new historicist scholarship employs a historical strategem linked methodologically not so much with the overthrow of the status quo as with its defense and revalorization. Antiquarianism is a conservative gesture historically even when it is used politically in behalf of an emancipatory project, which may help account for why so much of the new historicism of the new Americanists, like Pease's or, for different reasons, Tompkins's, is, or at least seems to be, politically divided within itself.[33] The second problem is that the new historicism's move to disenchant the past through a critique of its idealizations and deformations, unless one remembers Nietzsche's admonition to hold all three of these historical perspectives in constructive tension, may merely succeed in reducing the whole of the past to the same ideological level. This is what happens when the past is reduced to allegory, when the whole panoply of history can be restricted to a story of power and containment or consensus and dissensus.

*

Nowhere are these problems more in evidence than in what, by any measure, is the most ambitious response thus far to the new historicism in America, the *Columbia History of the Literature of the United*

States (hereafter called "the Columbia").[34] Variously described upon its appearance in 1988 as "the new authority," a rewriting of "the story of American literature," and "a pioneering work in the 'new historicism,'" the Columbia is, for all its merits—some of which are considerable—none of these exactly. A collaborative undertaking involving sixty-six contributors, five associate editors, four advisory editors, and a general editor, many of the articles it contains are too provisional in outlook and too uneven in quality to deserve the sobriquet "authoritative"; its editors reject the possibility of writing a unified or even a coherent narrative of American literary history in our time; and its contributions reflect considerably more of the old historicism than of the new. And even where exceptions can be noted—as in Philip Fisher's brilliantly relentless if also somewhat perverse reading of Mark Twain's bondage to the greed of what he and Charles Dudley Warner coined "The Gilded Age"—it would be more accurate to call its criticism "ideological" than "historical." Indeed, its editors explicitly dissociate themselves not only from any idea that its predecessors, such as the *Cambridge History of American Literature* and *The Literary History of the United States,* linked to the word "American," but also from the assumption that there is anything culturally distinctive, which is to say symbolically exoteric, about the literature, as the Columbia prefers to put it, "produced in that part of the world known as the United States."[35]

The Columbia's reluctance to embrace the notion of an American literature springs from two motives that are in themselves perfectly sound. One is a desire to avoid the pitfalls of the myth of American exceptionalism that risks confusing any one of the many literatures, and their supporting cultures, that have emerged in the history of the United States with the totality of them all. The second reflects a realization that terms like "history" and "literary" have become richly complicated in recent decades, and not least because we have learned how completely each term is implicated in the meanings of the other— how completely the figurative, the generic, and the tropological control our understanding of the historical; how notions like narrativity, historicity, and temporality determine our conception of literature. But the Columbia's admirable deference to the pluralism of the American literary landscape merely reminds one of what is wrong with the ideology of pluralism politically: variety is tolerated, even encouraged, precisely so that no one has to come to terms with it, much less to assess it critically.

What the Columbia needs, and what its sixty-six contributors cannot by themselves supply, is not so much a unitary conception of

American literature that would integrate the diverse narrative strands
of this literary history into one encompassing story, but rather a concept of discourse, to change the figure, sufficiently broad and various
enough to enable us to understand how, as the Columbia calls them,
"the varied voices within the one nation" have managed to develop a
comprehensible dialogue, or at least an intelligible conversation.[36]
Such a conversation need not be assumed to have ever possessed a
single subject or even a recurrent set of themes. But if this conversation
is to be understood as in any sense socially shared or shareable, which
is to say public, it must be perceived as a conversation many of whose
points of difference and even of disagreement still bear at least enough
of a family resemblance to one another to be construed as alternative
modes of speaking within a historically expanding range of discursive
possibilities. In short, it must be conceived as a series of individual
literary *paroles* that spring from some sort of shared cultural *langue.*

In this sense, then, and this sense only, what is needed still in American literary study, and what the Columbia as a whole does not begin
to furnish, is a working theory of its own subject, by which I mean
simply a conception of why and how these different works and writers
remain—or should remain—historically answerable to one another.
Such a theory is called for because, as so many of the Columbia's contributors attest, the relations among the writers and works associated
with the United States have now come to seem to us far more deeply
vexed and ambiguous, far more uncomfortably problematic, than
they appeared to be only twenty or thirty years ago. Yet such a theory
need possess no other aim than to conceptualize the nature of that
problematic in terms that strive for greater cultural generality and for
stronger narrative plausibility. What we have in lieu of such a theory is
a text whose disclaimers about the possibility of formulating such a
theory are oddly belied, though in contrasting ways, both by the fairly
traditional principles of its organization and by some of the more radically revisionist essays of which it is composed.

While, for example, the Columbia mentions literally hundreds of
writers and texts and seeks to reassess scores of others, few established
reputations are really altered. All sorts of groups are accorded new
respect, from women authors, colonial poets, immigrant writers,
and regionalist artists to Mexican-American, Asian-American, and
African-American writers, contemporary philosophers, fictional min-
imalists, and language poets, but, judging from the chapters reserved
for them, colonial American writing still seems to belong to Edwards,
Franklin, Jefferson, and, now, Cotton Mather; the American Renaissance continues to remain the preserve of Emerson, Hawthorne, Tho-

reau, Whitman, and Melville (though Poe, Irving, Bryant, Cooper, and the "Woman Author" all command chapters of their own that link them to such traditions as "Writers of the Frontier" or "Writers of the Old South"); and the post-Civil War period is again dominated by Dickinson, Mark Twain, and James, who have here been joined by Henry Adams.

In the modernist era, however, only Faulkner and, surprisingly, Frost merit chapters of their own, while Eliot is compelled to share space with Pound, Williams with Stevens, and, in what still feels like an odd ménage à trois, Hemingway winds up occupying a chapter with Fitzgerald and Stein. By comparison, the contemporary period affords an almost level prospect, where no individual writers quite seem to rise above the general average and must consequently find their place in chapters that, in addition to treating such traditional genres as poetry and drama, along with "the new philosophy" and "literature as radical statement," direct their attention to such historically specific developments as "neorealist fiction," "self-reflexive fiction," "fictions of the present," and "the avante-garde and experimental writing."

As it happens, some of the more exciting criticism in the Columbia is to be found in chapters that reassess these established reputations, but revisionist criticism of a high order—or, rather, historical writing that attempts to consolidate the gains that recent revisionist criticism has achieved—can also be found elsewhere in the Columbia, as in a variety of essays on the rise of the women author in the antebellum period, "women writers and the new woman" in the later nineteenth century, and the lost generation of woman writers "between the wars." Indeed, if the Columbia has succeeded in nothing else, it has demonstrated how much our understanding of American literature has recently been enhanced through the efforts of feminist criticism. But the Columbia includes a number of other strong chapters on a variety of related topics: colonial biography and autobiography, poetry in the early republic, regional humor, regionalism generally, the diversity of early-twentieth-century fiction, modern American criticism, the history of modern philosophy as it bears upon postwar intellectual developments that supported, and in some cases inspired, new discoveries in critical theory, and the third generation of modern American poets, which includes trenchant discussions of everyone from the New Formalists to the Beats, the confessional poets, Black Mountain or open-form poetry, deep-image poetry, and the New York school.

At least two of the essays in the Columbia propose implicitly what its editors claim to be currently impossible, namely, a theory of American literature as a whole. The first of these, possessing far more affinities with current historicisms than with past, argues that Puritan New World revisioning transformed subjective constructions into social rituals that continue to determine America's cultural—which is to say, its ideological—identity down to the present day. The second, which is just as thoroughly comfortable with the certainties of former historicisms, proposes that the transcendentalists and their adversaries, "fearing the determination of history and opposing the accumulations of institutional culture," established what remains, perhaps, the major theme in our literature through their idealist ambition to create a literature "in despite of culture." [37] Either way—and these essays portray it going in different, even opposed, directions—it is apparently possible to construct a theory of American literature even in an age of dissensus.

Because of the fairly traditional way the Columbia is organized—chapters on Renaissance literature of exploration and travel, on nineteenth-century nonfictional prose, and on the postmodernist literature of radical statement, not to mention those on social and intellectual backgrounds (even when they acquire "upscale" new titles like "Culture, Power, and Society [since World War II]"), still reflect academic distinctions—it is difficult, if not impossible, to obtain any clear sense of a host of important subtraditions in American writing and thought, much less of their own internal histories. Where, for example, can one find any extended treatment of nature writing, say, from Alexander Whitaker's *Good Newes from Virginia* or John Smith's *A Description of New England* to John McPhee's *Coming into the Country?* What about women diarists and memoirists from Anne Bradstreet through Mary Chestnut and Alice James to May Sarton and Audre Lorde? From the Columbia one would never learn that some of the most distinguished prose writing in America is to be found in personal letters by everyone from John and Abigail Adams, Emily Dickinson, and Henry Adams to William James, Henry James, the all-too-easily forgotten John Jay Chapman, and even Edmund Wilson. Nor would one be in a position to appreciate the importance of such genres as autobiography, confession, and testament (works like Maya Angelou's autobiography, Norman Mailer's *Armies of the Night,* James Agee's *Let Us Now Praise Famous Men,* and Theodore Rosengarten's *All God's Dangers: The Life of Nate Shaw* blur the distinctions between them) as well as that form of fiction known as the anatomy that defines what many critics take to be the dominant form not only of the greatest work of fiction in the nineteenth century, *Moby-Dick,* but also of the most remarkable narrative in the postwar period, *Gravity's Rainbow.* Also missing from the Columbia is any consideration of historical writing itself as an American literary genre, and particularly that curious metahistorical strain within it which sets out to define the meaning of the American experience, from George Bancroft, Francis Parkman, and Frederick Jackson Turner to Vernon Louis Parrington, Perry Miller, Daniel Boorstin, and David Hacket Fischer. Speaking of history, why no treatment of those verbal artists "whose writing," as James M. Cox has noted, "moved the world" but who "barely get a hearing in courses in American literature"—Jefferson, Madison, Lincoln, Grant?[38]

The Columbia lacks any sustained treatment at all of literary criticism and theory in the nineteenth century (E. P. Whipple and William Crary Brownell are not even mentioned in the index). Despite a chapter on modern philosophy, it also fails to devote any space to the extraordinary developments in critical theory that have not only permanently altered the face of contemporary American criticism but have also, as a consequence, generated most of the scholarship that made the creation of this volume something of a necessity. For a work that purports to be self-conscious about the historicity of literature, virtually no attention is paid to writing that was produced in direct response to actual historical events such as the Civil War, World War I, or the Vietnam War. Except in relation to the discussion of humor, the Columbia has almost nothing to say about American folk literature and the various cultural myths that sustain it, which in turn may account for its silence about so historically consequential a tradition as the art of black folk song and vernacular traditions in general.

In addition to confining the discussion of African-American literature—as of Mexican-American and Asian-American literature—to single chapters, and thus perpetuating the illusion, seriously challenged by several of the Columbia's other contributors, that African-American writing can be adequately comprehended in isolation from the larger medley of other American strains and kinds, the Columbia restricts the discussion of Native American writing to a brief essay about Amerindian orality at the beginning of the volume and thus omits the whole tradition of American Indian literature that ranges from the oratory of Chief Powhattan, Chief Logan, and Chief Pachgantschilias in the colonial period to the sayings and commentary of Chief Joseph of the Nez Perce, Black Elk, and Scott Momaday.

The Columbia is organized as though virtually all of the intellectual and moral culture transmitted to the New World during the first decades of settlement came by way of the British Isles. Far too little is made of the Hispanic contribution to this process, much less of the fact that during the first three generations of settlement, colonists in the northeastern part of the United States shared a mythology, as Howard Mumford Jones long ago reminded us, with the settlers of all the other "Americas" in the Western hemisphere.[39] And the cursory treatment of such topics as immigrant literature in the nineteenth century scarcely does justice to the contributions that other national traditions have made to the development of writing in the United States—of French intellectual and literary models in the era of the American Enlightenment, of German philosophy (and later the Higher Criticism) in the nineteenth century, and of various Continental movements from psychoanalysis and Marxism to existentialism and deconstruction in the twentieth.

There are other telling absences in the Columbia: contemporary southern writing has temporarily lost track of Harry Crews; Wright Morris has all but disappeared from the second generation of modern American fiction; and the extraordinary explosion of talent among contemporary black women writers fails to receive sufficient notice. Such lacunae are, perhaps, inevitable in an undertaking of this magnitude and complexity; yet one cannot help feeling that they could have been avoided if the editors had not so readily capitulated to the panorama not of dissensus so much as of divisiveness that typifies too much contemporary scholarship on American literature. It is no doubt true that we are currently in a period of turbulent reassessment in American literary study, that the canon is in process of reformation. But such periods do not necessarily require the suspension of all efforts to see the past, if not steadily, then at least, given the limits of one's horizons, entire. Yet to see the past in its entirety is neither to see it as completed and thus, as it were, finished, nor to see it unified. One does not need to know how it all hangs together to be able to delineate the most important elements that presently constitute it and the various controversies and concerns that still make it seem significant.

As an instance of the new historicism, then, or as an expression of the recanonization of American literature, the *Columbia Literary History of the United States* is something of a disappointment. If, on the one hand, it has managed to render an image of the American literary past that is more heterogeneous, complex, polyvocal, disparate, and sometimes dissonant, on the other, it has managed, despite the best efforts of many of its contributors, to make the actual warp and woof of that past, the cross-grained lines of force and vectors of energy that traverse it, more opaque, muddled, and inconsequential. In the name of their egalitarian pluralism, the editors not only argue implicitly that American writing lacks any common reference to a set of recurrent situations, discursive or otherwise; they tacitly imply as well that the differences among writers in the United States, both past and present, are essentially unassimilable to any common set of social practices, that the authors of the United States have ultimately produced no sustained communities of conversation. On this basis one would have to conclude that America doesn't have a literature at all, only a great welter of writers and writings.

*

Lawrence Buell has given the lie to this conclusion in what may well be the most successful—it is certainly the most ambitious—new historicist work of the last decade. If there is some irony in the fact that Buell might well find it uncomfortable to be placed in this company, there is no gainsaying that *New England Literary Culture* demonstrates more effectively than any other literary history I can think of precisely how social and political energies can be organized, expressed, and sometimes expanded by literary practices.[40] Indeed, *New England Literary Culture* may well be the most important study of the major writers of the mid-nineteenth century since *American Renaissance,* and one of the reasons it has achieved this distinction is the care with which Buell has thought through and presented the issues involved in any attempt to historicize fully the study of literature itself.

Buell is fully conversant with all the major intellectual challenges to any kind of literary historicism, both those posed from without and those posed from within. Those from without are posed either by older formalisms which, like the New Criticism, privilege the realm of the intrinsic over that of the extrinsic, or by the newer formalisms, like deconstruction, poststructuralism, and the New Semiotics generally, which presume that there is no other realm but the intrinsic. Those from within are posed by, among others, feminists and Marxists who in placing all discourse under the sign of gender or of material conditions risk dissolving history into just another culture-specific fiction. Buell, on the other hand, is still convinced that literary history can tell stories that are, in a pragmatic sense, "true," even though, like any other narrative forms, they must be construed as essentially an interpretive undertaking. Theoretically, he allies himself with a non-doctrinaire version of literary Marxism that "envisages language not merely as a relational system that conditions discourse, but also as [in the words of Clifford Geertz] 'articulated social presence,' itself the creature of the social reality it textualizes." By this he means that his study "will," as he puts it, "swim vigorously with the tide of fashion in approaching 'nonliterary' modes of discourse such as theology and historiography as fictionalized modes, yet it will also distinguish between these and more avowedly fictive constructs, and . . . will approach both as textualizations not only of cultural values but ultimately also of social reality."[41]

These "theoretical premises," as Buell calls them, lead him to conclude that any literary history must take some account of at least four different factors: periodization, canons and other demarcations of tradition, institutional controls such as genres, modes, historical kinds, and subgenres, and, finally, temporal sequences that suggest patterns of historical movement. Using these differentiations as structuring principles of his own text, Buell takes for his subject the creative literature produced by nearly 300 major and minor writers who either grew up in the New England states during the years 1770 to 1865, or spent the bulk of their adult life in New England, or, like Melville and Cooper, were clearly associated with it in outlook. These writers fall into five distinct but related generations whose succession enables Buell to show that the transitions from neoclassicism to romanticism and beyond to realism were by no means as sharp as traditional periodical schemes typically imply.

By lengthening the period under consideration and expanding his definition of literature to include all written and oral utterances that were intended to invite responses as verbal constructs, Buell is prepared to consider a much broader variety of both fictional and nonfictional writing than most previous studies of the era, and this, in turn, helps to realign and extend one's sense of the era's aesthetic achievement. Though Buell retains most of the figures from older canons—Emerson, Thoreau, Hawthorne, and, from a distance, Melville—he restores Emily Dickinson to her place among the others, elevates Harriet Beecher Stowe to a position alongside them, installs on a level equal to them all the hitherto neglected Elizabeth Stoddard, and attempts to reassess the reputations of a host of minor writers from St. John Honeywood to Tabitha Tenney.

If Buell's canon becomes enlarged in part because he is everywhere responsive to the discoveries of earlier scholarship, and particularly to the contributions of critical feminists, his reconception of the canon also derives from his sensitivity to the development of new genres and generic conventions within the period. Treating genre not as a hierarchical classification of fixed forms but as an evolving set of conventions that link various individual works together in highly complex and somewhat fluid networks of family resemblance, Buell shows how everything from New England oratory to literary scripturalism, from

Puritan historiography to romantic pastoralism and regional topophi-
lia (or the literature of place), served as ideological constraints influ-
encing literary production.

For all this, Buell is committed to an analysis that manages to operate on several levels simultaneously, on the socioeconomic level of
literary practice, the ideological level of aesthetic values, and the formal and generic level of the texts themselves. From this multilayered
approach emerge three large story lines or master narratives. One concerns the institutional development of New England literary culture
during these years. A second, reflecting "the transition from Neoclas-
sical to Romantic hegemony," involves a shift in the conception of the
artist from public citizen to private visionary without sacrifice of his
or her role as moral monitor of a cultural consensus that might at the
same time be seriously questioned. The third details the literary invention of New England itself as a cultural symbol system replete with its
own mythography of Puritan antecedence, its own iconography of the
village, its own form of landscape logocentricity, and its own traditions of the comic grotesque and provincial gothic.

The result is a literary history that challenges a number of the more
important assumptions controlling current practice in American literary studies, particularly among new Americanist historicists, and specifically as they pertain to a reexamination of the American Renaissance. Chief among them may be the view first proposed by Feidelson
that the mid-nineteenth-century writers were all, or mainly, proto-
modernists. Buell argues persuasively, I believe, and from extensive
examination of their stylistic practices and ideological preferences,
that they were at best premoderns, significant precursors of the writers
of our own century but by no means their advance party. Second, he
effectively counters the "accusatory" theory that criticizes even the
most socially and morally radical of these writers for complicity in the
maintenance of a rhetoric that supported cultural consensus by showing that this theory is based on too simple a model of consensus/dis-
sensus. Their varied achievement was in large part made possible,
Buell contends, by the same Whig-Unitarian cultural establishment
they had to confront and could never wholly escape but which, on
occasion, they nevertheless did manage successfully to displace, or at
least effectively to challenge. Third, Buell provides an entirely new
map of the age last surveyed with such meticulous care by Matthiessen
by confining his own examination, though not rigidly, to regional culture. Insisting that provincial consciousness is not "epiphenomenal"
for the American literary historian but "paradigmatic," his book affirms, as regional historians and critics have always known, that "to

conquer the nation, one must attack through the provinces." [42] Yet this assault would have proved ultimately futile if Buell had not been so assiduous in historicizing both his period and his own approach to it. Employing interpretive tools that are by turns Marxist, deconstructionist, feminist, generic, intellectual, and hermeneutic with admirable tact, he has, as his fourth major achievement, given new validity to the study of literary and cultural history by showing us how to dismantle the text, in Pierre Macherey's words, "in order to be able to reconstruct it *in the image* of its meaning, to make it denote directly what it had [only] expressed obliquely." [43]

★

One way of describing this last achievement is to say that it involves a recovery of what Hayden White calls "the context in the text." "The context in the text" represents not only the sedimented material sources of the text's production but also the traces of that to which the text's "historicality" is ultimately a response: what Paul Ricoeur designates as the tragedy of temporality. History is tragic because the human efforts it records to endow life with meaning must submit to "the corrosive power of time." But time works its corrosive power in full view of the human quest for meaning. Hence the pathos and paradox of that way of "being-in-the-world we call 'historical'" whose enigmatic quality can only be "grasped," so Ricoeur believes, symbolically and can only be made comprehensible, as White notes in a book far too subtle to do justice to here, "in those true allegories of temporality that we call narrative histories":

Their truth resides not only in their fidelity to the facts of given individual or collective lives but also, and most importantly, in their faithfulness to that vision of human life informing the poetic genre of tragedy. In this respect, the symbolic content of narrative history, the content of its form, is the tragic vision itself. [44]

To historicize is thus to be brought up against all that the self is exposed to within time because of time, by the odds against the self's continuance beyond time. [45] No historicism, new or old, that does not acknowledge the ultimate pathos of this predicament in the, among others, social and political contexts of human resistance to it deserves, on White's account, to be taken seriously. In addition, even if historicism is only another way of trying to get into and also out of history, as White says of Fredric Jameson's "political unconscious," no historicism that glosses the differences among the various tactics of historicization by which we try to do so can be regarded, so White implies,

as other than frivolous. There are real differences, that is, between jus-
tifying what Mircea Eliade once called the "terror of history" in the
name of the kind of antihumanism with which, in his earlier writing,
Foucault attacks the collusion between modern representations of historical discourse and the reconstitution of the human subject as a field
of study, and, say, Ricoeur's attempt to uncover the deep structures
that compel or at least control our need to render experience narratively in order to cope with the paradox it compels us to face but cannot help us wholly overcome, the paradox of temporality and its du-
ration, of time and eternity.

Elizabeth Bishop renders this paradox perfectly in some lines from
"At the Fishhouses," where she writes,

> It is like what we imagine knowledge to be:
> dark, salt, clear, moving, utterly free,
> drawn from the cold hard mouth
> of the world, derived from the rocky breasts
> forever, flowing and drawn, and since
> our knowledge is historical, flowing, and flown.

The hesitancy Bishop enforces by the comma she inserts between
"flowing" and "flown" registers with exquisite tact the paradoxical
character of our experience of the historical; becomes, in fact, a kind
of comment on the pathos of all historicisms, old and new. The continuous flux of experience, its remorseless change, encourages us to
believe that "historicity," or the "historical," is the chief attribute of
experience, and thus elicits in us the desire to re-present this "historicity" so that we can, if only temporally, arrest the movement of experience by inscribing ourselves, or rather our sense of the meaning of
this "historicity," in all its forms. But the inevitable passage of experience, its disappearance and loss, necessarily condemns as illusory and
fictitious any efforts to forestall its dissolutions through the inscription
of ourselves and our intuitions in such apparently stable structures as
history and narrative, and hence may only represent, curiously
enough, the form of our despair.

This is a paradox that can never be resolved, as Bishop shows; only
acknowledged and perhaps assimilated. "Historicality," "historicity,"
"historicism" therefore all refer merely to one (or more) among a variety of discursive practices for defining the odds against us and offer
us another set of terms—what Kenneth Burke would call "critical coordinates"—for, at the very least, calculating our chances, at the most,
attempting to enhance them. But the real issue isn't what we calculate
our chances to be—different critical systems furnish us with different

sets of calculations—or whether we can improve our margin; the crucial issue is how we go about our calculating. It essentially comes
down to a question of the "expense of spirit," to use Shakespeare's
phrase, that is being wagered in the process.[46] Those works of the
imagination and the intellect that raise the stakes for the human spirit
to the highest levels of cultural risk before making such measurements, and then make those measurements in the face of obstacles that
would normally be conceived to thwart, or at least to threaten, their
success—those works we call "major" or "classic." As White says with
the help of certain formulations from Jameson, "What the classic
achieves is an instantiation of the human capacity to endow lived contradictions with intimations of their possible transcendence."[47]

Thus White is prepared to claim that what distinguishes the classic
at any given time from all other similar works with which it might be
compared is not the universal truths that it is sensed to contain about,
say, the "human condition," but the models it provides for investigating the "human condition" and other such matters, both within the
text and beyond it, when the human condition, and the procedures for
investigating it, have been rendered particularly bewildering or perilous:

. . . the classic text, the master text, intrigues us, not because (or only because)
its meaning-content is universally valid or authoritative (for that is manifestly
impossible; in any event, it is a profoundly unhistorical way of looking at
anything), but because it gives us insight into a process that is universal and
definitive of human species-being in general, the production of meaning.[48]

Yet it does so, White insists, in its own way. The difference between
any text we think of as seriously "literary" or "classic" and all other
verbal constructs "has to do with the extent to which the classic text
reveals, indeed actively draws attention to, its own processes of meaning production and makes of these processes its own subject matter, its
own 'content'."[49]

It is this knowledge of literary texts not only as products of meaning but also as processes and models for producing and reproducing it
that is now at issue in the kingdoms of theory. How do we obtain such
knowledge? Why does such knowledge matter? What does such
knowledge do to our previous conceptions of literature? White's answer to this last question may not be the only answer, but it nicely
converges with Buell's thinking as well as with Jameson's, with Graff's
as well as with Ricoeur's:

Insofar as art and literature, across whatever local differences in their contents
occasioned by their production in concrete historical conditions, not only in-

stantiate the human capacity for imagining a better world but also, in the universality of the forms that they utilize for the representation of vision itself, actually provide us with models or paradigms of all creative productivity of a specifically human sort, they claim an authority different in kind from that claimed by both science and politics.[50]

The critical issue that the institutions of literary study in America can no longer evade or repress, as they once did, and that the historicism of the new Americanists has the potential to help them address, is what that authority amounts to and what sorts of empathy and empowerment it makes possible.

8

Interdisciplinarity and the Deepening of the American Mind

*

Damn braces. Bless relaxes.
William Blake

*

Interdisciplinarity has recently become a subject of considerable interest in the academy. No doubt some of its topicality derives from the perennial American fascination with borders, frontiers, and unexplored territories. Much of the current fascination with interdisciplinarity, however, now also derives from its appeal to a leftist ideology that associates intellectual disciplines with the institutional structures that create and empower them and that, in the hyperbolic mood of a good deal of critical discourse these days, is prepared to view the demarcation of intellectual territorialities as potentially a police tactic that is both imprisoning and oppressive. The radical response is to call for a revolt not only against disciplinary boundaries long held to be sacrosanct but also against the institutional hierarchies that protect and sustain them. This revolt is predicated on the possibility of developing greater self-consciousness about the fabricated and self-interested character of all disciplinary arrangements, but it must be extended—if it is to succeed in its professed work of liberation—to a challenge of the cartographic practices of the wider society that legitimates and shelters them.

Here is where the present leftist interdisciplinary project becomes noticeably more militant than the former liberal one. The liberal interdisciplinary project everywhere preserves the distinction between the academy and the world and merely wants to reform the way knowledge is produced and reproduced within the academy itself. The interdisciplinary project of the radicals, on the other hand, is based on the belief that the distinction between the academy and the world is itself political; the radicals therefore maintain that the only way to dismantle the boundaries that currently segregate one discipline from another is by challenging the structure of larger social articulations "within which the [disciplinary] articulations of the academy are rendered intelligible and seemingly inevitable."[1]

Stanley Fish, whose analysis I have been following, has produced an insightful critique of this radical project. "Being interdisciplinary is so very hard to do," as Fish points out in a recent article with this title, because the politics it professes is undercut by the epistemology on which it is premised. Its politics holds that if disciplinary boundaries can be dissolved, the mind will then be liberated to move into the gaps and discontinuities and new instabilities thus created and open discourse to process, relation, metamorphosis. By contrast its epistemology holds that no such intellectual freedom is ever possible because meanings are always produced from a position, or by a system, which exists as their unarticulated and unspecifiable ground. Hence to pretend that disciplinary emancipation and intellectual independence will follow from a demonstration that all disciplinary distinctions are historical rather than natural, contingent not given, is to presume that one can reveal the structures of knowledge from within an intellectual frame that is still hidden.

The more radical apologists for interdisciplinarity are not insensible of these difficulties but believe that there are at least two ways around them. The first is to realize that we always simultaneously occupy overlapping and conflicting disciplinary matrices that can be employed to check and criticize each other. The second is to cultivate an awareness of the conditions that authorize or legitimate a disciplinary practice, even as one practices it, in the hope of achieving what Bruce Robbins calls "productively divided loyalties."[2]

Fish is prepared to concede as much but remains unconvinced that this resolves anything. It would, perhaps, if the interdisciplinary construct could escape being contaminated by the techniques that produce it, but unfortunately this is impossible. For even when scholars import into their own disciplinary practice methods that are derived from some other, the "imported practice," as Fish calls it, "will always have the form of its appropriation rather than the form it exhibits 'at home.'"[3] Furthermore, because that "imported practice" is already marked by the practice or discourse that it is supposedly intended to open, it will not produce, as the leftists imagine it will, a set of loyalties that are conceptually and methodologically divided. As Fish puts it, the radical hope that you can achieve a reflective distance from the conditions of a disciplinary practice while at the same time engaging in that practice only means that you are now engaging not in that practice at all but rather in another—the practice, he calls it, "of reflecting on the conditions of a practice you are not now practicing." [4]

All this leads Fish to embrace the conservative view that while people cross disciplinary boundaries all the time, they do not thereby accomplish anything particularly interdisciplinary. Borrowing the methods of one field to get work done in another, or annexing the methods of other fields so that you can expand your own into their territory, or even establishing a new metadiscipline that studies disciplinarity itself—these activities, laudable as they are, do little or nothing to open, much less to alter, the mind. Far from reconstituting the material of knowledge by reconstruing the perspectives by which, and the purposes for which, it can be known, they merely represent various ways, Fish thinks, by which the mind can adjust its present forms of closure to new exigencies. This is what the mind practices when it is hedging its bets, or, to borrow the title of Fish's most recent book, "doing what comes naturally." But in this instance, "doing what comes naturally" amounts to defending the conservative, really reactionary, proposition that there is no possibility of learning anything at all, and this is a proposition that is rather spectacularly belied by the lesson of Fish's own critical practice.

Quite apart from its politics, there are several problems with this line of reasoning. The first is suggested by Derrida's response to the question of whether any intellectual practice can ever transcend the metaphysics of logocentricity without remaining hostage to the language of metaphysics. His well-known view is that the transcendence of metaphysics, or, for that matter, any other system of signification, is impossible because it would require a suspension of all the rules of determinate language. But this conviction has not prevented Derrida, along with other contemporary theorists, from problematizing this simplistic model of inside and outside or boundary and boundarylessness. To be dependent on any "hidden" system of signification, metaphysical or otherwise, Derrida notes, "does not mean that we are incarcerated in it as prisoners or victims of some unhappy fatality. It is simply that our belonging to, and inherence in, the language of metaphysics is something that can only be rigorously and adequately thought about from *another* topos or space where our problematic rapport with the boundary of metaphysics can be seen in a more radical light." [5]

Derrida has made the discovery of such a topos or space—what he calls "the non-place or non-lieu which would be the 'other' of philosophy"—the chief task of deconstruction itself. But the question for criticism is whether literature in distinction from philosophy has any

contribution to make to the accomplishment of this task. Fish obviously doubts that it does and regards the whole endeavor as perfectly
senseless; Derrida, on the other hand, is convinced that it can, though
the literature he has in mind is of a fairly special sort: "certain movements which work around the limits of our logical concepts, certain
texts [he is thinking of works by Blanchot, Bataille, and Beckett]
which make the limits of our language tremble, exposing them as di-
visible and questionable."[6] What is disclosed in such movements and
such texts is the possibility of an alterity that is, if irreducible to conventional linguistic forms, nonetheless capable of conception through
a perception of the limitations of their adequacy. Such a literature
keeps alive a sense of what lies beyond the horizon of our systems of
signification by dramatizing the failure of our systemizing attempts to
formulate it. As was noted in chapter 5, William James essentially
made this same argument from a pragmatist perspective but located
the source of our ability to see beyond the horizons of our systems of
signification somewhere else. One was not dependent on only those
very special and, from a historical point of view, very late forms of
literature that make language tremble to sense what lies beyond language's own significations; language was perfectly capable of performing this task by itself with its ordinary, everyday repertoire of conjunctive and relational words such as "and," "by," "with," "near,"
"toward," and so on.

The second problem with Fish's position is that his whole discussion is based on an essentially illusory opposition. The radical claim
that interdisciplinarity will serve to open the mind is no less misleading than the conservative claim that interdisciplinarity will leave the
mind as comfortably closed as it has always been. Both are based on a
spurious dualism. The issue that interdisciplinarity addresses is neither
how to free the mind nor how to fix it but rather how, as Melville put
it in *Moby-Dick,* to subtilize it. The opposite of subtilizing the mind is,
of course, to simplify it, and this, as we shall see, is the real enemy,
both political and epistemological, that interdisciplinarity is conceived
to combat. To subtilize the mind is neither to suppose that we can
dispense with disciplinary boundaries altogether nor to assume that
we have to accept those that have already been instituted. It is simply
to realize that while no literary study can occur without them, there is
nothing about the nature of boundaries themselves, disciplinary or
otherwise, that prevents one from seeing from more than one side of
them. This alone does not make for a more interdisciplinary environment, but it represents one of its most essential preconditions. Without the ability to see from different sides of various boundaries, there

is no possibility either of redrawing the boundaries themselves or, more crucially, of changing what can be seen as a result.

★

One of the chief obstacles to this realization is the view that interdisciplinary studies constitutes something like an independent field of studies, such as modernist studies or medieval studies, with interdisciplinarity its purported subject. Even if many scholars and critics think of their work as interdisciplinary, they do not, by virtue of this understanding, share anything like a set of common interests, common methods, or common problems. What they share instead, for want of a better term, is a predisposition to pursue their questions into areas of critical inquiry that cannot be mapped at all by the cartographic practices currently in disciplinary use. Students of interdisciplinary studies are thus marked by their willingness not simply to challenge, but also to cross, traditional disciplinary boundaries. Their hope, or at any rate their assumption, is that important dimensions of human experience and understanding lie unexplored in the spaces between them or in the places where they merge, overlap, divide, or dissolve.

It would be a mistake, however, to suppose that boundary crossing is either an infrequent practice in humanistic studies or a recent one. The humanistic practice of interdisciplinary excursions into foreign disciplinary territories goes all the way back in the West to classical antiquity, when Greek historians and dramatists drew on medical and philosophical knowledge, respectively, for clues to the reconception of their own material; and it has continued down to our own time where much social thinking has been "refigured," to use the coinage of Clifford Geertz, by encouraging social thinkers from a variety of disciplines to explore analogies between their own material and such aesthetic activities as play, ritual, drama, symbolic action, narrative, speech acts, games, and writing. In the Middle Ages, literary criticism put itself in the debt of systematic theology for its theories of interpretation and language. In the early modern period, the theologians, philosophers, and men of letters known as the "humanists" differentiated themselves as a semiprofessional class by adopting, over against the medieval schoolmen, the theories and practices of the classical Greek and Roman philosophers. The movement known as the Enlightenment in the eighteenth century could easily be described as a raid by the philosophes on the conceptions and methods of the physical sciences, and what we call nineteenth-century romanticism is only another term for what might be described as the intellectual appropriation, by fields such as theology, philosophy, literature, and the fine arts, of biologic and organic metaphors drawn from the natural sciences.

But if there is nothing unusual about humanists conducting sorties into alien "disciplinary" territory, there is nonetheless something quite distinctive and very exciting about the modern interest in such cross-field and cross-disciplinary peregrinations. This has to do with the reasons why, and the ways in which, contemporary literary scholars and critics have permitted such sallies to redefine both their subject matter and the kinds of questions they put to it. That is to say, the interdisciplinary move to explore the alien terrain of nonliterary genres and fields has amounted to considerably more than an attempt to draw different disciplines into conversational relations with one another, or to expand the horizons of one discipline by borrowing some of the insights and techniques of another. Even where the modern interdisciplinary impulse has been prompted by motives no more suspect than the desire to improve communication across territorial boundaries or to expand the parameters that define them, it rarely ends there. What may have begun as the simple promotion of a kind of good-neighbor policy, or an innocent adventure in exploring the exotic material of some "foreign" field, often results in something far less benign than boundary crossing and much more unsettling than boundary changing. What is at stake, to return to Geertz, is not just another redrawing of the disciplinary map but the principles of mapping as such. In this more contemporary sense, then, interdisciplinarity is not achieved through simple confrontations between specialized fields of knowledge—literature with history, chemistry with engineering, art history with the history of ideas—or through placing the insights and techniques of one discipline on loan to another—textual study borrowing the methods of computer science, history utilizing the techniques of demographers. Its effect, if not its purpose, is often nothing less than to alter the way we think about thinking.[7]

*

The process of interdisciplinary revisionism usually begins with a period of courtship between two distinct and often diverse disciplines that suddenly begin to discover spheres of mutual interest and complementary resources; then proceeds to a kind of marriage based on the belief that there are significant areas of compatibility between their respective methods and intellectual focus; and finally culminates in the production of offspring who share the parental genes and some of their dispositional features but possess a character all their own. Interdisci-

plinary exchanges thus depend on something more than ratcheting up
the level of sophistication with which one explores the relations between literature and something else—myth, psychology, religion,
film, the visual arts—by utilizing methods appropriate to the study of
each in some form of close, perhaps even symbiotic, cooperation. Interdisciplinarity requires instead an alteration of the constitutive question that generates such inquiry in the first place. Thus where relational studies proceed from the question of what literature (in its
traditions, its formal conventions, and its thematic concerns) has to do
with some other material (like music or social behavior) or some other
field (such as history, political science, or sociolinguistics), interdisciplinary inquiries proceed from the double-sided question about how
the insights or methods of some other field or structure can remodel
our understanding of the nature of the "literary," and, conversely,
about how literary conceptions and approaches can remodel our conception of the allied field and its own subject material.

An excellent example of this process can be found in the newly
emergent field of ethical criticism first explored by moral philosophers
like Iris Murdoch, Mikel Dufrenne, Bernard Williams, and Hilary
Putnam and now being developed by, among others, Martha Nussbaum and Wayne Booth. An outgrowth of a very ancient interest in
the relations between literature and philosophy that has been maintained for moderns by, among others, Friedrich Schiller, Samuel Tay-
lor Coleridge, Friedrich Nietzsche, Martin Heidegger, John Dewey,
Stuart Hampshire, Isaiah Berlin, Stanley Cavell, and Nelson Good-
man, the interdisciplinary challenge of ethical criticism is conceived to
be the transcendence of two related views. The first is that literature
possesses moral dimensions even though it is not a form of moral experience. The second is that philosophical conceptions of morality can
be illustrated by literary forms despite the fact that such forms are incapable of reflecting systematically on moral questions.

In *The Fragility of Goodness* and *Love's Knowledge,* Nussbaum in particular is concerned to revise both nostrums by arguing, first, against
most academic moral philosophers, that certain conceptions of the
good life, both individual and social, are simply not fully or adequately represented in forms of writing as abstract and affectless as
traditional philosophical disputation; and, second, against many literary critics and theorists, that the conventional aesthetic prejudice
against the ethically heuristic value of forms of writing like prose narrative or lyric poetry derives in part from a false assumption (widely
shared by most moral and other philosophers as well) that the emotions lack cognitive content even where they convey felt quality.

Her argument against both errors turns on their traditional resistance to the view that aesthetic forms play an educative as well as an illustrative role in processes of practical reflection on ethical issues, and it expresses itself in the assertion that while works of art often represent and express emotional effects, their deeper affective significance stems from the fact that their forms "are themselves the sources of emotional structure, the paradigms of what, for us, feeling is."[8] Nussbaum is therefore interested in developing a new structure of interdisciplinary inquiry that will, at one and the same time, demonstrate the extent to which certain kinds of moral reflection and insight are dependent upon narrative and other aesthetic structures and the extent to which practical ethical reasoning is in many instances a concomitant result of literary interpretation.

However, it must be added immediately that ethical criticism is by no means confined to Nussbaum's extremely adroit and compelling practice of it. The term—which has been the source of approbrium by critics as various as Northrop Frye and Fredric Jameson, and of praise by the likes of F. R. Leavis, Lionel Trilling, and David Bromwich—can also be applied more widely to various kinds of interdisciplinary study that go by different names—feminist criticism, African-American criticism, postcolonial criticism, ideological criticism, cultural studies—which also seek to submit literary forms to moral scrutiny or to challenge ethical reflection with metaphoric restructuration.

The interdisciplinary field of American Studies provides another example of how such inquiry reconfigures the constituent disciplines that compose it. Beginning in the 1930s as an attempt to link literary with historical studies—when literature was viewed by historians as little more than a set of illustrations of themes, ideas, and events from beyond the world of literature, and history was viewed by critics as merely the background of literature—American Studies very quickly turned into a much more complicated attempt to study the interactions between forms of collective mentality such as myths and archetypes, products of individual consciousness such as works of art and intellect, and social structures such as institutions and practices. In this interdisciplinary reformulation, the purpose of bringing literature again into relation with history and society—to say nothing of reconnecting social development with the politics as well as the poetics of mental constructs—was not so much to define, much less to valorize, the myths and other imaginative formations in which, and by means of which, their relations could be configured or even, to a considerable degree, imaginatively controlled; in the largest sense of the word, it was to find some way of criticizing the consequences of such configurations and controls. As Henry Nash Smith put it in *Virgin Land,* his chief object in writing a book about "the American West as symbol and myth" was to demonstrate how completely and destructively captive agrarian and frontier thinking were to the specious intellectual opposition they had inherited from the eighteenth century between "civilization" and the "wilderness." In like fashion, R.W.B. Lewis's purpose in submitting the myth of national innocence to intellectual and aesthetic examination in *The American Adam* was essentially to determine what, for good or ill, had been learned from its narrative applications.

In more recent years the notions of the literary, the social, and the historical in American Studies have been revised further in the interest of showing more empirically just how culture works. Thus in studies such as Lawrence Levine's *Black Culture and Black Consciousness,* Michael Gilmore's *American Romanticism and the Marketplace,* Cecilia Tichi's *Shifting Gears,* and Myra Jehlen's *American Incarnation,* critical attention is directed not simply to how cultural forms symbolically refract, or resist, or redirect social, political, and economic forces, but also to how, in some more material sense, they produce, represent, and sometimes misrepresent and distort them. If the best work of scholars in both of the most recent generations of American Studies centered around the meaning and function of the term "ideology" and set for itself a political task, they each nonetheless defined that task somewhat differently by virtue of the different sort of cohesiveness that they assumed the notion of ideology gives to the interdisciplinary study of cultural work itself. Where scholars of the earlier generation assumed that ideology constitutes that element of cultural coherence that the most morally significant forms of any culture simultaneously contain and resist, scholars of the later are more likely to view ideology as that component of cultural unity that the most morally significant or representative forms of any culture will at once absorb and camouflage.

Nonetheless, it has recently been asserted that the American Studies movement has largely failed because, however much it has revised conceptions of the literary, the historical, and the social, as well as of the relations between them, it never led to the creation of separate departments of American literature.[9] But this is to measure the success of an interdisciplinary field of inquiry in terms of whether it can achieve the kind of institutional recognition accorded the sorts of disciplinary structures that it is attempting to overthrow or at least to reconfigure. The success of the American Studies movement, like that of any other interdisciplinary undertaking, has derived rather from a variety of other more and less empirical measurements, such as the number of separate undergraduate programs and majors it has generated throughout the United States and the world, the kinds and quality of graduate programs it has produced, the new areas of research it has opened up, the professional associations it has sponsored, and, most important, the creativity, integrity, insight, and resilience of the scholarship that has been produced in its name.

But the key factor in any interdisciplinary undertaking is the success it has achieved in challenging previous interpretive paradigms and supplying new ones—in other words, in changing the way the newly configured disciplines now make sense of themselves to themselves. Judging by standards such as these, American Studies has proven as efficacious an interdisciplinary initiative as almost any other undertaken in American higher education in the postwar period. To cite but two examples, the cultural study of the colonial period in the United States is now rapidly ceasing to be treated as a staging area for the eventual creation of one or another version of the nineteenth-century American self, a self that was not only male and white but also middle class, and is instead being reconceived in more ethnographic terms as an interpretive site defined by the confrontation and often conflict between diverse cultures—Puritan versus Quaker, Calvinist versus Arminian or Antinomian, religious versus secular, European versus Native American, English versus French, Massachusetts Bay versus Connecticut Valley, New England versus Tidewater Virginia, city versus backwoods, male versus female, first generation versus second and third, and so on. In similar fashion, study of the cultural importance of the mid-nineteenth-century renaissance in literature and art has relinquished much of its Matthiessenian interest in the myth of the common man, and the possibilities of creating a literary and intellectual culture commensurate with America's democratic aspirations in favor of examining those explosive tensions often masked by such ambitions in the postwar era—tensions at once racial, sexual, social, religious, cultural, economic, and political—that erupted in a nation-rending civil war, a war whose history continues to remain unwritten, as Daniel Aaron argued more than twenty years ago, and thus to some degree still culturally unassimilated, down to the present day.

But this only indicates how difficult it is to demarcate precisely where, and how, to draw the boundaries not only *between* different kinds of interdisciplinary study but also *within* them. For American Studies, like feminist criticism, African-American criticism, or postcolonial criticism, is more of a composite methodological site where other interdisciplinary modes cross and recross—reader-response criticism, semiotic analysis, psychoanalytic inquiry, ethnic studies, social anthropology, cultural materialism, art history, gender studies—than it is a unitary mode of interdisciplinary study all its own. Furthermore, there are sharp and sometimes seemingly incommensurable differences between and among, say, feminist critics over whether to organize their research around models that are biological, psychological, cultural, or linguistic. What this suggests, to repeat, is that interdisciplinary studies may refer not to anything as specific or unified as a "field" in itself so much as to a distinctive predisposition to view all fields as potentially vulnerable to re-creation in the partial image of some other or others. This, in turn, renders the fields in question what Roland Barthes calls "transversals" whose reconfiguration seeks to produce or recover meanings that their formerly configured relations tended to blur, mask, or efface.[10]

★

As numerous students of interdisciplinarity in all fields can attest, the process of converting disciplines into transversals can not only be discomfiting but also potentially violent. When the parameters of traditional fields grow permeable or suspect under the pressure of questions that as presently constituted they cannot address, they grow ripe for infiltration, subversion, or outright assault. Such military metaphors may seem excessive but they are altogether apt. When the academic field now called anthropology first attempted to carve out a space for itself between history and sociology, it was described by one of its proponents, and not altogether inaccurately, as "a disciplinary poaching license." Thus images of encroachment, trespass, offense are inescapable: interdisciplinary studies risk disciplinary transgression in the name of interdisciplinary independence, disciplinary revisionism in the name of interdisciplinary emancipation and creativity.[11]

But the ideology of interdisciplinary freedom captures only those aspects of interdisciplinary activity that are potentially invasive and disruptive. There is another side to interdisciplinary practice that, according to some, is by contrast peremptory, juridical, prescriptive, and imperialistic. This threat derives from the fact that the redescriptive impulses of interdisciplinary studies almost of necessity place one discipline in a position of subordination to another. As a result, the subordinated discipline is not only destabilized but also threatened with subsumption in an anomalous, substitutionary structure that on the pretext of situating itself, as the prefix implies, between the two more traditionally constituted disciplinary matrices, actually manages to incorporate them both in some larger hegemonic framework. Whether one construes this new interdisciplinary formation as merely a product of the merger of the other two, or as itself a new metadiscipline beyond them, seemingly matters at all. A new methodological field has been produced, the imperiousness of whose procedures often runs counter to the redemptive heuristics used to justify it. Thus if interdisciplinarity is most often legitimated in the name of greater intellectual autonomy and openness, the transdisciplinary exploration it sanctions possesses the capability of disguising another form of meta-disciplinary despotism. To quote Barthes:

Interdisciplinary work is not a peaceful operation: it begins *effectively* when the solidarity of the old discipline breaks down—a process made more violent, perhaps, by the jolts of fashion—to the benefit of a new object and a new language, neither of which is in the domain of those branches of knowledge that one calmly sought to confront. . . . there now arises a need for a new object, one attained by the displacement or overturning of previous categories.[12]

Barthes defines this new mutational object as the *text,* arguing that it displaces or overturns the old "Newtonian concept of the 'work.'" By "text" Barthes means to refer less to a specifiable entity than to a site or intersection of productive activity, that is, to processes of signification rather than to forms of the signified. But whether the meta-discipline Barthes invokes is described as textual studies, or intertextuality, or—as certain contemporary critics now want to argue—cultural studies, his view that interdisciplinarity always supplants one set of disciplinary structures with another still more encompassing and dominant is by no means shared by all contemporary critics and scholars. What looks to Barthes like a new monolithic metadiscipline rising from the imperialistic subversion and partial fusion of two others appears to another group of scholars and critics rather more like a new integration of strategies, methods, and queries that acquire their particular sense of authority and empowerment from what the two disciplines on which heretofore they have traditionally drawn have customarily dismissed, repressed, or occluded. To cite but two examples, Feminist Studies arose initially as a protest against the false stereotypes that had been created about women in the literature written by men and has sought to recuperate the very different representations of their experience that women have furnished in their own writing. In like fashion, the successive stages of African-American criticism—from its inception in the Black Arts movement of the 1960s to its current attempt in the late 1980s and early 1990s to retheorize social and textual boundaries in all American cultural contexts and thus turn Black Studies into a critique of American Studies generally—demonstrates that African-American criticism arose in part out of new discoveries of what more conventional disciplinary inquiries had typically left out of account.

★

For purposes of the present discussion, it is perhaps enough to say, then, that there is a loose historical connection between the various associations that literature has for some time, and in some instances for many centuries, enjoyed with other fields or structured forms— forms like painting, film, sculpture, architecture, discursive argument, dogmatic and speculative theology, social thought, music, and, now, photography and the law; fields like jurisprudence, linguistics, anthropology, sociology, musicology, philosophy, religion, science, history, and politics—and the development of at least some interdisciplinary modes of approach to such interrelations. But this is an assertion that needs to be qualified to the bone. These developments have not followed any kind of orderly pattern; they are by no means fully descriptive of all the fields with which literature has possessed important conceptual and methodological filiations; and they are related very closely, as might be expected, to developments in literary and critical theory as well as to the emergence of new notions of textuality and intertextuality, particularly as they apply to the concept of culture itself. More exactly, modes of study that become genuinely interdisciplinary have usually developed through the crossing, displacement, or alteration of the boundaries between different forms of relational study, or have otherwise constituted themselves in the spaces between them as attempts to understand the asymmetrical relations between the protocols and perspectives that divide them.

As a case in point, deconstruction arose out of joining the philosophical interest in the critique of Western metaphysics with the new science of structural linguistics that in Ferdinand de Saussure's version of it stressed the fact that language is composed of signs that can be differentiated as to function. The material means of transmission, or acoustic image of any sign, Saussure called the "signifier"; the conceptual image, or intellectual referent, of any sign he took to be its "signified." This relationship between signifier and signified is what becomes problematic for the deconstructionist by virtue of his or her perception of the irreducible *differance*—as in differing and deferring— between them, and the inevitable suppression, repression, or dissemination of meaning to which this leads. Often misdescribed as a method or critical theory, deconstruction's chief aim is, in Derrida's view, to call into question and attempt to dismantle all the classical oppositions on which literary criticism (like theology and philosophy) is based—

between word and referent, language and being, structure and process, text and context—in order to see what such oppositions have traditionally veiled or concealed. By contrast, the new historicism has taken up methodological residence somewhere between deconstruction's preoccupation with the conflicting, if not self-canceling, forces of signification in any text and the neo-Marxist fascination with how processes of textualization not only reflect material circumstances and institutional patterns but also frequently, and often simultaneously, generate them.

But if interdisciplinary studies is sometimes formed by traversing inherited disciplinary boundaries, sometimes by transfiguring them, and sometimes by exploring the spaces between them, how is one to go about mapping its own contemporary permutations and forms? The simplest answer is probably to be found by reverting to the time-honored set of critical coordinates that have conventionally been employed to model literary texts—the author, the reader, the material or linguistic components of the text itself, and the world to which the text refers. This model, first delineated by M. H. Abrams in *The Mirror and the Lamp,* has been vastly complicated in recent years as our sense of each one of its coordinates has been expanded, but its use can nonetheless be instructive.[13] Such a model helps clarify immediately, for example, that much of the activity in interdisciplinary studies in recent years has been quite selectively focused. Given recent suspicions about the status of the author in contemporary criticism as well as the whole question of authorial intentionality, and the no less grave theoretical misgivings about the mimetic properties of art and the role of representation generally, interdisciplinary work has placed far less emphasis on the first and last coordinates of this literary model, the author and the world, and much more emphasis on the two middle coordinates, the reader and the work.

This selectivity is apparent everywhere. It is as clearly visible in all the contemporary variants of psychological criticism, which tend to be preoccupied with the mental and emotional states of individuals, even when they are taken to represent real-life psychological processes in the world, as it is in social and political criticism, which is typically concerned with the way the material environment serves either as a source of literary production, or as an object of literary representation, or as a determinant of literary reception and influence. Thus psychoanalytic criticism has for some time been considerably less interested in the psyches of individual authors, or the way literary texts mirror the psychological processes of persons and groups, than in how psychological structures, such as the unconscious, can be viewed as ana-

logues to literary structures like language, or in how strategies of literary typification and signification, such as metonymy, synecdoche,
and irony, can be read psychoanalytically both as representing and as
enabling processes of repression, displacement, transference, and
countertransference. Similarly, much of the most influential interdisciplinary criticism promoted by the newer Marxist theories has abandoned careful examination of the class background of writers, or the
sociopolitical verisimilitude of the world they create, in favor of exploring the manner in which works of literature and other art forms
not only reflect discursive traces of the class struggle and resolve social
conflicts symbolically but also inscribe stylistically the modes of production by which they were first legitimated.

Any map of interdisciplinary studies would look rather different,
however, if one were to use only one of these critical coordinates as the
cartographic axis. Take, for example, the new focus in recent criticism
on the reader, which provides a way of linking the phenomenological
criticism that Wolfgang Iser practices in *The Implied Reader* and *The
Act of Reading* with the *Rezeptionsästhetik* of Hans-Robert Jauss which
examines, in studies like *Toward an Aesthetic of Reception* and *Aesthetic
Experience and Literary Hermeneutics,* the changing responses of whole
peoples or communities over time. Nevertheless, under the same
heading one could also make room for the parallel, and much more
empirical, emphasis of critics like Nina Baym, in *Novels, Readers, and
Reviewers,* and Cathy N. Davidson, in *Revolution and the Word,* who
seek to rehistoricize the reading experience itself by examining the re-
corded responses of the actual readers of any text or the history of the
use of particular books, and align this kind of criticism with the new
emphasis that Frank Kermode in *The Classic* and Stanley Fish in *Is
There a Text in This Class?* have placed on the roles, respectively, of
interpretive institutions and interpretive communities. Such a map
would reveal that much of the interdisciplinary criticism in recent
years focusing on the experience of the reader has been propelled by a
grammar of ideological motives that are feminist, ethnic, or class-
oriented, but it would also disclose that some of this criticism—Norman Holland's *The Dynamics of Literary Response,* Barthes's *The Pleasures of the Text,* Gilles Deleuze's and Felix Guatarri's *Anti-Oedipus,* Julia Kristeva's *Powers of Horror,* Peter Brooks's *Reading for the Plot,* Mary
Jacobus's *Reading Women,* and Robert Scholes's *Textual Power*—has reflected interests that were psychoanalytic, structuralist, feminist, deconstructionist, semiotic, or a combination of all five.

On the other hand, were one to redraw the map of contemporary
interdisciplinary studies in relation to the critical coordinate of the text

itself, one could similarly highlight, as well as link, a variety of still other kinds of modern interdisciplinary studies. One point of departure for such a cartographic exercise might be the extraordinary interdisciplinary developments that followed upon the emergence of modern linguistics, a field that grew out of the convergence of work by Russian formalists, like Victor Shklovsky and Yuri Tynyanov, and Czech linguists associated with Jan Mukarovsky and the Prague School, with, again, the language theory of Saussure and the semiotics theory of Charles Saunders Peirce, all of which conspired to produce methods that applied linguistic insights to the study of all aspects of culture conceived as a system of signs. A key figure in these developments was Roman Jakobson who, in immigrating first from Moscow to Prague and then from Prague to the United States, helped bridge the gap between linguistics and semiotics and was thus in a position to lend encouragement to a great variety of interdisciplinary activity as widely differentiated as the stylistics criticism of Michael Riffaterre, the poetics analysis of Juri Lotman, and the narratological studies of scholars like A. J. Greimas, Tzvetan Todorov, Gérard Genette, Claude Brémond, and, now, Paul Ricoeur.

But the emergent field of linguistics also played an important role in promoting interdisciplinary work in fields quite distant from the study of the structure and properties of language. In one direction, it influenced the structuralist orientation that Claude Lévi-Strauss, and later Clifford Leech, brought to ethnographic studies and the development of modern social anthropology in general. In another, it helped shape formalistic and generic interests that run from the conservative, archetypal criticism represented by Northrop Frye's *Anatomy of Criticism* to the radical dialogical criticism associated with Mikhail Bakhtin's *Rabelais and His World* and *Problems of Dostoevsky's Poetics*.

Yet the field of linguistics and its many affiliations (indeed, far more than can be enumerated here) is only one of the interdisciplinary modes of study promoted by (even as it promoted) the study of the literary coordinate known as the text. To draw out the lines of interdisciplinary relationship that in modern literary study emanate from the textual coordinate, one would have to take into account everything from the modern development of hermeneutics (or interpretation theory), starting with the work of Wilhelm Dilthey and Martin Heidegger, and continuing through that of Hans-Georg Gadamer and Paul Ricoeur, to the new criticism of what Fredric Jameson calls "the political unconscious," with its roots in the work of Walter Benjamin and other members of the Frankfurt School (Theodor Adorno and Max Horkheimer), as well as the writings of Antonio Gramsci, and its expression in the writings of critics as various as Lucien Goldmann, Louis Althusser, Raymond Williams, Pierre Macherey, and Robert Weimann.

Still another way to map the varieties of contemporary interdisciplinary study would be to start with some of the new subjects it has helped make available for critical analysis—the history of the book, the materiality of body, the psychoanalysis of the reader and the reading process, the sociology of conventions, the semiotics of signification, the historicization of representation, the ideology of gender, race, and class, intertextuality, power, otherness, and undecidability— but it would be necessary to add that each of these topics, as presently, though variously, construed in contemporary studies, has also served both to attract and to project still further lines of interdisciplinary investigation. Studies of the body like Elaine Scarry's *The Body in Pain,* for example, have rewoven psychoanalytic, cultural, materialistic, neo-Marxist, and new-historicist strands of disciplinary interrogation; studies of representation such as Stephen Greenblatt's *Shakespearean Negotiations* have typically drawn into new combinations historicist, reader-response, cultural-materialist, hermeneutic, semiotic, and often deconstructionist inter- and cross-disciplinary modes. But in much of the newer interdisciplinary scholarship, studies of the body become studies of representation, and so the threading of disciplinary principles and procedures is frequently doubled, tripled, and quadrupled, and in ways that are not only mixed but also, from a conventional disciplinary perspective, often somewhat off center.

So described, the overlapping, underlayered, interlaced, cross-hatched affiliations, coalitions, and alliances toward which these cartographic operations lead can become truly baffling. Furthermore, insofar as they imply that disciplinary traditions of descent or influence always flow in one direction or in channels that are continously visible and hence continously traceable, such mapmaking exercises can also become deeply misleading, since the inevitable result of much interdisciplinary study, if not its ostensible purpose, is to dispute and disorder conventional understandings of the relationships between such things as origin/terminus, center/periphery, focal/marginal, inside/outside.

These observations raise an obvious question about whether the simplest, or at least the most coherent, way of conceptualizing the kinds of interdisciplinary studies that have emerged out of relational or interrelational studies might not be to focus directly on the associations that literature, or rather literary study, has developed with some of the other recognized, institutionalized fields of academic inquiry.

On this basis one could simply describe the different interdisciplinary endeavors that have grown out of the modern study of, say, literature and philosophy (phenomenological criticism, hermeneutics, deconstruction, neopragmatism, ethical criticism, the new rhetorical criticism), literature and anthropology (structuralism, ethnography or "thick description," folklore and folklife studies, myth criticism), literature and psychology (psychoanalytic criticism, reader-response criticism, anxiety-of-influence criticism, cultural psychology), literature and politics (sociological criticism, cultural studies, ideological criticism, materialist studies), literature and religion (theological apologetics, recuperative hermeneutics, generic and historical criticism, rhetorical studies), and literature and linguistics (Russian formalism, stylistics, narratology, semiotics).

However, what has to be borne in mind is that these correlate fields (anthropology, philosophy, religious studies, psychology, etc.) have themselves changed—and sometimes dramatically—during the last quarter-century, and one among a variety of factors generating that instability and revisionary ferment has been the success of the particular interdisciplinary initiatives they have either stimulated or helped sustain. It is also worth noting that less than half of the academic fields with which literature has historically enjoyed or established important ties are even mentioned here, and among those omitted, several, like law and science, are tethered to literature's earliest beginnings, and at least one, namely, film studies, is intimately connected to literature's future fortunes.[14]

*

But if relational and interrelational studies have precipitated and promoted the creation of certain kinds of interdisciplinary studies, they have clearly discouraged the development of certain others. Consider, for example, the case of the relations between literature and music. Study of the interrelations between literature and music goes back to the prehistory of literature itself, when verbal forms were still sedimented in sound and song. This interest has been expressed in a variety of ways over the ages, from the study of such musical elements of verbal form as rhythm, rhyme, alliteration, tone, voice, variation, balance, repetition, contrast, and counterpoint to the vast and complex historical relations between particular musical kinds, like the rondeau or the symphony, and the verse forms of Alfred de Musset and Algernon Swinburne or Thomas Mann's *Doctor Faustus* and Hermann Broch's *The Sleepwalkers*. The musicality of literature and the literariness of music are synonymous with works like Giuseppe Verdi's *Mac-*

beth and *Otello,* Alban Berg's *Wozzeck,* Benjamin Britten's *Billy Budd,* Franz Liszt's Dante and Faust symphonies, Richard Strauss's *Don Juan,* Claude Debussy's *Prélude à l'après-midi d'un faune;* and writers such as Jean-Jacques Rousseau, Denis Diderot, Novalis, Heine, E.T.A. Hoffmann, Giuseppe Mazzini, Nietzsche, André Gide, Bertolt Brecht, Aldous Huxley, James Joyce, and T. S. Eliot have all sought to translate musical technique into literary practice. Yet despite the eloquent arguments of critics like George Steiner that the quintessential form of art in literature is its music, or the testimony of distinguished musicologists like Leonard B. Meyers that music can never rid itself completely of the element of story, the venerable association of music with literature and literature with music, so intelligently interpreted in texts like Calvin S. Brown's *Music and Literature* and John Hollander's *The Untuning of the Sky,* has rarely led to the institutionalized development within literary studies of interdisciplinary approaches to the study of either the musicality of literary forms and meanings or the literary dimensions of music. The case within musical studies itself, however, is very different, as the interdisciplinary fields of opera studies, ethnomusicology, and even the aesthetics of music amply attest.

Similarly, despite countless distinguished examples, the long record of informed study of the interrelations between the visual and the verbal arts has only rarely resulted in the creation of interdisciplinary, as opposed to cross- or transdisciplinary, modes of study where, instead of merely bridging them, disciplinary boundaries are actually redrawn. While there have been numerous disciplinary exchanges between the literary and the plastic arts, there has been surprisingly little reconception of each in the image of the other. This is the more to be marveled at both because of the existence of various academic programs of study organized in behalf of the examination of this relationship, and also because of the brilliant interdisciplinary research in which it has issued in the work of people like Rudolph Arnheim, E. H. Gombrich, Erwin Panofsky, Meyer Schapiro, Richard Wollheim, Ronald Paulson, Arthur Danto, Barbara Novak, and Michael Fried. There are countless literary texts that treat works of visual art or the things they delineate, that employ visual techniques, that are linked to historical movements and manifestos associated with the visual arts, that call upon interpretive skills they have helped develop, or that otherwise inscribe visual modes of conception and assessment; but none of this has proved capable of overcoming either one of two kinds of resistance—the first to interpretation itself on the part of many art historians, the second to the intellectual power and percipience of the visual on the part of many literary scholars and critics. If art historians routinely eschew criticism for cataloguing, evaluation for description, literary historians and critics have typically treated all the fine arts as mere complements, adjuncts, illustrations of the verbal arts.

Striking evidence of this latter phenomenon can be found in Thomas Bender's *New York Intellect,* a study of the intellectual life of New York City from the middle of the eighteenth century to the middle of the twentieth. By the end of this period the culture of the city was recognized throughout the world for the eminence it had achieved in at least three of the fine arts—painting, dance, and music. By mid-century it had also assembled and nurtured an extraordinary group of critics known as the New York intellectuals who were associated with the *Partisan Review* and other magazines. Yet despite the cosmopolitanism of figures like Lionel Trilling, Philip Rahv, Alfred Kazin, Irving Howe, and Sidney Hook, virtually none of the New York intellectuals, with the occasional exception of Harold Rosenberg or Clement Greenberg, paid much attention at all to any of the artistic areas besides literature in which New York culture had achieved international recognition.

This is not to suggest, then, that there have been no interfield or transfield studies of literature and art or literature and music, much less to imply that these initiatives, when they have occurred, have failed to produce work of enormous and lasting value. Nor is it to claim that in the future they may not generate still more systematic and more institutionalized modes of interdisciplinary inquiry that reconstitute the materials and methods that currently compose them. It is merely to assert that a new confederation of practices, however salutary, is not a new configuration of methods, however experimental; and until a new configuration of methods produces a new refiguration of material, one does not have what can be called a genuinely interdisciplinary form of study. Interdisciplinarity involves a rethinking not just of conceptual frames, as Alan Liu has argued, but of their perceptual ground. What gets reconceived are not only the paradigms by which one discipline makes sense of itself to itself with the help of another but also the way such processes of reconception provide both disciplines with new ways of representing their own knowledge to themselves.[15]

★

Where did this new interest in interdisciplinarity come from? Was it the result of factors confined to the institutional culture of academic literary studies or the product of wider educational and social forces? Did it emerge all at once or in successive historical stages? What forms of resistance has the development of interdisciplinarity met? How is one to assess its benefits, and what sorts of problems is interdisciplinary study likely to confront in the future?

These are all difficult and important questions. They are also questions that are currently being vigorously contested. In addition to admitting of different and frequently conflicting answers, they are questions whose very form can be challenged as prejudicial. What they presume is that interdisciplinarity can be treated as a unified or coherent movement whose progress has typically been forward and uninterrupted, when its development seems more frequently to have described a course of successive, tentative, often uncoordinated, forays and retreats whose progress was more crabwise than linear. Another way to put this would be to say that just as intelligent theory always holds out the possibility of unintelligent practice, as Gilbert Ryle once observed, so it is equally possible that intelligent practice can sometimes be performed in the name of unintelligent, or at least unconscious or only half-conscious, theory. If this tells us anything, it should confirm the fact that forms of interdisciplinary study often emerge by accident. When not driven simply by the vagaries of fashion or the metaphysics of theory, they are most often occasioned by critical conundrums and simply offer themselves as workable solutions to practical problems. In other words, interdisciplinarity is the pragmatist's response to the dilemma of disciplinary essentialism.

Yet it must be noted that interdisciplinary study cannot flourish in an unfavorable environment. During the years following World War II, for example, when the pedagogy known in the United States as the New Criticism was in full sway, interdisciplinary literary studies were in a state of noticeable arrest and, where not arrested, were seriously eclipsed by other methodologies more formalistic and inward looking. But the ideology of interpretive refinement then epitomized by the New Criticism, or rather epitomized by its pedagogic practitioners in the schools—among its various proponents like John Crowe Ransom, Allen Tate, R. P. Blackmur, Kenneth Burke, Cleanth Brooks, and Robert Penn Warren, there were sharp and sometimes irreconcilable differences in poetics and procedure—had a much more deleterious effect (and still does) in England than in the United States. And even where similar prejudices were at work on the Continent, Europeans have always been more responsive to interdisciplinary initiatives than either the British or the Americans. Part of this is no doubt due to the looser departmental structure of the European university system, part as well to the role that philosophical discourse and ideas generally have traditionally played in European intellectual culture.

But generalizations like this are notoriously porous. The American university system in the twentieth century has been surprisingly hospitable to a variety of interdisciplinary curricular experiments without altering the way it organizes the structure of knowledge. As observed in the last chapter, this paradox has been explained by Gerald Graff as a result of the "field-coverage principle" by which departments of English retain their power and present organization by welcoming, as they are discovered and developed, all new fields and methods to the fold without permitting any one of them to challenge its own established hierarchies concerning the nature and teaching of literature.[16] The only problem with this explanation is that it may grant too much to the leftist view that identifies the modern American university with other institutions of the corporate state, and then postulates that its own expansion, like that of capitalism generally, derives from its ability to absorb the elements of conflict it produces. While there is no doubt that academic institutions exhibit something of the "repressive tolerance," as Herbert Marcuse called it, of late capitalism, it would be more accurate to say that the new movement toward interdisciplinary studies has actually resulted from many factors, both institutional and conceptual. If the "field-coverage principle" has proved influential in determining the way its intentions and achievements have been perceived and assimilated, the seismic theoretical shift that Roland Barthes first noticed from *work* to *text* has influenced the way interdisciplinary studies has, insofar as it can be said to possess an integrated vision at all, construed itself.

The discovery of the new world of textuality and intertextuality has served to question a number of interpretive shibboleths that controlled literary study for many decades. Among them are the following: that even where it is difficult to determine, all works of literature possess one and only one "definitive" meaning; that this meaning must be identical with the intentions of some transcendent Author; that to be understood properly, works must be read in independence of their relations, whether anxious or imperialistic, with other works; that it is appropriate to view reading as a process of reception and assimilation but never as a process of production and intervention; and that even when reading, interpretation, and criticism are seen as creative and not merely reflective activities, their operations must still be restricted to individual works and cannot be expanded to apply "literary" modes of analysis to the entire spectrum of cultural phenomena.[17]

Not surprisingly, recent exploration of the new world of the text has raised a whole series of fresh and troubling questions about the relations not only between one text and another but also between any text and its putative "context." If it has become increasingly difficult in a conceptual universe seamless enough to warrant description, in Julia Kristeva's phrase, as intertextual to determine just where one text leaves off and another begins, it is also difficult to know just what is a text and what isn't or can't be described as one. If all contexts are merely texts by another name, how useful or reliable is the practice of "contextualization," which would then seem merely to involve the interpretation of one interpretation by another equally unstable? Who or what legitimates or validates such interpretations of interpretation? Does this make culture anything other than an interlinked system of such legitimations and validations? How, in the face of such definitions, do cultures, and the contexts they represent, change? What forms or forces serve to curb, resist, or thwart such change? Is it possible to measure such things as change and resistance from within the context defined by any culture?

Questions such as these have not found ready, much less universally accepted, answers in contemporary criticism, but they have generated an enormously impressive amount of productive activity in search of them. One of the issues they have raised is whether the concept of culture itself has not possibly outlived its usefulness. As the anthropologist James Clifford has proposed, cultures are not only unstable, selective, contingent, strategic, and incompletely integrated; in actual historical experience, they also tend to function less as enduring forms than as, in Wallace Stevens' phrase, "Supreme Fictions," ways of creating collective identity in the face of forces that threaten it.[18]

New suspicions about the utility of the notion of culture have in turn precipitated fresh skepticism about the idea of the "West." This skepticism has naturally been aroused by the discoveries of social and cultural anthropologists, but it has also been generated by the results of postcolonial criticism (in the work of, to name only a few, Octavio Paz, Gayatri Spivak, Homi Bhaba, Edward Said, Stuart Hall, and Carlos Fuentes) and the new interest now beginning to be displayed by departments of English and comparative literature in writers from Central and South America, the Carribean world, Africa, Asia, the Middle East, the Indian subcontinent, and Eastern Europe. Causing further erosion of the boundaries between cultures and contexts, these new interdisciplinary undertakings have revealed how, when used comparatively, the idea of the "West" has been employed repeatedly to the disadvantage of its discursive opposites (the "Orient," the "Third World," "newly liberated peoples"), and how, when used normatively, as a broadly monocentric cultural entity, it has served to cloak many of the tensions, distortions, and injustices that have been performed in its name.

Taken together, these several factors have created a more pluralistic and, in some ways, more adversarial, or at least more disputatious, climate in criticism as a whole, a climate that has opened the way for what Paul Ricoeur once called "the conflict of interpretations." Aside from the fact that some observers, particularly on the right, now view such conflict as mere cacophony, what really has changed is not an increase in the level of discord so much as a growing realization that dialogue, contestation, diversity of opinion may be all that interpretation can ever attain. But if the achievement of interpretive consensus, or agreement, or uniformity has now come to be recognized as quite possibly an illusory ideal, then one can begin to appreciate how really crucial interdisciplinary studies is to that "refinement of debate," as Clifford Geertz's has called it, that may be achieved in its place.[19]

Interdisciplinarity will remain integral to this deepening of the discussion in the human sciences only so long as it remains determinedly suspicious of its own grounds, only insofar as it refuses to hypostasize or totalize its own methodological fascination with discrepancies, divergences, disjunctions, and differences. The threat of hypostasization or totalization in interdisciplinary studies comes from one of two temptations. The first is disciplinary reductionism, or the temptation to think that the methods of one field are sufficient to interpret the materials of many. The second is the appetite for metaphorical transfer, or the temptation to treat the material of one field as mere epiphenomena of the subjects of another. Needless to say, the future of interdisciplinary studies depends on avoiding such temptations. But it is also dependent on a number of other more institutional and material factors, such as the continued encouragement of administrators to devise new curricular experiments, the continued impatience of faculty and students with the present arrangements of knowledge, and the continued availability of financial resources to support the development of everything from new graduate programs, centers for study, summer institutes, and interdepartmental colloquia, to visiting and permanent professorships, outlets for publication, and scholarship aid.

Chief among these more empirical elements that will determine the future of interdisciplinarity is the ongoing controversy within the humanities (and beyond) about whether universities are to be defined principally, to employ Jonathan Culler's helpful distinction, as institutions devoted to the reproduction and transmission of culture or rather as institutions devoted to the critique and re-creation of culture.[20] While this is not a distinction anyone would have thought of making twenty or thirty years ago in American higher education, it is a distinction that presently shapes much of the debate about the reorganization of knowledge and the politics of the academy. Within the humanities itself, this debate centers on the nature and effect of cultural representations, and within interdisciplinary studies (if not also outside), it is divided rather sharply—to put it in terms somewhat different from those of Stanley Fish that were invoked earlier—between those who see the study of cultural representations as a political struggle over the sources and symptomatics of power and those who view the study of cultural representations instead as a hermeneutic struggle over the hierarchies and heuristics of value. In studying cultural texts, what are we trying to do: determine how and by whom the world should be governed, or which values should organize our experience of it?

While these questions are by no means unrelated, neither are they exactly the same. The long-term challenge for interdisciplinary studies is to remain undaunted by the tension between them without being seduced into thinking that this tension can be easily reduced or overcome. What is most productive intellectually in the current practice of interdisciplinarity is neither the utopian hope some radicals entertain that this tension can ultimately be erased nor the complacent belief which Fish maintains that it finally doesn't matter; what has been most productive is the inescapable fact of the tension itself and the deepened, pragmatic appreciation to which this has given rise: of how knowledge is always amenable to further interpretation and criticism, of how understanding is always susceptible to further correction and realization. The task is not to open the mind or to close it but to make it more penetrating and more discriminating at the same time.

9

Who's Zoomin' Who? Academic Pluralism,
Critical Public Discourse, and
American Civil Religion

★

Take another look, n' tell me, Babe,
Who's zoomin' who?

Aretha Franklin

★

In an omnibus review of recent works of contemporary critical theory, Denis Donoghue has provided a fairly accurate estimate of what I would take to be the general intellectual verdict on the relation between two of the three operative terms in my title. In Donoghue's view, academic pluralism has not been good for critical public discourse. If academic pluralism has encouraged the development of rival schools of criticism, it has also ensured their interiorization and marginalization. To invite a hundred flowers to bloom is, in contemporary American criticism at least, to permit them to talk more and more only to themselves, almost never to each other, and not at all to the general literate public.

Thus, in American literary criticism, for example, which has been so nearly academicized since the 1930s, we have seen a succession of alternatives—sociological criticism in the Depression, then the New Criticism, Chicago neo-Aristotelianism, and the cultural criticism of the New York intellectuals in the 1940s and 1950s, archetypal and myth-and-symbol criticism along with existentialism and phenomenology in the late 1950s and 1960s, and then in the 1970s and 1980s hermeneutics, reader-response criticism, literary structuralism and semiotics, deconstruction, psychoanalytic criticism, feminist criticism, black aesthetics and African-American criticism, and a new leftist criticism (with varying branches that are cultural materialist, new historicist, and postcolonial)—but too few of these alternatives have

212

ever engaged in serious conversation with their competitors, let alone with the lay readership of serious literature in our culture.

What these academicized critical options have achieved instead, according to Donoghue, is the creation of critical guilds centered around the worship, or at any rate the memorialization, of some founding figure and often associated with particular universities such as Duke, Yale, or the University of California at Irvine, as Donoghue adds somewhat ungenerously, "avid for publicity."[1] Appropriate devotion takes the form of a kind of rabbinic writing where the founder's words, already thickened with commentary generating its own exegesis—Marx can only be discussed through the filters of Lukács and Benjamin, complicated by Gramsci, Althusser, and, now, Jameson; Freud comes by way of Klein, Kohut, and Winnicott, or through Lacan, Kristeva, and Cixous; Heidegger requires a detour through Gadamer and sometimes Ricoeur; Derrida makes his way to us through de Man, Irigaray, Miller, Hartman, and Barbara Johnson—supports a journal of its own in which the texts of the faithful are regularly published but only fellow believers will be quoted.

Donoghue takes the aim of this spectacle of what Edward Said calls "traveling theory" to be nothing short of colonization: to infiltrate areas once assumed to be posted, such as law, sociology, ethics, religion, or philosophy, and thus begin to consolidate an empire. At this point, literary criticism is converted into critical theory, and critical theory then becomes a social practice like any other concerned, in this case, with the production and dissemination of meaning. Its only difference from such related social practices as the writing of poems, let us say, or the analysis of political campaigns, or the creation of computer programs is that critical theory is more self-conscious of its own processes and thus more amenable to correction, or at any rate to self-scrutiny.

One could easily extend this bleak picture to other fields of critical discourse supposedly more accountable to the public realm. Consider, for example, "social theory today," as Anthony Giddens and Jonathan H. Turner describe it in the title of a highly intelligent book they have edited which, once one moves beyond the classic schools represented by Marx, Weber, Durkheim, Pareto, Tönnies, Simmel, and Parsons, can be broken down into the titles they give their chapters—"Behaviorism," "Symbolic Interactionism," "The New Social Action Theory," "Analytical Theorizing," "Structuralism and Poststructuralism," "Ethnomethodology," "Structuration Theory," "World-Systems Analysis," "Class Analysis," "Critical Theory from the Frankfurt School to the Present," and "Mathematical Modeling."[2] There are, it is true, social thinkers from Christopher Lasch and Daniel Bell to George Kateb, Joseph Raz, and Sheldon Wolin who cannot be fitted into any of these molds, but they constitute the exception that proves the rule. Within the discursive practices of specific academic disciplines, as well as between them, there is a distressing hermeticism that seems, like so much of the wrong kind of scholarship, to pander to its own protocols, to serve only its own conventions rather than seeking communication with a broader world.

In this intellectual climate, much of the blame for what makes critical discourse private rather than public can be laid, and thus has been laid, at the door of academic pluralism. When the American university system responded to the political radicalism of the 1960s, so the argument proceeds, by opening up the educational curriculum, it created a new methodological and theoretical permissiveness that in the ensuing years has tended to confirm the indictment of conservatives and traditionalists that virtually anything goes in critical discourse and that nothing ultimately much matters. Thus one now hears prestigious critics claiming that there is fundamentally no difference between the invasive or transgressive nature of interpretation and any other act of political violence—as if reading a poem and, say, child abuse or terrorism were the same thing! The only parallel between the verbal situation these critics describe and the sociopolitical ones they invoke is to be found in the violence of the metaphorical exchange they practice, an exchange that permits them not simply to confuse realms of significance but also to debase the linguistic currency with which we discriminate, all the time and necessarily, among such realms on the basis of our assessment of their effects, whether potential or real.

*

But this picture can be overdrawn. It is just as easy—or at least almost as easy—to argue that the proliferation of critical languages within the academy has served to democraticize critical discourse rather than to privilege or privatize it. Not, of course, that the new critical practices, and their attendant modes of expression, have couched their appeals in the terms of general public discourse—as if what makes discourse public are the terms in which it is couched—but only, it could be argued, that the creation of such different, divisive, and sometimes alienating procedures as Derridean decentering or Foucauldian dehumanizing has proceeded from an interest in protecting what is specific, singular, divergent, or simply "other" from being effaced by more traditional, even more publicly approved, critical practices that have a political stake in discounting such things. Could it not be maintained, in fact, that if contemporary academic criticism has one single overriding concern, it is to defend the multitude of meanings, by no means all of them compatible, associated with the term "difference," and to defend them, finally, in the name of what is supposedly asserted by critics of whatever stripe—feminist, psychoanalytic, ethnic, Marxist, historicist, pragmatist—as a wider, or at least a more densely and particularly realized, sense of life?

Indeed, the possibility is worth entertaining that the real dispute among the defenders and apologists of the new critical practices and languages vouchsafed to us by academic pluralism may well be something quite different from the privileges of perspective or the self-mirroring characters that often we—and rather incredibly even they—associate with their own individual authority. The real dispute among them may well amount to a controversy of the broadest public import over just what constitutes "difference," politically, socially, sexually, racially, psychologically, religiously; which differences are commensurable with which; and how to understand and adjudicate their conflicting claims where these claims prove incommensurable.

By this I mean that the issue lying at the center of the arguments that divide the various critical schools and languages in America today could well turn on the nature and significance of otherness, a notion that is by definition social and thus public rather than private or personal, and, moreover, a notion whose problematic character is given, so to speak, with the idea of America itself. Even if the word could only function within a grammar of desire all too recognizably familiar, "America" comes into being conceptually, as a term of discourse for Europeans, as a way of imagining what was putatively "other," unexampled, divergent, unimaginable. The questions these debates mask or evade, then, have to do with how to conceive or represent "the Other" without succumbing to the false artificiality of oppositional thinking; with why the possibility of otherness has become so difficult to think, much less to accommodate institutionally, in a world as purportedly pluralistic or diverse as our own; with what to do when otherness becomes so radical, so detached, so estranged as to prevent interpretation or translation; and with how to complicate our curiosity about these conundrums in a way that acknowledges the potential for self-projection, for intellectual reflexivity, that is built into our attempt to theorize them.

This is not to say that the "interpretation of otherness" has not played a central role in critical discourse in the past.[3] It is only to argue that one might differentiate the public meanings, or at least the public implications, that critical discourse can achieve at the present moment, from whatever public meanings critical discourse may have possessed in the past, in terms of the seriousness with which contemporary criticism, both within the academy and outside (insofar as there is any real "outside"), is willing to take the question of otherness itself, and, furthermore, in relation to how much of its own authority critical discourse is willing to put at risk for the sake of formulating an adequate conception of and response to "the Other." But one could state this more simply. What apparently differentiates contemporary critical discourse from its modern precursors is the way it has reconceptualized the problem of the public *as* the problem of "the Other." On this reading, academic pluralism has thereby merely succeeded in turning contemporary criticism in a more public direction, thus paradoxically rendering it more democratic by, as it were, turning it in upon itself, or, rather, by turning contemporary criticism in upon the renovation of its own discourse for the sake of making that discourse more transparent if not answerable to alterity.

★

However, neither of these readings of the relations between academic pluralism and critical public discourse takes sufficient account of what is problematic about the terms themselves. If, for example, academic pluralism has generated a critical situation where everything is permitted discursively because nothing finally matters politically, then the whole notion of pluralism itself becomes academic indeed. Pluralism then simply becomes the description of an academic situation where what is construed as "difference" is encouraged precisely so that in the face of so much variety no one has to take any account of it. Pluralism so called then becomes simply another technique for tolerating or suppressing difference rather than for acknowledging and interacting with it.

By public discourse, then, I mean discourse whose terms are not simply conversable with one another but are developed for the sake of producing further conversation and deepened understanding, of leading to enhanced conversation. But it could easily be argued that the term "public" is in fact even more problematic than the phrase "academic pluralism." One person's "public" may be another person's "elite," and even when the term "public" can overcome the onus of privilege and exclusion it sometimes acquires, it nevertheless always implies selectivity. "Public" always refers to something that is both multiple and polyphonic; its monolithic nature is a myth and, like other mythic ideas, is highly susceptible to manipulation. Think only of Lionel Trilling's famous gesture toward a public world through the reference his criticism constantly made to a generalized "we," which merely turned out to be a code word for what he otherwise referred to, and meant to flatter, as "our educated classes." [4]

Christopher Lasch has placed yet greater critical pressure on this notion by arguing that Americans in fact no longer even believe in a world that is "public." Instead, as Lasch observed in an essay devoted to the historical prescience of George Orwell's *1984,* we now live in "a curiously insubstantial world, a world of images and abstractions in which organized expertise has replaced practical experience and images of things have become more vivid than things themselves." Many people attribute this situation to the way social roles have now become more complex and contrived, thus leading to a greater diffusion of personal identity and a more uncertain sense of self. When selves no longer occupy fixed social stations, belief in a public world that is "reassuring in its solidity" and "which outlasts an individual life and passes some sort of judgement on it" becomes almost impossible. Hence it is scarcely surprising that the creation and development of a sustained sense of personal identity gives way to what Lasch calls "the deliberate management of impressions," to what Irving Goffman referred to in the title of his well-known book as "the presentation of self in everyday life." [5] Whereupon social conversation becomes the exhibitionist controversy of the TV talk shows, in which different perspectives, no matter how banal, are entertained and exploited not for the sake of reminding us that there are private voices that deserve to be heard in public, but only to keep us, their audience, constantly diverted and disengaged.

But Lasch warns that this way of putting it may place the cart before the horse. Though it is tempting, he admits, to deduce from this that the problem with personal identity in America derives chiefly from the fact that society has become more fluid and theatrical, Lasch believes that the real source of trouble lies elsewhere. The real problem, as he sees it, is not that selves now inhabit universes of meaning that are primarily metaphoric and perform activities that are mainly symbolic but that people "no longer inhabit a world that exists independently of themselves and that survives their own passing." [6] The true critical task, Lasch asserts, has become an oddly conservative one: to resist the erosion of those foundations, at once cultural, psychological, and ethical, that stabilize the self in reality so that we can once again confirm

its sense of belonging to a world beyond and outside its own consciousness to which the self, in the measure of its own freedom, is
responsible.

But this immediately raises a question of some import ontologi-
cally. What if our sense of a world distinct from the self, a world that,
so to speak, stands over against the self and passes judgment on the
self, is itself symbolic, or at any rate composed of symbols, and symbols that are not only enormously unstable and protean but also unusually self-reflexive and potentially solipsistic? Such at least is the testimony of a host of American artists and intellectuals from Ralph
Waldo Emerson, Margaret Fuller, and Herman Melville to W.E.B.
DuBois, James Baldwin, Flannery O'Connor, and Elizabeth Hardwick. In *The Crying of Lot 49,* Thomas Pynchon's Oedipa Maas succumbs to a temptation familiar to them all when, looking down from
a neighboring hillside on the configured patterns of suburban sprawl
that comprise the town of San Narciso, she confuses the patterns of
tract housing on which she gazes with the image of the first printed
circuit she had ever seen in the back of a transistor radio, and then
proceeds to discern in those "outward patterns a hieroglyphic sense of
concealed meaning, an intent to communicate." [7] Oedipa's is the temptation to inscribe herself in the spectacle she contemplates and then to
compound matters by imagining that the spectacle, or object of perception, reciprocates. Just as Emerson's speaker in *Nature* risks confusing the Spirit he believes to be incarnate in the world beyond the self
with the energy that suffuses his own soul, so Oedipa is in danger of
discerning in the patterns of meaning that surround and nearly suffo-
cate her a set of symbolic weavings which she herself has made and
which only secure more completely her imprisonment in the tower of
her own egotism.

But neither Emerson nor Oedipa reveals the worst effects of these
epistemological symbolics and the cultural narcissism that attends
them. For that one must repair to the figure of someone like Captain
Ahab in *Moby-Dick,* or Thomas Sutpen in *Absalom, Absalom,* or Simon
Legree in *Uncle Tom's Cabin,* all representatives of the kind of malevo-
lent blindness that befalls anyone who is prepared to make over the
whole of the public as well as the personal world into an image of
compensation for his or her own outraged or injured sense of identity.
Sutpen, Legree, and Ahab, we like to think, are exceptions, mutations, monstrosities, but it can scarcely be said that they are unfamiliar
ones. Indeed, in their willingness to sacrifice whole worlds—whole
publicly constituted, physically exigent worlds—to vindicate the
claims of their own aggrieved sense of self, they merely carry to an

extreme what the political scientist Michael Paul Rogin claims to have been the interpretive practices of the last incumbent in the White House.

★

As Rogin demonstrates in *Ronald Reagan the Movie,* leadership of the American government was for eight years in the hands of a person who not only reduced life in all of its concrete, complex, conflicting particularities to a set of symbolic forms (what Anthony Lewis coined as "an anecdotal view of the world") but also converted those forms into symbolic projections—and, in his case most especially, simplistic, self-serving, narcissistic projections—of an oddly vacant, curiously embittered, clearly adolescent self. Reagan always "had the best lines," as the *New York Times* once quipped, because all of his responses to domestic and foreign crises were lifted from his old films.

Thus the symbolic subsumption of public meanings—indeed, the symbolic swallowing of the public world—is far from remaining a matter of pure conjecture in America. And it is worth remarking that eight years of this behavior by the president of the United States, behavior in which, to speak plainly, the American public and most of its more visible organs of expression—the media, the educational system, and the churches and synagogues—were complicit, has done little to curb American appetites for symbolic self-flattery and self-delusion. If anything, the transformation of the Oval Office into a screening room for the rerun of B movies has only further undermined public confidence in the existence of a public world by demonstrating once again that in America what Quentin Anderson once termed "the imperial self" can dispose and redispose the constituents of the real about as effortlessly as a woman rearranges her skirt.[8]

Jean Baudrillard's term for the process I have been describing is "simulation," and in the Reagan years simulation became established as one of the chief modes of governance. Simulation describes a cultural world in which, as Mark Poster has noted, objects and discourses have no origin, no ground or foundation, no real reference but themselves.[9] It is a world that could only have been produced because of the technological breakthroughs of late corporate capitalism, where the media come to dominate the forms of production, where controlling the flow of information becomes the key to power, and where symbols, or "symbolic capital," become the chief commodity of consumption.[10] But these symbols, or, better, simulacra, having no other referent but themselves, completely dissolve the relationship between

appearance and reality, presence and absence, imaginary and real. Public policy, like private obsession, can then be driven, as in the case of
the defense system known as "Star Wars," by personal fantasy, and
reality, or the world purportedly beyond consciousness and presumably defined over against it, can be reduced to a series of images of
nostalgic longing for what never was.

Milan Kundera calls this process by another name. He calls it *kitch*,
in this case political kitch, which in any case is something quite different from poor taste and its aesthetic equivalent, junk art. As Kundera
points out, there is a "kitch attitude," "kitch behavior," even "the
kitchman's need for kitch," which he defines as "the need to gaze into
the mirror of the beautifying lie and to be moved by tears of gratitude
at one's own reflection."[11]

By whatever name we call it—*simulation, kitch, cliché*—it becomes
apparent that the chief threat to critical discourse may not lie, as Lasch
thinks, in our lack of belief in a public world many of whose meanings are shared in common, but rather in the fact that there are now
almost no worlds we can inhabit at all whose meanings are not only
shared by everyone else but also shared in a manner that thwarts the
possibilities of communication, or at least trivializes rather than en-
riches them. The space reserved by symbols for a world or worlds
we might call "public" is a space that, if not empty altogether, has
been emptied of the content of difference, has been rendered trivial and
vapid.

In so humanly desiccated a space, it could be argued, criticism is
compelled to relinquish all its public pretensions to keep open the
channels of communication among peoples and positions and content
itself merely with learning how, like Oedipa Maas, to wait—"if not
for another set of possibilities to replace those that had conditioned the
land to accept any San Narciso among its most tender flesh without a
reflex or a cry, then at least, at the very least, to wait for the symmetry
of choices to break down, to go askew," wondering all the while "how
it had ever happened here, with the chances once so good for diversity?"[12]

Oedipa doesn't get an answer to this question. All she can do is hope
that she has somehow, inadvertently,

stumbled onto a secret richness and concealed density of dream; onto a network by which X number of Americans are truly communicating whilst reserving their lies, recitations of routine, arid betrayals of spiritual poverty, for
the official government . . . system; maybe even onto a real alternative to the
existlessness, to the absence of surprise to life, that harrows the head of every-
body American you know, and you too, sweetie.[13]

But the danger is that Oedipa is merely hallucinating this other public in America, or that someone has mounted a plot to make her think so, or that she is simply hallucinating such a plot. In other words, Oedipa, like the rest of us, is caught in a circular maze of symbols, of signs, of simulations, and the harder she tries to escape it, the more desperately she becomes entangled inside it.

The question to be asked—and it is being asked in many of the disciplines of criticism (social, political, literary, and cultural) as well as in the departments of art—is whether there is any way to overcome the circularity of this epistemological predicament, where the harder one tries to break out of the spiral of increasingly vacuous and self-flattering symbolic simulation in America, and in the world generally, in the direction of some more concrete, independent arena of public experience standing over against it, the more one discovers that the only world or worlds that can be called public are composed of symbols as well, and very often symbols of a kind that no one but those who manufacture and manipulate them like. If there is any public world beyond our symbols, a world about which we can possess shared beliefs, a world in response to which we can develop a common language, that world is not likely to be revealed in answer to the Laschian question about whether the realm of the public and the political can once again achieve, or reachieve, dominion over the realm of the symbolic and the insubstantial. It will only be disclosed in response to the problem of how to make the symbolisms of public life and civic responsibility once again determinative (insofar as they ever actually were) of our social constructions and spiritual aspirations. This issue is not about whether public worlds should have priority over symbolic preferences so much as about how to reintegrate and reincorporate the meaning of such terms as "public," "civic," and "responsibility" in our symbolic restructuration. Hence to reenvision America critically is not at all to remove this process from the realm of symbols but to reconceive the nature of the symbolic realm itself and of the potentially critical as well as expressive, not to say ethical, processes that go on inside it.

★

One might plausibly argue that the most serious attempt to reincorporate the symbolism of public life and civic responsibility into the processes of cultural restructuration in the United States has been underway throughout most of the postwar period and is to be associated with the widely reported discussion concerning the existence and profile of what has come to be called an American civil religion.

Conceived as a spiritual alternative to America's various inherited or-
thodoxies, American civil religion, or at least the debates about its nature and meaning, has a long history that goes back to the controversies surrounding the establishment of the First Amendment to the
Constitution of the United States and the contradictory theological
traditions of Puritanism and Republicanism, of evangelical Calvinism
and the Enlightenment, that have continued to fuel them. The divisions between those traditions have created an ambiguous and continuing interpretive crisis in which the First Amendment seems simultaneously to guarantee protection against civil involvement in
religious affairs and to authorize the establishment of a strong religious
heritage for the United States. Thus to some, the "no establishment
clause" encourages a secularism incompatible with the religious pro-
pulsion evident in the entirety of American history. To others, the
"free exercise" clause promotes an implicit support of religion that
conflicts with the constitutional tradition of separation between
church and state. Still others view the First Amendment provisions as
the guarantee of a religious and social pluralism which they regard as
the social and religious hallmark of American democracy; while yet
still others recoil from the very idea of pluralism and support instead a
public theology that not only sees the Constitution grounded on religious beliefs but also views the function of First Amendment guarantees as a protection of the religious beliefs that underpin it.

As if these divergences of opinion were not enough, there is a serious difference between what most Americans say they believe about
the relation between church and state and how they act. Most Americans say they believe in the constitutional "wall of separation," as Jefferson termed it, between the civil and the ecclesiastical, but in actual
experience they keep confusing the two, and often purposely. Thus
while the courts, and occasionally the legislatures, are busy guarding
against civil preference for any religious group, the coins of the realm
are inscribed with the motto "In God We Trust," the Congress of the
United States makes use of the services of a chaplain, the president and
other officials regularly seek divine support for public policies, and the
Supreme Court has concluded, in what was a memorable if uncharac-
teristic opinion delivered by Justice William O. Douglas, that Americans are a religious people whose system of government presupposes a
Supreme Being.

These discrepancies between constitutional professions of belief and
actual social and political behavior are no accident. They are the result
of the wide latitude of interpretation to which the provisions of the
First Amendment have historically always been susceptible, and they

point to the fact that, for a variety of reasons, the place of religion in American life has proved resistant to legal adjudication. At the root of these controversies and confusions is the fact that religion in American society has enjoyed no single or simple definition, that American society has been of different minds at different times (and within different constituencies) as to the social importance of religion, and, finally, that the social importance of religion can be variously construed by the First Amendment.

Anyone interested in the relationship between the civil order in America and the moral responsibility that its citizens share for its maintenance and legitimation thus quickly finds him- or herself asking a widening set of questions: In a nation so committed to preserving the separation between the civil and the sacred, how does one account for the continuing reference to the United States as a Christian nation, much less for the perennial eagerness of American leaders to seek divine sanction for public policies? What is the role of religious symbols in American social and political life? How can the state remain neutral in religious matters when so many of its decisions impinge upon the interests of particular religious communities and traditions? Has the doctrine of state neutrality led paradoxically to the creation of a de facto religious establishment, or civil religion, in the United States? Is such a de facto civil-religious establishment in the United States compatible with the pluralism of American society and the diversity of American religious practices?

★

These are the kinds of questions that found themselves back in fresh circulation in the United States following the Allied victories in Europe and Asia, when the nation's new geopolitical prominence in the world revived interest in those spiritual traditions from its past which might help, if not to account for the spectacular increase in America's present fortunes in the world, at least to assist the ship of state in negotiating the hazardous waters of its new global responsibilities. The first person to explore such issues in the postwar period was the sociologist Will Herberg who, in a book published in 1955 entitled *Protestant Catholic Jew,* argued persuasively that the coherence of American society and the vigor of its people was due in no small measure to the existence of a common set of beliefs, widely shared by most of its citizens, both about and in "the American way of life." Insisting that these beliefs were religious to the core, Herberg nonetheless dissociated them from anything that could be construed as a simple distillation of the creeds of all American sects and other ecclesiastical formations. Belief in "the American way of life" was not be confused with some common denominator of religious affirmation in America because it was clear that a number of religious groups in the United States still resisted assimilation to "the American way," most notably churches of "ethnic immigrant background," religious bodies (whether orthodox, liberal, or neoorthodox) with strong theological coloration and what were once referred to as "the religions of the disinherited, such as pentecostal, millenarian, and holiness sects."[14] Indeed, this American public religion did not even encompass all the beliefs found in the more mainline or conventional religious bodies or faiths because, according to Herberg, it possessed a distinctive theological structure all its own that was influenced by, and at the same time also exerted strong influence upon, both Christianity and Judaism. At the heart of this religious Americanism, Herberg found an underlying commitment to the values of democracy which actually took a variety of different expressions. When these democratic values were translated into political terms, they resulted in allegiance to the Constitution; when translated into economic terms, they expressed themselves as adherence to the free-enterprise system; when translated into social terms, they amounted to an affirmation of equalitarianism; when translated into philosophical or theological terms, they issued in a preference for idealism.

Not surprisingly, the claim that America's public religion amounted to little more than a wholesale embrace of "the American way of life" in its entirety, or at least in the entirety of its postwar expressions, was quick to find its critics in those who perceived in such an assertion an unacceptable element of jingoism, of naked spread-eagleism. But it wasn't until 1963, and the publication of Sidney Mead's *The Lively Experiment,* that a real civil alternative to traditional Christianity—and, for that matter, to orthodox, conservative, and reform Judaism—was defined. Mead identified this alternative to traditional Christianity not with the democratic revolutions of the nineteenth century but with the movements of the Enlightenment in the Europe and America of the later seventeenth and early eighteenth centuries. Thoroughly monotheistic in character—Mead was fond of referring to it wittily as a monotheism of the First Person—this new public or civil religion, Mead argued, was premised on the existence of a creator God who had left evidence of his intentions in the orderly patterns of the book of Nature. While this book was by no means easy to read, God in his wisdom had not left human beings without hermeneutic resources. By endowing them with the capacity to reason, he had thereby provided human beings with the potential to discern his will. If no single individual was capable of fathoming the whole of that will, nonetheless every individual was in a position to discern some aspect of it if all individuals remained free to participate in a true social and political republic of opinions.

Mead believed with good reason that this set of beliefs described the religion of James Madison and Benjamin Franklin no less than that of Thomas Jefferson and most of the other Founding Fathers, but in *The Old Religion in the Brave New World* he added quite persuasively that this civil, public faith was eventually to precipitate a religious reaction in the Second Great Awakening from which American culture has never recovered. The results of this reactionary evangelical enthusiasm were ultimately to sever religious life in America from intellectual life—thus bequeathing to us the present situation where the former has become institutionalized in the denominations, the latter in the universities—and consequently to eviscerate the public realm. The two spiritual traditions that might have combined to contribute to the continual revisioning of American civil religion then withdrew from the public realm altogether, leaving the space of civic affairs to drift in a sea of expediency and self-justification.

Concerned explicitly about that sense of drift, Robert Bellah several years later sought to carry the discussion of American civil or public religion and its discursive responsibilities one step further. Agreeing with Mead that a religious alternative to historic Christianity and Judaism developed in the eighteenth century, Bellah nonetheless indicated, in his well-known 1967 article on "Civil Religion in America," that he shared with Herberg the view that this alternative religion is by no means confined to the intellectual period or set of ideas known as the Enlightenment and that it never conceived itself, however distinct its structure, as a substitute or replacement for more traditional faiths. According to Bellah, American civil religion simply set for itself a series of tasks somewhat different from those assumed by its more traditional counterparts, though these tasks or functions were equally differentiable from any associated with "the American way of life." On Bellah's reading, civil religion in America does not promote the worship of "the American way of life" or of any of its more representative institutions, such as the free-enterprise system or democratic equalitarianism. Instead, he maintains, the American civil religion—drawing freely on such Jewish and Christian themes as the myth of the chosen people, the New Jerusalem, and the errand into the wilderness, and applying them to America's own sacred occasions and holy places, such as the Fourth of July and the Gettysburg battlefield—seeks to resituate the nation's entire cultural experience, and not just some selected aspects of it, in a transcendent or ultimate perspective.

So conceived, American civil religion refers to a rather vague but nonetheless coherent set of beliefs and rites that exists alongside of, but remains distinct from, the traditional historical religions in America. Neither a sectarian offshoot of American Protestantism nor a sacralized version of American democracy, civil religion in America constitutes a system of national symbols and rituals that construe the American political experiment in representative government as a decisive event in what Old Testament theologians were once fond of calling "the mighty acts of God." Documents like the Declaration of Independence, the Constitution of the United States, Jefferson's Second Inaugural, Lincoln's Gettysburg Address, and other presidential statements serve as the sacred scriptures of this social and political religion, and George Washington, who is often doubled with everyone from Jefferson himself to Theodore Roosevelt, Woodrow Wilson, John Fitzgerald Kennedy, and Ronald Reagan, is often cast in the role of its American Moses leading his people out of the bondage of English tyranny (or the threat of any other kind of foreign domination, not merely of the country itself but subsequently of any of its dominions and markets or even of its so-called interests) and into the new world of American liberty and independence.

With its Tillichian echoes of "ultimate concern," Bellah's heavily Protestantized version of American public religion was to stimulate various revisions of its own, the most notable being John Murray Cuddihy's *No Offense: Civil Religion and Protestant Taste,* published in 1978. Cuddihy objected to the attempt to confer the authority of ultimacy on American civil religion by arguing that in fact such a sociopolitical construct was merely a religion of civility whose sole object is to accommodate religious differences. This becomes evident, Cuddihy maintains, only when we no longer ask with Herberg, Mead, and Bellah what the American civil religion presumably professes but inquire instead after the nature of its practices. What it practices, Cuddihy insists, is a code or etiquette of decorum that not only legitimates religious diversity but also choreographs, as it were, the rites of toleration. Founded on the rock of American cultural pluralism, the only heresies of this civil-religious tradition are sectarian divisiveness and religious exclusiveness, the only orthodoxy theological accommodation. According to the canons of this new civil piety, there is no other spiritual ideal but religious amiability, no other ethical norm but good taste, no other critical aim but meliorism.

But if this religion of civility is therefore more preoccupied with good manners than with adequate morals and metaphysics, Cuddihy is nonetheless convinced, in opposition to Bellah, that it has no intention to keep its place. From the perspective of the more traditional and unassimilated faiths that make up the spectrum of American religious life, the behavior of American public religion strikes Cuddihy as, on the contrary, positively indecorous and uncivil, since it is always invading the sacrosanct precincts of the more traditional faiths and rendering them religiously inoffensive, even innocuous.

By this point in the debate, the historian John Wilson had become convinced that the argument about the existence of a civil religious framework designed to legitimate the American public realm and legislate discursively what goes on there had become religiously questionable itself. Not only was the theological as well as the political bias of its various participants clearly in evidence; the entire discussion seemed to him to be occurring against a background of cultural and political crisis. More specifically, the intensity of the whole debate about the existence of a public religious consensus in America seemed paradoxically to reflect an underlying anxiety not only about the stability and cohesion of that consensus but also about the integrity of the wider sociopolitical order. Furthermore, it seemed to mask—though none too effectively—an interest in reviving that same discursive tradition of consensus for the sake of at once relegitimating the reality of the public sphere and remapping the ethical obligations it entails for all its citizens. To Wilson this made the whole civil religion debate, and the discursive practices it sponsored, begin to look like nothing so much as what the social anthropologist Anthony F. C. Wallace calls a "revitalization movement." [15]

Revitalization movements arise during periods of rapid and distressing social change, when one set of cultural meanings is in the process of being challenged and possibly supplanted by another. Their purpose is to save the endangered culture by repossessing those traditions and values within it that are felt to express its deepest significance. Viewed in this light, the various definitions of American civil or public religion look to Wilson like responses to the postwar erosion of faith in the American system of values and represent attempts to restore confidence in that system by reinterpreting its ultimate meanings against a background of broadly social and political symbols and events. American civil religion thus becomes a defense mechanism for shoring up American cultural consensus.

★

But where, in fact, did these social and political systems investing the public order with religious significance come from? What are the origins of the American tendency to valorize the public order by sacralizing it? For a full answer to this question, one would need to return to the age of sixteenth- and seventeenth-century discovery and exploration and trace the evolution of a process of sacralization that began long before the migration of European peoples to the Western hemisphere and has been continually nourished by groups and individuals—from native-American Indians and African slaves to East European, Latin American, and Far Eastern immigrants—who initially felt alienated from it, frequently excluded from it, and often repelled by it. Named only three centuries later by Walt Whitman, that process describes the quest for what he called a "New World metaphysics." [16] Whitman first coined the phrase in *Democratic Vistas* to designate the spiritual foundations on which he believed a new American literature—really a new American culture—must be based. However, the notion of a New World metaphysics need not be, and should not be, restricted to Whitman's fairly specific use of it to designate the superstructure of democratic thinking in America. It can and must be extended to refer to any spiritual vision inspired by reflection on the symbolic problem of how to construe the "idea of order" implied by the term "America" in a manner congruent with the ethical possibilities of living in the symbolic location it describes. Considered in this light, the quest for a New World metaphysics is—and always has been—a potentially religious undertaking, and one synonymous with, and socially and politically constitutive of, the symbolic meaning of America itself.

If Whitman was scarcely the first writer or thinker to associate the development of a distinctive society and culture in America with a distinctively symbolic and religious conception of America's meaning, neither was he the last. The correlation of the sacred symbol of America with the conception of a public realm organized in behalf of the moral responsibilities it defines for its citizens can be found throughout the whole range and extent of the American experience: in James G. Gatz's attempt to found a new religion of wonder and awe out of the meretricious symbols of American success in *The Great Gatsby* no less than in William Bradford's *Of Plymouth Plantation* written to display the record of God's direction and support in the building of the Plymouth colony; in Hart Crane's desire in *Brooklyn Bridge* "of the curveship [to] lend a myth to God" no less than in Chief Joseph's eloquent speech to Congress in 1879 protesting the harsh and deceitful treatment the Nez Percé suffered at the hands of the American government and pleading for the freedom of his people; in William Shakespeare's depiction of the New World in the colors of Arcadian enchantment no less than in the folksongs of African-Americans which describe a land of tribulations that can be met with joyous faith, a New World of sorrow that nonetheless evokes humor and courage.

Evidence of this same phenomenon can be found within the more orthodox precincts of seventeenth-century religion itself, when many of America's first European settlers used the Bible to define the meaning of their colonial enterprise. As has been observed elsewhere, the New England Puritans originally turned to the Bible to obtain scriptural warrant for their "errand into the wilderness," but it was only a comparatively short, though fateful, step from reading the Bible as an explanation of the unfolding pattern of events occurring in America to interpreting the unfolding symbolic pattern of events occurring in the New World as a fulfillment, whether potential or actual, of the divine promises made in Holy Writ. And once this "interpretive turn" was made, the process of American revisioning that had initially been merely proposed in the Bible, and in that sense "authorized" by it, threatened almost completely to absorb the Bible itself. Not only were the Old and New Testaments in danger of being reduced merely to a kind of National Testament and the biblical *Heilsgeschicte,* or history of salvation, transformed into the American salvation of history; America itself was threatened with metamorphosis from an empirical and social and political reality into an exclusively symbolic reality, and the symbol of America was rapidly hypostasized into a kind of revelatory template or New World scripture.[17]

To put this somewhat differently, where the Bible had initially been perceived as providing the rationale for the colonization of America, the colonization of America came in time to be regarded as a rationalization and realization of the scriptural template, became, in fact, the principal text to be read, the Bible itself. Either way, events, processes, perceptions that could as easily have yielded a sense of reality as public and "other" gave way under the impress of colonial revisioning to the belief that reality, and particularly the public reality that seems, in Lasch's formulation, "to stand over against us," is an affair of texts and tropes, of signs and significations, the only real issue being not whether they are true or false, or even objective as opposed to illusory, but rather whether they are sacred or merely profane.

But the historian Henry F. May has recently argued that we may not have to go so far back to find the roots of this American tendency to sacralize the secular and thus to legitimate spiritually the ethical obligations entailed in occupying American public space.[18] The ideological content of the revitalization movement known as American civil religion, he points out, comes directly out of the nineteenth-century heritage of American Christianity and can be summarized under the headings "Patriotic," "Progressive," and "Protestant." While these attributes can by no means be associated with all the sectarian and denominational traditions that made up the mosaic of American religion in the nineteenth century, May contends that they still gave religion in America whatever coherence and distinctiveness it possessed up to the end of that century and thus comprised the religious legacy that is still felt to be central and decisive in the civil religion discussion.

But this only suggests that the revisionary quest for an American civil religion creative of a discursive consensus that was public and critical at the same time may have been doomed from the start. Like Fitzgerald's Jay Gatsby, it was striving to awaken in the future an image of an America that was in some sense already lost to the past. Yet there is sufficient reason to believe that even if it were not lost to the past, the experiment in civil religious revisionism bent on making the symbolism of public life and its concomitant discourse once again constitutive of our social constructions was likely to fail for two other reasons: first, because, as has already been stated, the experiment was never without an apologetic, which is to say a self-reflexive if not self-serving, prejudice of its own; and, second, because, as an attempt to lend the authority of ultimacy to a public world over against the self, the quest for an American civil religion never succeeded in showing that Americans actually believe in a public world genuinely independent of the self, a world "reassuring in its solidity" that "outlasts an individual life and passes some sort of judgement on it."

★

If there exists any such world that stands over against the symbolic solipsism of the religion America has made of its own civic celebrations and renders a judgment on its self-absorption, that world—or at least a sense of it—does not exist wholly independent of what Kenneth Burke describes as "the troublous genius of symbolism" but has been evoked in pragmatic response to it.[19] That is, far from existing apart from the realm of symbols, a public world designed in part to pass judgment on the sentimentality of our civil religion and its ritual machinery has achieved a new social and even political palpability only as a kind of symbolic counter-force to it. The world to which I refer (though I do not mean to close off the possibility that there are others as well) is one that has drawn on the rich veins of vernacular suspicion and humor that thread so much of American oral and literary culture and have been created in reaction to the public world of official America to puncture its pomposities. The rhetoric of this "other" world is essentially comic and earthy and often scatological, and it specializes in deflating all attempts to sacralize the meaning of "America" and to valorize its practices ethically. It is a world mentally and emotionally inhabited by all those who have been oppressed by such usages, and it is typically characterized by a discourse or rhetoric that in theory if not always in expression is public, communal.

Thinking of authors as notably mainstream—but also as culturally alienated from what Peter Berger once referred to as "the noise of solemn assemblies," such as Emerson, Whitman, Melville, Mark Twain, and Hemingway—Leo Marx has argued, in an essay too little known in American religious as well as literary circles, that this rhetoric or discourse constitutes "the uncivil response of American writers to civil religion in America." Exhibiting an impatience with all the theological forms of cultural pretension, it is designed as a reminder that over against all the proud commodores and custodians of our pretended virtues, both national and individual, there is a collective world of the vulgate, the ordinary, of what, in the "The American Scholar," Emerson referred to as "the common," "the familiar," "the low," and "the vulgar," that is capable, at least discursively, of by turns comic or ironic transgressions against their supercilious solemnities. This more prosaic world is prepared to view all attempts to turn New World metaphysics into a legitimation of New World pieties and puerilities as, in the words of Marx's title, "Noble Shit." [20]

The phrase is actually Norman Mailer's, though it originally belonged to a skinny G.I. in World War II who, upon returning from a Filipino rice paddy one morning after relieving himself with a beatific smile on his face, taught Mailer by his own admission something of what there was to love about his country. It was not the obscenity of the young G.I.'s explanation of what he had just "taken" that so touched Mailer but the way that, as he puts it in *Armies of the Night,* "all the gifts of the American language came out in the happy play of obscenity upon concept, which enabled one to go back to concept again. What was magnificent about the word shit is that it enabled you to use the word noble." [21] Such linguistic flexibility, and the ability to use it fluently, testifies, so Mailer thinks, to "what editorial writers [are] fond of calling the democratic principle with its faith in the common man." But what Mailer discovered in the army, and what the editorial writers still rarely mention, is that "that noble common man was obscene as an old goat, and his obscenity was what saved him. The sanity of said common democratic man was in his humor, his humor was in his obscenity." [22]

For all of its crudeness, then, the exclamation of the American G.I.

in the rice paddy, like the platoon verdict that the overconscientious officer who has to be saluted with back stiffened and eyes erect is "chickenshit," is actually therapeutic and regenerative, according to Marx, recuperating for the word "noble" some of the dignity that has been evacuated from it through overuse and trivialization. But even more important to Mailer is the essentially egalitarian nature of such humor and its recuperative effects. Based on "a reductive philosophy which looked to restore the hard edge of proportion to the overblown values overhanging each small military existence," Mailer finds in such humor "a blow . . . struck for democracy and the sanity of good temper." [23]

Some readers may nevertheless feel that the gamy rhetoric of what here might be called the excremental sublime seems like an absurdly inadequate, not to say uncouth, defense against the discursive engines of official ideological bombast (or, as is more often the case, ideological ooze), and Marx is clearly aware, as Mailer is not, that such language is often found in the mouths of people who care hardly at all about democratic principles. But at the same time one should not underestimate either the critical shrewdness of such rhetoric or its historical resilience. Its genealogy goes back on the one side, one might call it the elevated or transcendental side, to the great passage in *Walden* about the melting railroad bank. This is Thoreau's image for the way Nature consummates itself, where the artistry at its heart, and the surest evidence of its transcendence of all the conventional oppositions of thought and feeling, of reason and propriety, of "Higher Laws" and "Brute Neighbors," is to be found in Nature's ability to mix the fecal with the felicitous, dung with divinity, thus creating a wilderness or New World where we "witness our own limits transgressed, and some life pasturing freely where we never wander." [24]

On the other side—the, so to speak, low or popular side—one can trace the roots of this rhetoric back to the kind of sentiment expressed by Timothy Root in a rarely remembered anecdote that Perry Miller included in his great biography of Jonathan Edwards. The story concerns the embarrassment suffered by Edwards himself when children presumed to be reading Scripture during the Great Awakening were found instead to be poring over a book written for midwives and known vernacularly as "The Granny Book." In the investigation that followed, it was solemnly determined that the names of the guilty should be published and their crime described for the community to remember. But one of their number was not intimidated by this threat of exposure. Indeed, far from being cowed by the prospect of public humiliation, Timothy Root actually defied it by standing up to the committee, and to Edwards, and to the whole Northampton social and ecclesiastical establishment, with the words: "They are nothing but men molded up of a little dirt; I don't care a turd, I don't give a fart for any of them." [25]

It is no coincidence that this anecdote closes an essay by Elizabeth Hardwick on recent American televangelism called "Church Going." On a superficial reading, Hardwick's essay belongs to what might be designated the genre of revenge criticism; she is out to give these video pastors their due. From the oily and imperturbable fatuity of Pat Robertson and the antic but inconsequential apocalypticism of Oral Roberts to the bullying, backwoods bluster and salacious longing of Jimmy Swaggart, she sees little in these ministers of the meretricious but a sleazy appeal to conscience and heaven that not only puts "no distance between themselves and the Holy Trinity" but also fails to hide what amounts to the sale of indulgences on a scale "that would shame a Borgia Pope," and she tells it like it is: "it's a fearful infiltration of the Godhead, an oozing into the sacred sources, blatant as an updated campaign of the Antichrist." [26]

Hardwick's loathing of the religious right is so splendidly arrayed in the rhetoric of righteous indignation that it very nearly manages to muffle the literary echo of her title. That echo is of a poem by the British poet Philip Larkin which, in addition to sharing the same title with Hardwick's piece, similarly treats contemporary religion, at least for the disbelieving intellectual, as a kind of tourist attraction. But even if one allows for differences between England and the United States, much has happened to organized religion in the thirty-odd years between the founding of "the Movement," as Larkin's group is called in England, and this latest episode in the history of American evangelicalism. Where Larkin found only a genial kind of death— "Once I am sure there's nothing going on," his poem reflectively begins, "I step inside letting the door thud shut"—Hardwick discovers a lurid new life, though a life not of faith so much as of what Henry James termed, in *The American Scene,* "the triumph of the superficial and the apotheosis of the raw." [27]

Larkin's gentle satire leads to nothing darker than the wistful admission that "this cross of ground" once "held unspilt/So long and equably what since is found/Only in separation—marriage, and birth,/ and death, and thoughts of these—," and before he finishes, his nostalgia, were it not accompanied by so much final irony, almost manages to turn this realization into something salubrious:

A serious house on serious earth it is,
In whose blent air all our compulsions meet,
Are recognized, and robed as destinies.
And that much never can be obsolete,
Since someone will forever be surprising
A hunger in himself to be more serious,
And gravitating with it to this ground,
Which, he once heard, was proper to grow wise in,
If only that so many dead lie round.

Hardwick's excoriation produces instead the prospect of a complete rout of the traditions of belief, the ritual supports, and the symbols of solace to which the practice of churchgoing once exposed the faithful. American televangelism replaces the sanctuary with Swaggart's Family Worship Center, which is no more than "a large theatre for audience" where "the high performer himself," surrounded by a choir of one hundred voices, shares center stage, microphone in hand, with occasional soloists and visiting clergy flanked by the Great Man's Family.

Protestant denuding of setting and symbol can go no further; there is no altar, no communion rail, no face of Jesus in a frame, no baptismal font, and, naturally enough, no Stations of the Cross, no Ark of the Covenant. These preachers do not perform marriages, visit the dead, and so no "dead lie round" in the parking lots. There is no symbol at all except the highlighted star, the beseeching main attraction.[28]

To Hardwick this is retrograde religion, or as Mark Twain put it in his indictment of the religion of nineteenth-century racist sentimentality, "soul-butter and hogwash." These media ministers betray no feeling for the noble sanities and difficult complexities of the Scriptures, no awareness of "the dense and painful, morally painful, studies and disputes of centuries past"; their focus is wholly on the perfervid forms they have put in their place, forms that seem bent on nothing so much as separating the widow from her mite and securing their own self-deification. It is a spectacle that once warmed the pen of H. L. Mencken, but Hardwick shares none of Mencken's contempt for the substance of Christianity, merely for the venalities of its economic exploitation. To be sure, Hardwick can be as unsympathetic with the hardscrabble background of this media religion, by turns uxorious and bellicose, as Mencken ever was, but her greatest disdain is reserved not for the faith they trivialize but for these hawkers of the holy themselves, who see the spiritual needs of others as so much commercial tender. Indeed, her disdain is so appealing precisely because it positions itself in relation to that culture-wide crisis of belief whose gravity is measured so thoughtfully in a poem like Larkin's.

Such critical discourse as Hardwick's is thus a severe, and sometimes even coarse, but effective reminder that while we cannot get beyond the world of symbols, we can sometimes reconfigure the elements that compose it, traverse the grain of the images that make it up, take up residence, so to speak, in the spaces between its circuitry, suspended like Pynchon's "other" Americans among the matrices of that world in some "lineman's tent like caterpillars, swung among a web of telephone wires, living in the very copper rigging and secular miracle of communication, untroubled by the dumb voltages flickering their miles, the night long, in the thousands of unheard messages."[29] These "remembered drifters," as Oedipa calls them, are "Americans speaking their language carefully, scholarly, as if they were in exile from somewhere else invisible yet congruent with the cheered land she lived in." Like the "walkers" she recalls from her youth "along the roads at night, zooming in and out of your headlights without looking up, too far from any town to have a real destination," these "other" Americans are in search of a place, really a spiritual site, beyond what is conventionally recognized in America as a destination of that sort.[30] To find it, they seem to realize (and Oedipa almost manages to say), requires an eye for the discrepant, an appreciation of the incongruous, a nose for the innocuous.

But the aim of such practices is not necessarily deflationary, much less deprecatory. Even where they enact a ludic, or, for that matter, a potentially offensive refusal to be bamboozled by the world of officialese, even when they convert downward rather than upward, their aim is essentially sanitive and curative and, yes, even after their fashion, regenerative. Such "comic correctives," to use Kenneth Burke's pregnant phrase, produce a form of moral "bookkeeping" that specializes in how to "make 'assets' of our 'liabilities.'" Dependent above all on learning how to see "the world's rich store of error . . . as *a genuine aspect of the truth*"[31] and on encouraging people *"to be observers of themselves, while acting,"*[32] it enables people to "transcend" themselves by noting their own foibles, to improve the "human barnyard" by becoming expert in their own fallibilities.[33] This is a form of human cost accounting as familiar to Ralph Ellison's Invisible Man, turning the experience of "the blues" into an idiom by which to defend and strengthen himself against the injuries of history, as it is to Toni Morrison's Baby Suggs, teaching the people who come to her in the consecrated Clearing, laughing, dancing, and crying together, that the only grace they can obtain is the grace that they can imagine.

Just as there is nothing about these critical practices that compels them to be debased or degrading, so there is something unmistakable about them that is inherently egalitarian and demotic, not to say democratic. Indeed, it might not be too much to say that they are a way of reenacting what is perhaps the oldest dream of America itself: that there exists a *terra nuova*—some have called it a "New World"—where in all its diversity and division and difference humankind can live out its imagination of self-realization, not in isolation from other persons but rather in reaction to them, often in resistance to them, always in relation to them, relying chiefly on the resources of its own obdurate unwillingness to become captive either of its own categories and closures or of anyone else's. The possibility of critical public discourse in America—and thus the possibility that there is any public world beyond the pretensions of our beliefs—depends in large measure on the obduracy of this vernacular intransigence, this wily stubbornness, this "wariest of wary reasonings," as Clifford Geertz calls it, "on all sides of all divides." [34] Fiercely independent and yet yearning for community, it constitutes one of America's richest, though now most deeply endangered, spiritual assets, an asset that for better and worse continues to play itself out, if nowhere else in American life, in our critical compulsion to "counterstate," our pragmatic recourse to symbolic revisioning.

Notes

*

Chapter 1

1. William James, *Pragmatism: A New Name for Some Old Ways of Thinking* (New York: Longmans, Green, 1907), 96.

2. Cited in Ralph Barton Perry, *The Thought and Character of William James,* vol. 2 (Boston: Little, Brown, 1935), 479.

3. Wilfrid Sellars, "Empiricism and the Philosophy of Mind," in *Minnesota Studies in the Philosophy of Science,* vol. 1, ed. Herbert Feigl and Michael Scriven (Minneapolis: University of Minnesota Press, 1956), 300.

4. Pierre Bourdieu, *In Other Words: Essays Towards a Reflexive Sociology* (Stanford, Calif.: Stanford University Press, 1990), 29. In this connection, it is interesting to observe that Barbara Herrnstein Smith has drawn very sharp criticism of her latest book, *Contingencies of Value,* for resorting to economic idioms to discuss questions of value and other serious matters.

5. Some of the following points were made, with his usual astuteness, in a personal letter to me by Denis Donoghue. Donoghue is himself a sympathetic and extremely lucid student of the history of American pragmatism, at least through the writings of Kenneth Burke, but there is considerable evidence that his reservations about the subsequent history of pragmatic reflection in the United States are shared by a number of other thoughtful interpreters of the contemporary critical scene.

6. "Few issues have expressed as powerful a hold over the thought of this century as that of 'The Other.' It is difficult to think of a second theme, even one that might be of more substantial significance, that has provoked as widespread an interest as this one; it is difficult to think of a second theme that so sharply marks off the present—admittedly a present growing out of the nineteenth century and reaching back to it—from its historical roots in the tradition. To be sure the problem of the other has at times been accorded a prominent place in ethics and anthropology, in legal and political philosophy. But the problem of the other has certainly never penetrated as deeply as today into the foundations of philosophical thought—the question of the other cannot be separated from the most primordial questions raised by modern thought." Michael Theunissen, *The Other,* trans. Christopher Macann (Cambridge: M.I.T. Press, 1984), 1.

7. Cited in John McDermott, ed., *The Writings of William James* (Chicago: University of Chicago Press, 1977), 134.

8. Bell Hooks, "marginality as site of resistance," in *Out There: Marginali-*

zation and Contemporary Cultures, ed. Russell Ferguson, Martha Gever, Trinh T. Minh-ha, and Cornel West (New York and Cambridge: The New Museum of Contemporary Art and The MIT Press, 1990), 343.

9. The phrase comes from Richard Poirier's book *Robert Frost: The Work of Knowing* (New York: Oxford University Press, 1977).

10. The book is *Gone Primitive: Savage Intellects, Modern Lives* by Marianna Torgovnick (Chicago: University of Chicago Press, 1990), though I take considerable liberties in the way I develop her central idea.

11. This is not to deny that Western primitivism has taken certain more positive forms, or that the Western history of going primitive might have taken a markedly different trajectory than it has. Torgovnick has some very acute things to say about both these matters, 246–48.

12. Peter Homans, *The Ability to Mourn: Disillusionment and the Social Origins of Psychoanalysis* (Chicago: University of Chicago Press, 1989)—a brilliant rethinking of the vexed interrelations among the psychobiography of Freud's own self-analysis, the development of the psychoanalytic movement, and the emergence of a psychoanalytic theory of culture. I cannot begin to do justice either to this book's importance for our understanding of the sociological dimensions of the Freudian revolution or to the intricacy of its arguments about a vast number of issues pertinent to cultural as well as psychological studies. My chief interest in this book here—from whose wealth of insights I borrow selectively and interpret freely, even loosely, for my own purposes—is to explore the convergence between what Homans views as the psychic destiny, or, better, vocation, of the successfully "analyzed" self and the interpretive space pragmatism tries to open up and turn to moral account in cultural discourse.

13. Philip Rieff, *The Triumph of the Therapeutic: Uses of Faith after Freud* (London: Chatto & Windus, 1966), 1–27.

14. Homans, *Ability to Mourn,* 5.

15. Ibid.

16. As Lionel Trilling once pointed out, the irony is that in his last work Freud was working toward a view of the mind that was figurative through and through: *The Liberal Imagination* (1950; New York: Harcourt Brace Jovanovich, 1978), 33–55.

17. Kenneth Burke, *Terms for Order,* ed. Stanley Edgar Hyman (Bloomington: Indiana University Press, 1964), 63.

18. Ibid., 55–56.

19. Ibid., 65.

20. Homans, *Ability to Mourn,* 9.

21. This view is not dissimilar to the one expressed by Cato and cited by Hannah Arendt at the end of *The Human Condition* (Chicago: University of Chicago Press, 1958), 325: "Never is [man] more active than when he does nothing, never is he less alone than when he is by himself."

Chapter 2

1. Walter Benn Michaels, *The Gold Standard and the Logic of Naturalism* (Berkeley: University of California Press, 1987), 18. This, as we shall see, is an odd way to put it, especially for a "new historicist" like Michaels. In addition to supposing that theology is something other than a cultural form, it implies that there is some kind of reflective practice or theoretical discourse that could or does exist above history.

2. Sacvan Bercovitch and Myra Jehlen, eds., *Ideology and Classic American Literature* (Cambridge: Harvard University Press, 1986), 1.

3. Giles Gunn, *The Culture of Criticism and the Criticism of Culture* (New York: Oxford University Press, 1987), 19–40.

4. Edward W. Said, *The World, the Text, and the Critic* (Cambridge: Harvard University Press, 1983), 291.

5. Quentin Anderson, *The Imperial Self* (New York: Alfred A. Knopf, 1971).

6. Said, *The World, the Text, and the Critic*, 241.

7. Ibid., 29.

8. Said's position is most fully adumbrated in the two chapters from *The World, the Text, and the Critic*, entitled "Introduction: Secular Criticism" and "Conclusion: Religious Criticism"; Culler's in an article entitled "Comparative Literature and the Pieties," in *Profession 86* (New York: Modern Language Association, 1986), 30–32, and in the chapter entitled "Political Criticism: Confronting Religion," in his book, *Framing the Sign: Criticism and Its Institutions* (New York: Basil Blackwell, 1988), 69–82. Of the two, Said's seems the more moderate. At times he speaks as though "secularity" involves little more than a skeptical, self-consciously situated criticism "reflectively open to its own failings" and by no means value free. At other times, however, he speaks of "secular" or "oppositional criticism" as one which is not only suspicious of all totalizing, reifying, dominating habits of mind, but also wholly defined by its "difference from other cultural activities and from systems of thought or of method." The more the identity of this kind of criticism is based upon self-consciously maintained differences from every other mental activity or form, the more it succumbs, because of its wholly oppositional nature, to a totalization of its own.

9. Jacques Derrida, *Writing and Difference*, trans. Alan Bass (Chicago: University of Chicago Press, 1979), 95.

10. Said, *The World, the Text, and the Critic*.

11. Sacvan Bercovitch, "The Problem of Ideology in American Literary History," 636.

12. Ibid.

13. Ibid., 635.

14. Ibid.

15. Ibid., 636.

16. Ibid., 645.

17. Fredric Jameson, *The Political Unconscious: Narrative as a Socially Symbolic Act* (Ithaca: Cornell University Press), 57.

18. Leo Marx, "Pastoralism in America," in Bercovitch and Jehlen, *Ideology and Classic American Literature,* 40–41.

19. See Edmundo O'Gorman, *The Invention of America* (Bloomington: Indiana University Press, 1961), and Giles Gunn, *New World Metaphysics* (New York: Oxford University Press, 1981), esp. xix–xxii, 3–37.

20. Michaels, *The Gold Standard,* 18.

21. Quoted, in ibid., 19.

22. This observation is drawn from an unpublished paper by Gerald Graff entitled "Criticism among the Crocodiles: Ideology, Literary History, and the Students."

23. Sacvan Bercovitch, *The Puritan Origins of the American Self* (New Haven: Yale University Press, 1975), 136–86.

24. For an excellent study of the difference, see Donald G. Mathews, *Religion in the Old South* (Chicago: University of Chicago Press, 1976), 185–250.

25. Kenneth Burke, *Counter-statement* (Berkeley: University of California Press, 1968), 163.

26. See Raymond Williams, *Marxism and Literature* (Oxford: Oxford University Press, 1977), 101–14.

27. Sacvan Bercovitch, "The Problem of Ideology in American Literary History," *Critical Inquiry* 12 (1986), 648.

28. The phrase "New Americanists" has been devised by Frederick Crews to describe the scholars chosen by Sacvan Bercovitch to contribute to the next major canonical undertaking in American literary study, the new five-volume *Cambridge History of American Literature* of which he is the general editor, now due for publication in the early 1990s. Employing an exclusively generational and, as Crews implies, ideological standard of selection, Bercovitch has restricted his list of twenty-one scholars to "Americanists trained in the sixties and early seventies" who, being somewhere between "tenure and the age of forty-five," can be accounted "spokespersons for dissensus." See Frederick Crews, "Whose American Renaissance?" *New York Review of Books,* October 27, 1988, 68–81.

29. See James T. Kloppenberg, "The Virtues of Liberalism: Christianity, Republicanism, and Ethics in Early American Political Discourse," *Journal of American History* 74 (June 1987), 9–33.

30. William James, *Pragmatism and Other Essays* (New York: Washington Square Press, 1972), 168.

31. Ibid, 169.

32. Ibid.

33. Ibid.

34. Michel Foucault, *Power/Knowledge: Selected Interviews and Other Writings, 1972–1977* (New York: Pantheon, 1980), 133.

35. Michel Foucault, *The History of Sexuality,* vol. 1: *An Introduction,* trans. Robert Hurley (New York: Random House, 1978), 95–96.

36. William James, "The Teaching of Philosophy in Our Colleges," *Nation* 23 (1876), 178.

37. Edward Said, *The World, the Text, and the Critic* (Cambridge: Harvard University Press, 1983), 241; Raymond Williams, *Politics and Letters: Interviews with New Left Review* (London; New Left Books, 1979), 252.

38. Said, *The World, the Text, and the Critic,* 225.

39. Hayden White, *The Content of the Form* (Baltimore: The Johns Hopkins University Press, 1987), 144.

40. Henry Samuel Levinson, "Religious Criticism," *Journal of American Religion* 64 (January 1984), 41–48.

41. Barbara Herrnstein Smith, *Contingencies of Value* (Cambridge: Harvard University Press, 1988), 169.

Chapter 3

1. Edwards A. Park, "The Theology of the Intellect and That of the Feelings," *Memorial Collection of Sermons by Edwards A. Park,* comp. Agnes Park (Boston, 1902), 108.

2. The following comprises a list of his chief titles: *What Constitutes the State* (New York: J. Allen, 1846); *Tracts for the New Times. No I, Letter to a Swedenborgian* (New York: J. Allen,, 1847); *Moralism and Christianity: Or, Man's Experience and Destiny* (New York: J. S. Redfield, 1850); *Lectures and Miscellanies* (New York: J. S. Redfield, 1852); *Love, Marriage, Divorce, and the Sovereignty of the Individual: A Discussion between Henry James, Horace Greeley, and Stephen Pearl Andrews* (1853; New York: B. R. Tucker, 1889); *The Nature of Evil* (New York: D. Appleton, 1855); *The Church of Christ Not an Ecclesiasticum* (London: W. White, 1856); *Christianity, the Logic of Creation* (New York: D. Appleton, 1857); *The Social Significance of Our Institutions* (Boston: Ticknor Fields, 1861); *Substance and Shadow: Or, Morality and Religion in Their Relation to Life: An Essay on the Physics of Creation* (Boston: Ticknor Fields, 1863); *The Secret of Swedenborg: Being an Elucidation of His Doctrine of the Divine Natural Humanity* (Boston: Fields, Osgood, 1869); *Society the Redeemed Form of Man, and the Earnest of God's Omnipotence in Human Nature* (Boston: Houghton, Osgood, 1879); *Portraits of Places* (Boston: Houghton Mifflin, 1883); and *The Literary Remains of the Late Henry James,* ed. and intro. William James (Boston: Houghton Mifflin, 1884).

3. *Letters of Charles Eliot Norton* (Boston: Houghton Mifflin, 1913), 2:379.

4. Daniel Aaron, *Men of Good Hope* (New York: Oxford University Press, 1961), 133.

5. William James, *The Literary Remains of the Late Henry James,* 15.

6. *Life and Letters of Edwin Lawrence Godkin,* ed. Rollo Ogden (New York: Macmillan, 1907), 2:117–18.

7. Ibid., 118.

8. See Austin Warren, *The Elder Henry James* (New York: Macmillan, 1934); Ralph Barton Perry, *The Thought and Character of William James* (Boston:

Little, Brown, 1935), 1:3–169; F. O. Matthiessen, *The James Family* (New York: Alfred A. Knopf, 1947), 3–69; Frederick Harold Young, *The Philosophy of Henry James, Sr.* (New York: Bookman Associates, 1951); Leon Edel, *Henry James, the Untried Years: 1843–1870* (Philadelphia: J. P. Lippincott, 1953), 19–56; R. W. B. Lewis, *The American Adam: Innocence, Tragedy, and Tradition in the Nineteenth Century* (Chicago: University of Chicago Press, 1955), 54–63; Quentin Anderson, *The American Henry James* (New Brunswick, N.J.: Rutgers University Press, 1957), 3–28, 51–124; Richard Poirier, *A World Elsewhere: The Place of Style in American Literature* (New York: Oxford University Press, 1966), 22–26, 111–13; Jean Strouse, *Alice James* (Boston: Houghton Mifflin, 1980), 6–9, 12–19, 17–20, 42–47, 64–68, 205–13; *Henry James, Senior: A Selection of His Writings,* ed. Giles Gunn (Chicago: American Library Association, 1974).

9. Henry James, *Notes of a Son and Brother* (New York: Scribner's, 1914), 230.

10. *The Secret of Swedenborg,* vi–vii.

11. Cited in Gunn, *Henry James, Senior,* 130.

12. Richard Poirier first drew my attention to the importance of this passage in *A World Elsewhere,* 25; also cited in Gunn, *Henry James, Senior,* 130.

13. Cited in Gunn, *Henry James, Senior,* 133.

14. Quoted in Perry, *The Thought and Character of William James,* 1:47.

15. See ibid., 13.

16. See R. W. B. Lewis's discussion of "the fortunate Fall" and "the party of Irony" in *The American Adam,* 54–63.

17. *The Literary Remains of the Late Henry James,* 216.

18. *Notes of a Son and Brother,* 234.

19. *The Literary Remains of the Late Henry James,* 391.

20. *Substance and Shadow,* 220.

21. Ibid., 222.

22. Matthiessen, *The James Family,* 6.

23. Cited in Gunn, *Henry James, Senior,* 92.

24. William's crisis occurred as he was entering a dressing room in March 1870, "when suddenly there fell upon me without warning, just as if it came out of the darkness, a horrible fear of my own existence. Simultaneously there arose in my mind the image of an epileptic patient whom I had seen in the asylum, a black-haired youth with greenish skin, entirely idiotic, who used to sit all day on one of the benches . . . with his knees drawn up against his chin. . . . The universe was changed for me completely" (*Varieties of Religious Experience,* 1902, New York: The Modern Library, 1927), 157.

Alice's crisis occurred in the summer of 1878, as she was to note in her *Diary:* "I have been dead so long, and it has been simply such a grim shoving of the hours behind me as I faced a ceaseless possible horror since that hideous summer of '78 when I went down to the deep sea, and its dark waters closed over me, and I knew neither hope nor peace" (*The Diary of Alice James,* ed. Leon Edel [1934; New York: Penguin, 1964], 230).

Henry, Junior's occurred most probably in 1910 during a nightmare, when he found himself on the other side of the bedroom door trying to resist its invasion by some frightful presence. Seized by an "unutterable fear," James nonetheless reports his still more remarkable "thought that I, in my appalled state, was probably still more appalling than the awful agent, creature or presence, whatever he was, whom I had guessed . . . to be making for my place of rest" (*A Small Boy and Others* [New York: Charles Scribner's Sons, 1913], 348). And when Henry finally managed to expel the intruder, he discovered that the long hall through which he was chasing him was the Louvre's Gallerie D'Appolon.

25. *Society the Redeemed Form of Man*, 45.

26. Ibid., 74.

27. Ibid., 53.

28. Quoted in Perry, *The Thought and Character of William James*, 1:27.

29. Quoted in Edel, *The Untried Years*, 35.

30. Quoted in Gunn, *Henry James, Senior*, 249.

31. Quoted in ibid., 245–46.

32. Quoted in Perry, *The Thought and Character of William James*, 83.

33. *The Literary Remains of the Late Henry James*, 424.

34. Perry, *The Thought and Character of William James*, 1:64.

35. Ibid., 133–34.

36. *Society the Redeemed Form of Man*, 333–34.

37. *The Literary Remains of the Late Henry James*, 75–76.

38. *Notes of a Son and Brother*, 229.

39. See Leon Edel, "Introduction: A Portrait of Alice James," *The Diary of Alice James*, 1–22; Ruth Yeazell, Introduction, *The Death and Letters of Alice James: Selected Correspondence*, ed. Ruth Yeazell (Berkeley: University of California Press, 1981); Jean Strouse, *Alice James*.

40. *The Diary of Alice James*, 96.

41. William's paper appeared in Scribner's in March 1890; Alice's journal entry, which reflects admiration rather than irritation, is dated October 26, 1890.

42. *The Diary of Alice James*, 146.

43. William James, "Author's Preface," *The Meaning of Truth in Pragmatism and Other Essays* (New York: Washington Square Press, 1963), 138.

44. See Richard Poirier, *The Renewal of Literature* (New York: Random House, 1988), 9–10.

45. *The Diary of Alice James*, 160.

46. Ibid.

47. Ibid., 196.

48. Quoted in Gunn, *Henry James, Senior*, 308.

49. James sent yet another recollection of his father's influence, this one more personal, to his wife soon after his father's death (*The Selected Letters of William James*, ed. Elizabeth Hardwick [New York: Farrar, Straus and Cudahy, 1961], 118–19): "For me, the humor, the good spirits, the humanity, the faith in the divine, and the sense of his right to have a say about the deepest reasons of the universe, are what will stay by me. I wish I could believe I should transmit some of them to our babes. We all of us have some of his virtues and some

of his shortcomings. Unlike the cool, dry thin-edged men who now abound, he was full of the fumes of the *ur-sprunglich* human nature; things turbid, more than he could formulate, wrought within him and made his judgements of rejection of so much of what was brought [before him] seem like revelations as well as knock-down blows. . . . I hope that rich soil of human nature will not become more rare! . . ."

50. Quoted in Gunn, *Henry James, Senior,* 308.

51. Quoted in Perry, *The Thought and Character of William James,* 1:71.

52. Quoted in Matthiessen, *The James Family,* 680.

53. *Notes of a Son and Brother,* 229.

54. Henry James, *The Future of the Novel: Essays on the Art of Fiction,* ed. Leon Edel (New York: Vintage Books, 1956), 12.

55. William James, *A Pluralistic Universe* (London: Longmans, Green, 1909), 20–21.

56. Cited in *The Writings of William James,* ed. John J. McDermott (Chicago: University of Chicago Press, 1977), 134.

57. William James, *Essays in Radical Empiricism* and *A Pluralistic Universe,* ed. Ralph Barton Perry (New York: E. P. Dutton, 1971), 25.

58. William James, *Pragmatism and Other Essays,* 5.

59. Ibid.

Chapter 4

1. Richard Rorty, *Consequences of Pragmatism* (Minneapolis: University of Minnesota Press, 1982); Richard J. Bernstein, *John Dewey* (New York: Washington Square Press, 1966); John J. McDermott, *The Culture of Experience: Philosophical Essays in the American Grain* (New York: New York University Press, 1976); Sidney Hook, *John Dewey: An Intellectual Portrait* (New York: John Day, 1939); John Herman Randall, *Nature and Historical Experience* (New York: Columbia University Press, 1958); Morton White, *The Origin of Dewey's Instrumentalism* (New York: Columbia University Press, 1944).

2. John Dewey, *Reconstruction in Philosophy* (New York: H. Holt, 1920), p. 186.

3. John Dewey, *Individualism Old and New* (1929; New York: Capricorn Books, 1962), 165.

4. John Dewey, *The Public and Its Problems, John Dewey, The Later Works, 1925–1953,* vol. 2, ed. Jo Ann Boydston (Carbondale: Southern Illinois University Press, 1984), 329.

5. See Richard Rorty, *Contingency, Irony, and Solidarity* (Cambridge: Cambridge University Press, 1989); Richard J. Bernstein, "Dewey, Democracy: The Task Before Us," in *Post-Analytic Philosophy,* ed. John Rajchman and Cornel West (New York: Columbia University Press, 1985), 48–59; John J. McDermott, *Streams of Experience: Reflections on the History and Philosophy of American Culture* (Amherst: University of Massachusetts Press, 1986); James T. Kloppenberg, *Uncertain Victory: Social Democracy and Progressivism in European and American Thought, 1870–1920* (New York: Oxford University Press, 1986): Cornel, West, *The American Evasion of Philosophy: A Genealogy of Prag-*

matism (Madison: University of Wisconsin Press, 1989); Robert B. Westbrook, *John Dewey and American Democracy* (Ithaca and London: Cornell University Press, 1991).

6. *The Public and Its Problems,* in *John Dewey: The Later Works,* 2:327–28.

7. John Dewey, *Democracy and Education* (1916; New York: Macmillan, 1944), 99.

8. John Dewey, "Creative Democracy—The Task Before Us," in *The Philosopher of the Common Man: Essays in Honor of John Dewey to Celebrate His Eightieth Birthday,* ed. Sidney Ratner et al. (New York: Greenwood Press, 1968), 393.

9. *Democracy and Education,* 322.

10. George Kateb, "Arendt and Representative Democracy," *Salmagundi* 60 (Spring-Summer, 1983), 59.

11. Quoted in Benjamin DeMott, "The Twentieth Century 1900–1976," in *America in Literature,* vol. 2, ed. Alan Trachtenberg and Benjamin DeMott (New York: John Wiley, 1978), 808.

12. Ibid., 807–8.

13. For a fuller discussion of Dewey's theory of mind and its relation to the creation of culture, see Giles Gunn, *The Interpretation of Otherness: Literature, Religion, and the American Imagination* (New York: Oxford University Press, 1979), 134–37.

14. Quoted in John Dewey, *Experience and Nature* (1925; La Salle, Ill.: Open Court, 1929), 10.

15. Ibid., 11.

16. Ibid., 12.

17. Ibid., 24.

18. Ibid., 38.

19. Ibid., 39.

20. Ibid., 40.

21. John Dewey, *Art as Experience* (1934; New York: Perigee Books, 1980), 13.

22. Ibid., 14.

23. Ibid.

24. Ibid., 56.

25. Ibid., 14.

26. Ibid., 15.

27. Ibid., 60.

28. Ibid.

29. Ibid., 15.

30. Ibid.

31. Ibid., 59.

32. *Experience and Nature,* 306–7.

33. Ibid., 291.

34. Ibid.

35. Ibid., 314.

36. *Art as Experience,* 3.

37. Ibid., 3–4.

38. Immanuel Kant, *Critique of Judgement*, quoted in M. H. Abrams, *The Mirror and the Lamp* (1953; New York: W. W. Norton, 1958), 327.

39. *Experience and Nature*, 306.

40. See Giles Gunn, *The Culture of Criticism and the Criticism of Culture* (New York: Oxford University Press, 1987), 8–18.

41. *Art as Experience*, 48.

42. Ibid., 137.

43. *Experience and Nature*, 291.

44. *Art as Experience*, 270.

45. Ibid., 273–74.

46. *Experience and Nature*, 138.

47. *Art as Experience*, 144, 148.

48. Quoted in DeMott, "The Twentieth Century 1900–1976," 808.

49. *Experience and Nature*, 323.

50. For a fuller discussion of Dewey's view of criticism as "the discipline of severe thought," see Gunn, *The Culture of Criticism and the Criticism of Culture*, 13, 73–74.

51. *Experience and Nature*, 330.

52. *Art as Experience*, 348.

53. Ibid., 347.

54. *Experience and Nature*, 326.

55. Quoted in *Art as Experience*, 347.

56. *Experience and Nature*, 10.

Chapter 5

1. Francis Bacon, *Bacon's Novum Organum*, ed. Thomas Fowler (Oxford: Clarendon Press, 1878), Book 1, Aphorisms 38–59.

2. Ibid.

3. See Stanley Fish, "Consequences," in *Against Theory: Literary Studies and the New Pragmatism*, ed. W.J.T. Mitchell (Chicago: University of Chicago Press, 1985), 106–12,

4. Barbara Herrnstein Smith, *Contingencies of Value* (Cambridge: Harvard University Press, 1988), 179.

5. Walter Benn Michaels and Stephen Knapp, "Against Theory," in *Against Theory: Literary Studies and the New Pragmatism* (Chicago: University of Chicago Press, 1985), 11–30.

6. C. B. McPherson, *The Political Theory of Possessive Individualism: Hobbes to Locke* (London: Oxford University Press, 1962).

7. Wallace Stevens, *Opus Posthumous* (London: Faber and Faber, 1957), 198.

8. Richard Rorty, *Contingency, Irony, and Solidarity* (Cambridge: Cambridge University Press, 1989), 16.

9. Ibid., 22.

10. Ibid., 6.

11. Ibid.

12. Ibid., 21.

13. Ibid.

14. Cited in ibid., 29, 73.

15. Cited in ibid., 29.

16. Ibid., 39–40.

17. Ibid., 125.

18. Ibid., 82

19. Ibid.

20. Ibid., 63.

21. Ibid., 84.

22. Ibid., 15.

23. Ibid., 15.

24. Cited in ibid.

25. Ibid., 80.

26. For Rorty's rejection of the metaphysical side of Dewey, see Richard Rorty, *Consequences of Pragmatism* (Minneapolis: University of Minnesota Press, 1982), 72–89.

27. Quoted in F. O. Matthiessen, *American Renaissance* (New York: Oxford University Press, 1941), 222.

28. Ibid., 93.

29. Richard Rorty, "Postmodern Bourgeois Liberalism," *Journal of Philosophy* 80 (October 1983), 583–89.

30. Clifford Geertz, "The Uses of Diversity," *Michigan Quarterly Review* 25 (Winter 1986), 111.

31. Richard Rorty, "On Ethnocentricism: A Reply to Clifford Geertz," *Michigan Quarterly Review* 25 (Fall 1986), 534.

32. Geertz, "The Uses of Diversity," 121.

33. Rorty, "On Ethnocentricism," 533.

34. Ibid.

35. Geertz, "The Uses of Diversity," 120.

36. Quoted in Geertz, ibid., 114.

37. Ibid., 112.

38. Ibid., 114.

39. Rorty, "On Ethnocentricism," 533.

40. Ibid., 533, 534.

41. Ibid., 533.

42. Rorty, *Contingency, Irony, Solidarity,* 190.

43. "An Exclusive Talk with Salman Rushdie," *Newsweek,* February 12, 1990, 49.

44. Carlos Fuentes, "Time For *Our* Sinatra Doctrine," *Nation,* February 12, 1990, 185, 198–203.

45. *Collected Papers of Charles Saunders Peirce,* ed. Charles Hartshorne and Paul Weiss, 6 vols. (Cambridge: Harvard University Press, 1931–35), 1:52.

46. Geertz, "The Uses of Diversity," 113.

47. Quoted in Ralph Barton Perry, *The Thought and Character of William James* (Boston: Little, Brown, 1935), 2:328–29.

48. William James, "Is Radical Empiricism Solipsistic?" in *William James,* ed. Bruce Kuklick (New York: Library of America, 1987), 1204.

49. William James, ibid., 1205.

50. John Dewey, *Human Nature and Conduct* (New York: Modern Library, 1950), 263.

51. Ibid., 263–64.

52. James Agee, *Let Us Now Praise Famous Men* (Boston: Houghton Mifflin, 1941, 1969), 11.

Chapter 6

1. There is, of course, considerable historical inaccuracy in so selective a procedure. Even if one grants the dominance of Protestantism in early American Christianity, Roman Catholicism was not an inconsequential presence in some of the colonies, and by the time of the American Revolution Judaism had established a modest foothold in Rhode Island and South Carolina.

2. *Henry F. May, The Enlightenment in America* (New York: Oxford University Press, 1976).

3. See Crane Brinton, *Ideas and Men* (Englewood Cliffs, N.J.: Prentice-Hall, 1950), 369–408; *A History of Western Morals* (New York: Harcourt, Brace, 1959), 297–98, 306–7, 374–75, 450–79.

4. Jonathan Mayhew, "A Discourse Concerning Unlimited Submission," in *Pamphlets of the American Revolution, 1750–1776,* ed. Bernard Bailyn, vol. 1, 1750–65 (Cambridge: Harvard University Press, 1965), 213.

5. Alan Heimert, *Religion and the American Mind, from the Great Awakening to the Revolution* (Cambridge: Harvard University Press, 1966).

6. Robert A. Ferguson, "We Hold These Truths," in *Reconstructiing American Literary History,* ed. Sacvan Bercovitch (Cambridge: Harvard University Press, 1986), 24.

7. For this formulation of the innermost assumption of Enlightenment belief, I am indebted to remarks made by Schubert M. Ogden at a symposium on "Knowledge and Belief in America," sponsored by the Woodrow Wilson Center for International Scholars at the Smithsonian Institution in Washington, D.C., April 18–20, 1990. This formulation also possesses a distant relation to Henry May's association of Enlightenment faith with all those who believe the following two propositions: "first, that the present age is more enlightened than the past; and second, that we understand nature and man best through the use of our natural faculties" (May, *The Enlightenment in America,* xiv).

8. Of the two, the Enlightenment is probably the easier to define simply because the historical movement to which it refers, however various its expressions, was confined to a much smaller group of people who were far narrower in interests and enjoyed such dominion as they achieved for a decisively shorter period of time. Thinking of a collection of intellectuals that included Voltaire, Locke, Hume, Moses Mendelssohn, Montesquieu, Rousseau, Diderot, Turgot, Helvetius, Condorcet, Adam Smith, Jefferson, and Paine,

Isaiah Berlin has provided perhaps the most satisfactory summary of the consensus that linked their diverse views in the following statement, which must be quoted entire ("Joseph de Maistre and the Origins of Fascism," *New York Review of Books,* September 27, 1990, 60):

> But sharp as the genuine differences between these thinkers were, there were certain beliefs that they held in common. They believed in varying measure that men were, by nature, rational and sociable; or at least understood their own and other's best interests when they were not being bamboozled by knaves or misled by fools; that, if only they were taught to see them, they would follow the rules of conduct discoverable by the use of the ordinary human understanding; that there existed laws which govern nature, both animate and inanimate, and that these laws, whether empirically discoverable or not, were equally evident whether one looked within oneself or at the world outside. They believed that the discovery of such laws, and knowledge of them, if it were spread widely enough, would of itself tend to promote a stable harmony both between individuals and associations, and within the individual himself.
>
> Most of them believed in the maximum degree of individual freedom and the minimum of government—at least after men had been suitably reeducated. They thought that education and legislation founded upon the "precepts of nature" could right almost every wrong; that nature was but reason in action, and its workings therefore were in principle deducible from a set of ultimate truths like the theorems of geometry, and laterly of physics, chemistry, and biology.
>
> They believed that all good and desirable things were necesarily compatible, and some maintained more than this—that all true values were interconnected by a network of indestructible, logically interlocking relationships. The more empirically minded among them were sure that a science of human nature could be developed no less than a science of inanimate things, and that ethical and political questions, provided that they were genuine, could in principle be answered with no less certainty than those of mathematics and astronomy. A life founded upon these answers would be free, secure, happy, virtuous, and wise. In short they saw no reason why the millennium should not be reached by the use of faculties and the practice of methods that had for over a century, in the sphere of the sciences of nature, led to triumphs more magnificent than any hitherto attained in the history of human thought.

9. Richard Brodhead, "Literature and Culture," in *The Columbia Literary History of the United States,* ed. Emory Elliott et al. (New York: Columbia University Press, 1988), 472–73.

10. Henry Adams, *The Education of Henry Adams* (Cambridge: Houghton Mifflin, 1961), 7.

11. Serious objections to the primacy Miller accords the mind, and the role of cognition generally in Puritan spirituality, begin with Alan Simpson's *Puritanism in Old and New England* (Chicago: University of Chicago Press, 1955) and continue down to the present day in Andrew Delbanco's *The Puritan Ordeal* (Cambridge: Harvard University Press, 1989). Important challenges to Miller's focus on New England in early-American cultural settlement can be found in a number of studies from Daniel J. Boorstin's *The Americans: The Colonial Experience* (New York: Random House, 1958) to Jack P. Greene, *Pursuits of Happiness: The Social Development of Early Modern British Colonies and the Formation of American Culture* (Chapel Hill: University of North Carolina

Press, 1989), and David Hacket Fisher, *Albion's Seed: Four British Folkways in America* (New York: Oxford University Press, 1989).

12. Kenneth Murdock, *Literature and Theology in Colonial New England* (New York: Harper and Row, 1949, 1963), 208.

13. Van Wyck Brooks, *America's Coming-of-Age* (Garden City, N.Y.: Doubleday Anchor Books, 1958), 3; D. H. Lawrence, *Studies in Classic American Literature* (Garden City, N.Y.: Doubleday Anchor Books, 1951), 26.

14. Herman Melville, "Hawthorne and His Mosses," in *Moby-Dick,* ed. Harrison Hayford (New York: W. W. Norton, 1967), 540.

15. Terrence Martin, *The Instructed Vision: Scottish Common Sense Philosophy and the Origins of American Fiction* (Bloomington: Indiana University Press), 60–76.

16. This trend has beginnings as early as F. O. Matthiessen's *American Renaissance,* and its persistence can be seen even in works that problematize the understanding of the form, such as Michael Davitt Bell's *The Development of American Romance* (Chicago: University of Chicago Press, 1980), or that seemingly address different traditions, such as Eric J. Sundquist's "The Country of the Blue," in *American Realism,* ed. Eric J. Sundquist (Baltimore: The Johns Hopkins University Press, 1982), 3–24.

17. *The Education,* 457–58.

18. Alfred Kazin, *An American Procession* (New York: Alfred A. Knopf, 1984).

19. Some of the most obvious treatments of religion in the postwar period would include F. O. Matthiessen's *American Renaissance: Art and Expression in the Age of Emerson and Whitman* (New York: Oxford University Press, 1941); Charles Feidelson's *Symbolism and American Literature* (Chicago: University of Chicago Press, 1953); Richard Chase's *The American Novel and Its Tradition* (Garden City, N.Y.: Doubleday Anchor Books, 1957); R.W.B. Lewis's *The American Adam: Innocence, Tragedy, and Tradition in the Nineteenth Century* (Chicago: University of Chicago Press, 1955); Leslie Fiedler's *Love and Death in the American Novel* (New York: Dell, 1960); Roy Harvey Pearce's *The Continuity of American Poetry* (Princeton: Princeton University Press, 1962); John F. Lynen's *The Design of the Present* (Princeton: Princeton University Press, 1969); Sacvan Bercovitch's *The American Jeremiad* (Madison: University of Wisconsin Press, 1979); David Reynolds's *Beneath the American Renaissance: The Subversive Imagination in the Age of Emerson and Melville* (New York: Alfred A. Knopf, 1988); and, most recently, the last chapter of Andrew Delbanco's *The Puritan Ideal.*

20. Lewis P. Simpson, *The Brazen Face of History* (Baton Rouge: Louisiana University Press, 1980), 55.

21. Richard Chase, *The American Novel and Its Tradition* (Garden City, N.Y.: Doubleday Anchor Books, 1957), 11.

22. Tony Tanner, *City of Words* (New York: Harper and Row, 1971), 15.

23. Ibid.

24. For an example of the first, see Quentin Anderson, *The Imperial Self* (New York: Alfred A. Knopf, 1971); for an example of the second, see Nina

Baym, "Melodramas of Beset Manhood: How Theories of American Fiction Exclude Women Authors," in *The New Feminist Criticism*, ed. Elaine Showalter (New York: Pantheon Books, 1985), 63–80.

25. A related but somewhat different narrative emerges from the study Tania Modleski has made of models of feminist self-description and ideological resistance offered by popular artforms such as gothic novels, Harlequin romances, and daytime soap operas in *Loving with a Vengeance: Mass-Produced Fantasies for Women* (New York: Methuen, 1982).

26. Elizabeth Fox-Genovese, "American Culture and New Literary Studies," *American Quarterly* 42 (March 1990), 21.

27. Ibid., 22.

28. May, *The Enlightenment in America*, 360.

29. Reynolds, *Beneath the American Renaissance*.

30. An excellent discussion of the cultural metaphysics of this tradition can be found in John McWilliams, "Poetry in the Early Republic," in *Columbia Literary History of the United States*, ed. Emory Elliott et al. (New York: Columbia University Press, 1988), 156–67.

31. See Giles Gunn, *The Interpretation of Otherness: Literature, Religion and the American Imagination* (New York: Oxford University Press, 1979), 161–74.

32. Feidelson, *Symbolism and American Literature*, 34.

33. This way of reading the book has been richly informed by Tony Tanner's Introduction to *Moby-Dick* (Oxford: Oxford University Press, 1988), vii–xxviii.

34. Daniel Hoffman, *Form and Fable in American Fiction* (New York: Oxford University Press, 1965), 233–78.

35. Tanner, Introduction to *Moby-Dick*, xxvii.

36. *The Writings of William James*, ed. John J. McDermott (Chicago: University of Chicago Press, 1977), 45.

37. Cited in Richard Poirier, *The Renewal of Literature: Emersonian Reflections* (New York: Random House, 1987), 142.

38. William James, "Author's Preface to *The Meaning of Truth*," in *Pragmatism and Other Essays* (New York: Washington Square Press, 1963), 138.

39. Richard A. Hocks, *Henry James and Pragmatistic Thought* (Chapel Hill: University of North Carolina Press, 1974), 27.

40. May, *The Enlightenment in America*, 109.

41. For exceptions to this rule, see F. O. Matthiessen, *The James Family* (New York: Alfred A. Knopf, 1961), 315–45, 673–84; Henry Bamford Parkes, "The James Brothers," *Sewanee Review* 56 (1948), 323–28; Eliseo Vivas, *Creation and Discovery* (Chicago: Henry Regnery, 1955), 21–41; Richard A. Hocks, *Henry James and Pragmatistic Thought*; Kazin, *An American Procession*, 211–34; Ross Posnock, "William and Henry James," *Raritan* 8/3 (Winter 1989), 1–25.

42. Matthiessen, *The James Family*, 343.

43. Ibid., 345.

44. Ibid., 92.

45. For Cavell, see *In Quest of the Ordinary: Lines of Skepticism and Romanti-*

cism (Chicago: University of Chicago Press, 1988); for Poirier, see *The Renewal of Literature*.

46. Poirier, *Renewal of Literature*, 202.

47. Ibid., 203.

48. Ibid.

49. See the response of a feminist critic like Nina Baym, *New York Times Book Review*, March 22, 1987, 37.

50. Poirier, *Renewal of Literature*, 131.

51. Ibid., 178.

52. Stanley Cavell, *This New Yet Unapproachable America* (Albuquerque, N.M.: Living Batch Press, 1989), 116.

53. Poirier, *Renewal of Literature*, 202.

Chapter 7

1. See E. D. Hirsch, *The Aims of Interpretation* (Chicago: University of Chicago Press, 1976), 73–92, 124–45.

2. Gerald Graff, *Professing Literature: An Institutional History* (Chicago: University of Chicago Press, 1987).

3. Wesley Morris, *Toward a New Historicism* (Princeton: Princeton University Press, 1972).

4. Michel Foucault, *The Archaeology of Knowledge,* trans. A. M. Sheridan Smith (New York: Harper Colophon, 1972), 117.

5. Quoted in Graff, *Professing Literature,* 86.

6. Graff has subsequently turned this insight into the animating principle of a new project for pedagogical and curricular reform in the humanities that accentuates "teaching the conflicts." It is one thing, however, to note that suppression or neglect of the conflicts that define the humanistic curriculum at any given historical moment and influence the teaching of the texts and topics that comprise it impairs their heuristic values and quite another to assert, as Graff's new proposal seems to, that those conflicts should or do comprise the main contents of that curriculum. Graff's most extensive defense of this proposal to date can be found in "Other Voices, Other Rooms: Organizing and Teaching the Humanities Conflict," *New Literary History* 21 (Autumn 1990), 817–39. The most searching critique of this approach that I know of is to be found in David Bromwich, "The Future of Tradition," *Dissent* 36 (Fall 1989), esp. 554–57.

7. The philosopher George Santayana, who was a member of that faculty, held a different opinion: "Did the members of the Harvard Faculty form an intellectual society? Had they any common character or influence? I think not. . . . I never heard of any idea or movement springing up among them, or any literary fashion. It was an anonymous concourse of coral insects, each secreting one cell, and leaving that fossil legacy to enlarge the earth." Cited in Graff, *Professing Literature,* 98. For a more judicious view, see Bruce Kuklick, *The Rise of American Philosophy: Cambridge, Massachusetts, 1860–1930* (New Haven: Yale University Press, 1977).

8. Graff, *Professing Literature*, 252.

9. Ibid., 5.

10. Ibid., 258.

11. Kermit Vanderbilt, *American Literature and the Academy* (Philadelphia: University of Pennsylvania Press, 1986), 520.

12. The strongest proponent of this view is probably Jane Tompkins, *Sensational Designs* (New York: Oxford University Press, 1985).

13. Charles Feidelson, Jr., *Symbolism and American Literature* (Chicago: University of Chicago Press, 1953), 3.

14. Ibid., 4.

15. Graff, *Professing Literature*, 10.

16. Edmund Wilson, *Axel's Castle* (New York: Scribner's, 1931), x.

17. Alfred Kazin, *Contemporaries* (Boston: Little, Brown, 1962), 497.

18. Alfred Kazin, *An American Procession* (New York: Alfred A. Knopf, 1984), 36.

19. Ibid., 141.

20. Ibid., 88.

21. Ibid., 163.

22. Ibid., 338.

23. Ibid., 362.

24. Cited in ibid., 63.

25. Alan Trachtenberg, "Comments on Evan Watkins' 'Cultural Criticism and the Literary Intellectual,'" *Works and Days* 3 (1985), 36.

26. Fredric Jameson, *The Political Unconscious* (Ithaca: Cornell University Press, 1981), 81.

27. Ibid., 57–58.

28. Donald E. Pease, *Visionary Compacts* (Madison: University of Wisconsin Press, 1987), 204.

29. Ibid., ix.

30. For a description of the difference between the way Matthiessen interpreted the five writers he deemed of major significance in the period—Emerson, Thoreau, Whitman, Hawthorne, and Melville—and the way, for example, they were being interpreted in the late sixties and early seventies, see Giles Gunn, *F. O. Matthiessen: The Critical Achievement* (Seattle: University of Washington Press, 1975), 131–32.

31. Pease, *Visionary Compacts*, 247.

32. Graff, *Professing Literature*, 223.

33. In *Sensational Designs,* Tompkins finds the agency of female empowerment in the antebellum period in an ideology of Protestant religious orthodoxy that now as then had at heart, whatever its occasional effects, the subordination of women within a framework of patriarchy.

34. This will no doubt change when the new four-volume *Cambridge History of American Literature* under the general editorship of Sacvan Bercovitch is published.

35. *Columbia Literary History of the United States,* ed. Emory Elliot et al. (New York: Columbia University Press, 1988), xix.

36. Ibid., xxii.

37. Michael J. Colacurcio, "Idealism and Independence," in ibid., 226.

38. James M. Cox, *Recovering Literature's Lost Ground* (Baton Rouge: Louisiana State University Press, 1989), 8.

39. See Howard Mumford Jones, *O Strange New World* (New York: Viking Press, 1964), 1–70.

40. See Stephen Greenblatt, *Shakespearean Negotiations: The Circulation of Social Energy in Renaissance England* (Berkeley: University of California Press, 1988), 1–20, 40.

41. Lawrence Buell, *New England Literary Culture* (Cambridge: Cambridge University Press, 1986), 10.

42. Ibid., 22.

43. Cited in ibid., 17.

44. Hayden White, *The Content of the Form* (Baltimore: The Johns Hopkins University Press, 1987), 181.

45. Warner Berthoff, *Literature and the Continuances of Virtue* (Princeton: Princeton University Press), 1986.

46. Berthoff's term for this process is "virtue." Anything but a simple moral category to be confused with the four, seven, eight, or twelve virtues defined by various religious and ethical systems, or some "teachable moral goodness" (124), virtue is for Berthoff "a kind of anthropological quid"; that is, an "effect-producing property of being and acting specific to human beings" (16). It is Berthoff's word for the showing forth or reenactment of human capacity in the teeth of resistance. As found in works of literature, where it is always displayed "under the conditions taken as regulating it" and becomes persuasive in direct proportion to "its participation in those 'forms of life' . . . we feelingly know or remember knowing, intuiting, in ourselves" (14), virtue is known simply as that potency or force or presence that "regularly eludes the expectations of scheduled understanding" (124). From this Berthoff concludes, "our deepest imaginative interest in virtue is thus not in what it *is* but in what its life and answering power may be in temporal reality, what effects it is palpably capable of, and most of all whether and how it can, against odds, effect its own further existence and so give itself, and everything it empowers, *continuance*" (18).

47. White, *The Content of the Form,* 157.

48. Ibid., 211.

49. Ibid.

50. Ibid., 144.

Chapter 8

1. Stanley Fish, "Being Interdisciplinary Is So Very Hard to Do," in *Profession 89* (New York: MLA, 1985), 17.

2. Bruce Robbins, "Professionalism and Politics: Toward Productively Divided Loyalties," in *Profession 85* (New York: MLA, 1985), 49–54.

3. Ibid.

4. Ibid., 20.

5. Jacques Derrida, "Deconstruction and the Other," in *Dialogues with Contemporary Continental Thinkers,* ed. Richard Kearney (Manchester: Manchester University Press, 1984), 112.

6. Ibid.

7. Clifford Geertz, "Blurred Genres: The Refiguration of Social Thought," *American Scholar* 49/2 (Spring 1980), 165–66.

8. Martha Craven Nussbaum, "Narrative Emotions: Beckett's Genealogy of Love," *Ethics* 98 (January 1988), 236.

9. Jonathan Culler, *Framing the Sign: Criticism and Its Institutions* (New York: Basil Blackwell, 1988), 8; Gerald Graff, *Professing Literature* (Chicago: University of Chicago Press, 1987), 211.

10. Roland Barthes, "From Work to Text," in *Textual Strategies: Perspectives in Post-Structuralist Criticism,* ed. Josue V. Harari (Ithaca: Cornell University Press, 1979), 75.

11. Fish, "Being Interdisciplinary Is So Very Hard to Do," 15–17.

12. Barthes, "From Work to Text," 73–74.

13. See, for example, Paul Hernadi, "Literary Work: A Compass," *Critical Inquiry* 3 (Winter 1976), 369–86.

14. Some of the others mentioned, for example, in the Modern Language Association's *Interrelations of Literature,* ed. Jean-Paul Barricelli and Joseph Gibaldi (New York: MLA, 1982), include myth, folklore, sociology, law, science, music, and the visual arts.

15. For this insight as well as several others in this chapter, I am indebted to an unpublished paper by Alan Liu entitled "Indiscipline, Interdiscipline, and Liberty: The Revolutionary Paradigm."

16. Graff, *Professing Literature,* 6–9.

17. For some of this discussion of the new world of the text, I am indebted to Richard Macksey, "A New Text of the World," *Genre* 16 (Winter 1983), 307–16.

18. See James Clifford, *The Predicament of Culture* (Cambridge: Harvard University Press, 1988), 21–54.

19. Clifford Geertz, *The Interpretation of Cultures* (New York: Basic Books, 1973), 29.

20. Culler, *Framing the Sign,* 33–36.

Chapter 9

1. Denis Donoghue, "In Their Masters' Steps," *Times Literary Supplement,* December 16, 1988, 1399.

2. *Social Theory Today,* ed. Anthony Giddens and Jonathan Turner (Stanford: Stanford University Press, 1987).

3. See Giles Gunn, *The Interpretation of Otherness: Literature, Religion, and the American Imagination* (New York: Oxford University Press, 1979).

4. Lionel Trilling, *The Liberal Imagination* (New York: Harcourt Brace Jo-

vanovich, 1978), 89. Trilling referred by this phrase to "those people who value their ability to live some part of their lives with serious ideas."

5. Christopher Lasch, "*1984* Are We There?" *Salmagundi* 65 (Fall 1984), 60.

6. Ibid., 6l.

7. Thomas Pynchon, *The Crying of Lot 49* (New York: Bantam Books, 1961), 13.

8. Quentin Anderson, *The Imperial Self* (New York: Alfred A. Knopf, 1971), 13.

9. Mark Poster, ed. *Jean Baudrillard: Selected Writings* (Stanford: Stanford University Press, 1988), 1–9.

10. Pierre Bourdieu, *Distinction: A Social Critique of the Judgement of Taste,* trans. Richard Nice (Cambridge: Harvard University Press, 1984), 291.

11. Milan Kundera, *The Art of the Novel,* trans. Linda Asher (New York: Harper and Row, 1988), 135.

12. Pynchon, *The Crying of Lot 49,* 13.

13. Ibid., 128.

14. Will Herberg, *Protestant Catholic Jew* (New York: Doubleday and Co., 1955), 78.

15. See John Wilson, *Public Religion in American Culture* (Philadelphia: Temple University Press, 1979).

16. See Giles Gunn, ed., *New World Metaphysics: Readings on the Religious Meaning of the American Experience* (New York: Oxford University Press, 1981).

17. See Sacvan Bercovitch, "The Biblical Basis of the American Myth," in *The Bible and American Arts and Letters,* ed. Giles Gunn (Philadelphia: Fortress Press, 1983), 219–29. Some of the sentences in this and related paragraphs are taken from my Introduction to this volume.

18. See "The Religion of the Republic," in Henry F. May, *Ideas, Faith, and Feelings: Essays in American Intellectual and Religious History, 1952–1982* (New York: Oxford University Press, 1983), 164–72.

19. Kenneth Burke, quoted in William H. Rueckert, *Kenneth Burke and the Drama of Human Relations* (1963; Berkeley: University of California Press, 1982), 161.

20. "'Noble Shit': The Uncivil Response of American Writers to American Religion," in Leo Marx, *The Pilot and the Passenger* (New York: Oxford University Press, 1988), 261–90.

21. Norman Mailer, *Armies of the Night* (New York: New American Library, 1968), 48.

22. Ibid., 47.

23. Ibid.

24. Henry David Thoreau, *The Illustrated Walden,* ed. J. Lyndon Shanley (Princeton: Princeton University Press, 1973), 318.

25. Cited in Elizabeth Hardwick, "Church Going," *New York Review of Books,* April 12, 1988, 21.

26. Ibid., 20.

27. Henry James, *The American Scene* (Bloomington: Indiana University Press, 1968), 465.

28. Hardwick, "Church Going," 18.

29. Pynchon, *The Crying of Lot 49,* 135.

30. Ibid.

31. Kenneth Burke, *Attitudes toward History,* 3d ed. (Berkeley: University of California Press, 1984), 172.

32. Ibid., 171.

33. Ibid.

34. Clifford Geertz, "Blurred Genres: The Refiguration of Social Thought," *American Scholar* 49 (Spring 1980), 179.

Index

★

259